Praise for the First Edition of *The New Rules of Retail*

"Takes a real approach to describe why some retailers prospered and others failed through each wave of retail history. Lewis and Dart's use of case examples brings the book to life, clearly spelling out how customers and the competitive environment have changed and how retailers today must connect with their customers and take control of their value chain to not only be successful, but survive."

—*Ken Hicks, Chairman and CEO, Foot Locker, Inc.,*
and former COO of JCPenney

"*The New Rules of Retail: Competing in the World's Toughest Marketplace* is an important and instructive read for industry veterans and newcomers alike. Lewis and Dart provide a practical roadmap for success in the rapidly evolving environment, along with an assessment of the retailers who 'get it.' With the authors' dire prediction that 50 percent of retailers will be unable to survive the transition to Wave III, this is a must-read for everyone in the business today!"

—*Jane Elfers, President and CEO, The Children's Place*

"This book is an essential read for anyone who is interested in a history of what drives 70 percent of the U.S. economy and the many challenges expected to be faced in the future. Like we are now seeing in politics, the voter/consumer is in the driver's seat, and those serving her had better take heed."

—*Allen Questrom, former CEO, JCPenney,*
Federated Department Stores, and Barney's

"*The New Rules of Retail* is a must-read for students of contemporary retailing. Full of meaningful insights about the current environment, the authors chart the course for a successful retail future."

—*Paul Charron, former CEO of Liz Claiborne*

"Lewis and Dart have written an interesting and thoroughly researched book that traces the evolution of the retail business from the distant past to the looming future. Clearly, they know and understand all the players—well worth reading."

—*Marvin Traub, former President and CEO, Bloomingdale's*

"*The New Rules of Retail* is an incredibly interesting and a provocative read. I thoroughly enjoyed the authors' insight on past events. I look forward to debate and dialogue about their predictions for the future."

—*Tom Wyatt, President, Old Navy*

"Lewis and Dart give a very accurate view of the past history of retailing. But more importantly, they offer an insightful and strategic view of the consumers and business models needed to support its future."

—*Claudio Del Vecchio, CEO, Brooks Brothers*

"*The New Rules of Retail* shows how to win in an unprecedented environment where consumers have instant access to hundreds of choices for everything they need. Lewis and Dart's recommendations are dramatic, but they show that the consequences for those who stick with the status quo will be dire. A highly original and insightful book."

—*Mark Sarvary, CEO, Tempur-Pedic International Inc.*

"Lewis and Dart have so many thought-provoking ideas that I used up a box of paper clips marking the pages I wanted my various department heads to read. And they're easy to follow—I understood the concept of a 'neurologically connective experience' right away. All future decisions in retailing and wholesaling will be influenced by this book."

—*Bud Konheim, CEO, Nicole Miller*

"Lewis and Dart have shown once again that they have their fingers on the pulse of both consumer needs and the ever-changing retail industry. *The New Rules of Retail* is a must-read for anyone who wants to not only survive but to thrive in the decades to come."

—*Kevin M. Burke, President and CEO, American Apparel & Footwear Association*

"*The New Rules of Retail* is a powerful analysis of the tectonic shifts that have transformed this industry, and it reveals the secrets of succeeding in today's new economic and digital environment. Authors Robin Lewis and Michael Dart know retailing inside and out and their thought-provoking book, with its incisive perspective, proves it."

—*Tracy Mullin, former President and CEO, National Retail Federation*

THE NEW RULES OF RETAIL

COMPETING IN THE WORLD'S TOUGHEST MARKETPLACE

SECOND EDITION

ROBIN LEWIS AND
MICHAEL DART

St. Martin's Press
New York

THE NEW RULES OF RETAIL, SECOND EDITION. Copyright © 2014 by Robin Lewis and Michael Dart. All rights reserved. Printed in the United States of America. For information, address St. Martin's Press, 175 Fifth Avenue, New York, N.Y. 10010.

www.stmartins.com

Designed by Letra Libre, Inc.

Library of Congress Cataloging-in-Publication Data

Lewis, Robin, 1940–
    The new rules of retail : competing in the world's toughest marketplace / Robin Lewis and Michael Dart.—Second edition.
        p.   cm.
    ISBN 978-1-137-27926-2 (hardcover)
    1. Retail trade. 2. Retail trade—Management. 3. Retail trade—Technological innovations. 4. Wholesale trade. 5. Consumer satisfaction. I. Dart, Michael. II. Title.
HF5429.L4854   2014
658.8′72—dc23
                                                                                        2014003487

Our books may be purchased in bulk for promotional, educational, or business use. Please contact your local bookseller or the Macmillan Corporate and Premium Sales Department at (800) 221-7945, extension 5442, or by e-mail at MacmillanSpecialMarkets@macmillan.com.

First published by Palgrave Macmillan, a division of St. Martin's Press LLC

First St. Martin's Press Edition: August 2014

10 9 8 7 6 5 4 3 2

To Martha and Cloe

To Janine, Alison, and David

And a special dedication to Judith Russell,
who kept us organized and on time,
edited our sometimes incorrect grammar,
and offered her brilliance in many parts of the book

CONTENTS

ACKNOWLEDGMENTS

As we began to finalize this updated edition, and the expansion of our original thesis to include the full-on, explosive effects of the "technology era," we spent many hours and days poring over what seemed like tons of research, digging for supportive nuggets and even whole veins to back our logic and strengthen our vision of how the transformation of the industry is going to play out.

In the middle of this yeoman's quest, we realized that between us we had another untapped and enormously rich resource: our past and current professional colleagues; a great number of C-level and senior executives throughout the retail and other consumer-facing industries whom we had become friendly with over the years; many academicians; and various industry association leaders.

We sought many of them out and received not only great insight, much of it profound, but also, more importantly, their positive support and sincere interest in reading our final product.

Others who were not directly involved with our efforts, and many who were simply business colleagues over the years, nevertheless provided knowledge and strategic insights that later became useful in the shaping of our thesis. We want to thank them as well.

At the end of the day, by the time we put pen to paper or fingers to keyboard, we knew not only that our expanded, technology-altering thesis was on track for driving the transformation but also that it was made even more robust through all our past knowledge sources as well as our direct conversations with the executives whose businesses were in the middle of the fundamental changes taking place.

More importantly, we were honored that these great friends, colleagues and professional associates, both past and present, were interested enough to give of their time to provide us with invaluable perspectives and knowledge.

Angela Ahrendts, former CEO, Burberry

David Bell, Operating Adviser, Pegasus Capital Advisors; Senior Adviser, AOL Inc.

Phil Black, former Publisher, *The Apparel Strategist;* CNN correspondent

Frank Blake, CEO, The Home Depot

Heather Blonkenfeld, Marketing Director, Kurt Salmon Associates

Pete Born, Executive Editor, Beauty, *Women's Wear Daily*

Pauline Brown, Chairman, North America, LVMH

Kevin Burke, former President and CEO, American Apparel and Footwear Association

Tom Burns, Senior Vice President, Doneger Inc.

Vanessa Castagna, former CEO, JCPenney; former Executive Chairwoman, Mervyn's

Paul Charron, Chairman and CEO Emeritus, Liz Claiborne, Warburg Pincus Non-operating Chairman, Campbell's Soup Company

Michael Coady, CEO Emeritus, Fairchild Publications

Bruce Cohen, Partner, Kurt Salmon Associates

Mark Cohen, Professor of Marketing, Columbia University Graduate Business School; former Chairman and CEO, Sears Canada

Neil Cole, CEO, Iconix Brands

Kathryn Cordes, Director, Global Marketing and Operations, Deloitte

Bill Crain, former Vice Chairman, VF Corporation

Bill D'Arienzo, Founder and CEO, Wm. D'Arienzo Associates

Claudio Del Vecchio, Chairman and CEO, Retail Brand Alliance; owner of Brooks Brothers

John Donahoe, Director, President and CEO, eBay

Jane Elfers, CEO, The Children's Place

Joe Ellis, author of *Ahead of the Curve;* former Partner, Goldman Sachs

Pamela Ellsworth, Professor, Department of International Trade and Marketing and Chairperson, Global Fashion Management Graduate Program, FIT

Kathy Elsessor, Managing Director and Head of Consumer Retail Group, Goldman Sachs

Jim Fielding, CEO, Claires Inc., former President, Disney Retail

Ruth Finley, Founder and President, Fashion Calendar

Ben Fischman, CEO and President, Retail Convergence Inc. brand Rue La La

Mike Fitzgerald, former President, Delta Galil

John Fleming, CEO of e-commerce, Uniqlo

Neal Fox, President and CEO, the Cross brand

Don Franceschini, CEO emeritus, former Vice Chairman and CEO, Personal Products; retired, Sara Lee Apparel

David Freschman, CEO, FashInvest, Managing Principal, Innovation Capital Advisors

Michael Gould, former Chairman and CEO, Bloomingdale's

Nick Graham, Founder and former CEO, Joe Boxer

Bob Grayson, Founder, Robert C. Grayson & Associates / The Grayson Company

Rob Gregory, former COO and President, VF Corporation

Joe Gromek, former Director, President and CEO, Warnaco

Mindy Grossman, CEO and Director, HSN

Gilbert Harrison, Founder, Chairman and CEO, Financo

Ken Hicks, CEO, Foot Locker, Former COO, JC Penney

Clark Hinkley, CEO Emeritus, Talbots

Brendan Hoffman, CEO, The BonTon

David Jaffee, President and CEO, Ascena Brand Group

Ron Johnson, Former President and CEO, JC Penney

Roy Johnson, Instructor, Department of
    Communication Studies, Baruch
    College, City University of New York
Andy Kahn, Chairman Emeritus, Kahn
    Lucas Lancaster, Inc.
Harvey Kanter, Chairman, President and
    CEO, Blue Nile
Sonia Kashuk, Founder and owner, Sonia
    Kashuk beauty brand
Bud Konheim, Cofounder and CEO,
    Nicole Miller
William Lauder, Executive Chairman,
    The Estée Lauder Companies
Margot Lewis, Founder and CEO,
    Platform Media NY
Claire Liu, Former consultant, Kurt
    Salmon Associates
Walter Loeb, Consultant and Retail
    Expert
Terry Lundgren, Chairman, President
    and CEO, Macy's
Dan MacFarlan, former Vice Chairman,
    VF Corporation
Margaret Mager, former Managing
    Director and Business Unit Leader—
    Retail Industry, Goldman Sachs
Arthur Martinez, Chairman,
    Abercrombie & Fitch, former
    Chairman and CEO, Sears
Alexis Maybank, Co-Founder, Gilt
    Groupe
Mackey McDonald, former Chairman
    and CEO, VF Corporation
Mindy Meads, CEO, Calypso
Bob Mettler, former Chairman and CEO,
    Macy's West
Carol Meyrowitz, CEO, TJX
    Companies
Larry Mondry, former CEO, CSK Auto
    Corporation
Tracy Mullin, former President and CEO,
    NRF
Karen Murray, President, Nautica brand
Tom Murry, President and CEO, Calvin
    Klein
Ed Nardoza, Editor-in-Chief, Fairchild
    Fashion Group
Chuck Nesbit, Former Executive VP and
    COO, McMurray Fabrics, Inc.
Blake Nordstrom, CEO, Director and
    President, Nordstrom
D. Scott Olivet, Operating Partner,
    Altamont Capital, former Chairman,
    Collective Brands,
Kirk Palmer, CEO, Kirk Palmer &
    Associates

Cindy Palusamy, Consultant, CP Strategy
    Inc. Partners & Colleagues, Kurt
    Salmon Associates
Deborah Patton, Editor, *The Robin
    Report*
Frank Pickard, Vice President and
    Treasurer Emeritus, VF
    Corporation
John Pomerantz, CEO Emeritus, Leslie
    Fay
Stefan Preston, former CEO, Bendon
    Intimates
Allen Questrom, CEO Emeritus,
    Federated Department Stores,
    JCPenney and Barney's
Madison Riley, Principal, Kurt Salmon
    Associates
Bruce Roberts, former President, Textile
    Distributors Association
Rick Roberts, Cofounder and Partner,
    Cynthia Steffe Designs
Ellen Rohde, former President, Vanity
    Fair Intimates
Doug Rossiter, Vice President and
    Program Director, The Advantage
    Group International, Toronto
Matt Rubel, former CEO, Collective
    Brands
Judith Russell, Marketing Consultant;
    Partner, *The Robin Report*
Kevin Ryan, Co-Founder, Gilt Groupe
Peter Sachse, Chief Stores Officer, Macy's
Steven Sadove, former CEO, Saks Inc.
Mark Sarvary, CEO and President,
    Tempur-Pedic
Chris Schaller, former CEO, Forstmann
    & Co.
Denise Seegal, President and CEO,
    Magaschoni, Inc., former President,
    Liz Claiborne
Mike Setola, President and CEO,
    MacGregor Golf Co.
Warren Shoulberg, Editorial Director,
    Progressive Business Media
Jane Singer, Marketing Consultant
Joseph Spellman, Senior Consultant, The
    Estée Lauder Companies
Tony Spring, CEO, Bloomingdale's
Marty Staff, Consultant, former CEO,
    Hugo Boss and Joseph Aboud brand
Cynthia Steffe, Cofounder and Partner,
    Cynthia Steffe Designs
Michael Steinberg, former CEO, Macy's
    West; Director, Fossil Inc.
Trudy Sullivan, former President & CEO,
    Talbots

Burt Tansky, former CEO, Neiman
  Marcus
Jock Thompson, Executive Vice
  President, Scope Apparel
Miranda Tisdale, Consumer Research
  Manager, Kohl's
Carol Tome, CFO, The Home Depot
Mike Ullman, Chairman and CEO,
  JCPenney
Paco Underhill, Founder, CEO and
  President, Envirosell

Jeanette Wagner, Consultant and former
  Vice Chair, The Estée Lauder
  Companies
Kenneth Walker, Managing Director,
  Republic of Innovation
Dee Warmath, Senior Vice President,
  Global Product Developments, NPD
Manny Weintraub, founder and CEO,
  Emanuel Weintraub Associates
Eric Wiseman, CEO and President, VF
  Corporation

Lastly we would like to give a very special thanks to our agent, Edward Necarsulmer IV. Without his belief in the relevancy and timeliness of our thesis, and his dogged, unyielding determination to find a publisher for the first edition of our book, this edition would still be but a dream.

And, of course, the ultimate thanks to the editors and staff at Palgrave Macmillan, the publisher that actually made it happen.

PROLOGUE

IN SEARCH OF THE FUTURE

The Past Is Not Prologue

On the morning of January 25, 2012, in an event that felt like a cross between a Fashion Week extravaganza and one of Apple's famous product launches, JCPenney's newly appointed CEO, Ron Johnson, took the stage at New York's Pier 57. More than seven hundred industry executives, designers, merchandisers, members of the media and other luminaries had assembled there to hear Johnson lay out his plans to reinvigorate the venerable retailer.

It was a potentially Woodstock-like defining moment for a new era of retailing, with Johnson as JCPenney's Jimi Hendrix. Everyone present felt that they were part of something groundbreaking. Years from now, they'd be able to say, "I was there."

Crisply, clearly and logically, Johnson explained how he and his team were going to completely transform the department store into "America's favorite store, period."

He recalled how, back in the 1960s, department stores had it all. Using the Dayton-Hudson department store as an example of an "unbelievable experience," he described how families would spend the entire day shopping, dining and enjoying fashion shows and other festivities. He then recounted the share loss of the department-store sector as a whole over the past twenty years— much of it to specialty stores, because consumers prefer those brands and the experience over what he referred to as "tired stores," "stale presentations," "not the newest products" and "zero integrity in pricing."

He continued: "Department stores have all the competitive advantages: low real estate, big marketing budgets, lots of space," before concluding, "Something is fundamentally wrong here." Another comment was a lead-in to one of his transformative strategies: "In an Internet age where you can have exactly what you want with one keyword, people won't tolerate big stores. You have to break it down for them. When we want a great product today, we go to a specialty store like J. Crew or H&M."

Johnson's plan was to transform about seven hundred of Penney's eleven hundred stores into small, JCPenney-branded enclosed "mini-malls." A new, architecturally modern layout would house what he called "streets of branded boutiques or shops," with one hundred strong, modern brands, all in their own image—meaning JCP would be shedding about three hundred of the brands it then carried, as well as some of its own private-label brands. Johnson said, "We want private brands, not private labels." Ironically, this new approach took much of its inspiration from the very stores that stole the department store's thunder over the past thirty to forty years: the specialty chains.

The most exciting and fun attraction in this new shopping extravaganza promised to be what Johnson called a "Town Square," located in the center of the store. Here there would be events, fashion shows, eateries, cooking and other classes, a place of learning (Genius Bar, anyone?), music, videos, and so on. The surrounding "streets," in addition to shops, would be scattered with seating, coffee stands, gelato stations, popcorn vendors and more. The whole JCPenney brand would be transformed into a compelling experience so consumers would come more often, stay longer and spend more. And more importantly, if successful, JCP would become a leading example of a neurologically connecting shopping experience so compelling that it would preempt consumers from buying online—by giving them a reason to come to the fun place called JCPenney.

Penney's new business model was intended to capture a different core consumer—young millennial families—which meant it would, by design, lose part of its current customer base, particularly lower-income and older customers. Additionally, the new concept would be applicable in only about seven hundred doors. However, in those doors it was projecting a productivity rate of $300 per square foot compared to their current rate of $120, and it would be poised for growth rather than slipping into maturity and decline, which had been the case upon Johnson's arrival.

Johnson, architect of the vaunted Apple retail stores, had big plans for technology in all its forms, not only for an omni-channel strategy but also for every aspect of JCP's value chain, from sourcing to building to empowering salespeople.

A final key part of his transformative strategy was to be a bold, revolutionary "fair and square" pricing model, designed to abruptly terminate all discounting. In Johnson's opinion, "fake prices" were driving the consumer crazy in hundreds of different ways. "The fundamental flaw of department stores is the pricing strategy," he said at one point. In the prior year, Penney had held 590 separate sales, while the average customer purchased only four times a year. "So customers ignored us 99 percent of the time," he said. In their analysis, Penney found that on average, consumers were forcing prices back down to their pre-markup levels. Noting that about 75 percent of its products were selling at a 50 percent discount, Johnson said, "I thought to myself, this is desperation."

This led him to a three-pronged "fair and square" pricing strategy: (1) pricing all goods about 40 percent lower than where they currently start; (2) holding themed promotions twelve times a year, not 590; and (3) launching "Best Price Fridays," promoting sales on the first and third Fridays of every month to clear slow movers.

This grand vision, he declared with great confidence on that big stage in New York, would be initiated pretty much simultaneously, despite the barely recovering economy. He explained that simultaneous implementation was necessary because all the pieces were interconnected; if they were acted upon sequentially, it would be much more complex and possibly deleterious to achieving the whole vision. And, as evidenced by the very public disclosure of his entire strategy, there would be no quiet testing.

Across the entire JCP enterprise, the transformation began on February 1, 2012.

The first step was his revolutionary pricing strategy. Almost overnight, the company shut down all discounting, enacting the formula outlined above. And, indeed, a revolution it became. The first of thousands, maybe even millions, of JCPenney customers, who would ultimately represent billions of dollars in lost sales, walked out the door and never returned.

Scarcely a year after his Steve Jobs–like big-stage launch presentation, after JCPenney's sales had shrunk by more than $5 billion and earnings had plunged by almost $1 billion, Johnson was gone.

What was to be the biggest transformation in the history of the industry became its biggest, fastest and most-discussed failure.

There is nothing in retailing's past that would serve as a prologue to this book and to the future of retail. We are entering what we call retailing's Wave IV, in which its leaders, grappling with a new, fully birthed technology era, are attempting to address the enormous challenges it brings, hoping to turn them into equally immense opportunities. To borrow from the mantra of Amazon CEO Jeff Bezos, Wave IV is "Day One" of the future of retail. It is characterized by the explosive expansion and disruption of technologies and the Internet, with smartphones and millions of apps as its primary accelerants. It is a time of unprecedented competition, overcapacity, price deflation and uncertainty. And it is the era of the all-powerful consumer.

It was during this time, the very beginning of Wave IV, that JCPenney attempted to massively and fundamentally transform itself. However, while most experts agreed at the time that Johnson's vision was strategically transformative, its implementation was a cataclysmic failure.

Johnson made the risky bet that consumers were ready to kick their bargain-addiction habit—*cold turkey*. Worse, he introduced the new pricing strategy before the great new brands or the fully redesigned and laid-out stores with all the wonderful envisioned experiences were even in place. Thus, even if consumers were inclined to swap "deals" for "fair value," there was no new visible value in place for them to choose.

This untested pricing initiative launched overnight was arguably the primary reason for the rapid collapse of the business, which JCPenney's former CEO, Mike Ullman, is now trying to turn around.

From our perspective, since *The New Rules of Retail* was first published in 2010, we could see and totally understand Ron Johnson's vision for transforming the department-store business model. It aligned with the New Rules we laid out in that book. We discussed its similarity to what Selfridges department store had accomplished in London in the 1990s, and how the department stores in Wave I, called "palaces of consumption," provided the same kind of experiences Johnson was pursuing.

Today, as we observe the evolutionary (as opposed to revolutionary) transformation of Macy's and its Bloomingdale's division, as well as Nordstrom and a few other traditional department-store models in this book, we believe that these retail brands are actually achieving much of what Johnson had envisioned—but in a more methodical, strategically sensible way.

In this more expansive and technology-inclusive revision of the book, we strongly advise that such transformations must take place in Wave IV across all retail sectors, and that the only way they can succeed is through our (now technologically enhanced) New Rules, by creating powerful neurologically connecting experiences—online, offline and on the move; preemptively distributing one's value, digitally, physically and on multiple other platforms, 24/7; and totally controlling one's value chain—the only way to achieve the first two Rules.

We invite you to join us, then, as we charge forward into Wave IV, identifying the awe-inspiring technological enablers, enhancers and wholly new business concepts that are further empowering not only already-omnipotent consumers but retailers as well. We will take you from Johnson's "Day One" well into the future, providing a view of what new strategies and business models will be required to delight the changing and totally empowered consumer. And while the Rules (neurologically connecting experiences, preemptive distribution and value-chain control) have not changed strategically since the release of our first edition in 2010, they have been immensely expanded upon, reflecting the full-on power of the digital age.

It will quickly become obvious that nothing in retailing's past provides an adequate prologue for the transformation businesses must now go through. And transform they must, or they will be no more.

Welcome to the new *New Rules of Retail,* and enjoy the read.

PART 1

DEFINING THE FOUR WAVES OF RETAILING

CHAPTER 1

WAVE I

PRODUCER POWER

The Emergence of Organized Retail

In the late 1800s, the population of the United States was about 60 million, spread out across thirty-eight states, with 65 percent living on farms or in small towns. There were only a dozen or so cities with 200,000 or more residents, and yearly national income was about $10 billion. The Wild West was still wild, even as rail was being laid to follow the migrating population.

Despite suffering from the "Long Depression"—not as deep as the Great Depression, but longer, stretching from 1873 to 1897—the country nevertheless generated enough capital to spawn the so-called Gilded Age (1865–1900), with its infamous industrialist tycoons (called "robber barons" by some) like Jay Gould, John D. Rockefeller, Leland Stanford, Andrew Carnegie and many others, who built our railroads, drilled and distributed our oil, made our steel, launched our banking system and built the foundations of our manufacturing infrastructure. America was just beginning to understand how to harness the use of electricity and new industrial processes to accelerate production in order to provide the growing population with the products and services it really needed.

The phonograph, typewriter, telephone and electric light were introduced, and after Karl Benz's invention of the first combustion-engine automobile in

Germany in 1886, Henry Ford created the Model T Ford, ultimately replacing horse-drawn carriages. In 1913, Ford developed the concept of the assembly line, for which he was labeled the father of mass production. By the Roaring Twenties, Ford was selling hundreds of thousands of Model Ts, and still he couldn't keep up with demand.

Compare that to today, when every household has two or three cars in the driveway, yet the Big Three—General Motors, Ford and Chrysler—are not only cutting capacity but also fighting numerous global competitors for market share.

Ford's inability to keep up with demand in the 1920s occurred for several reasons. During the early years of Wave I in the mid-nineteenth century and well past the turn of the century, the period of vast industrialization, transportation and communications infrastructure-building was still in its infancy. There was limited access to goods and services because supply-side growth could not keep up with growing consumer demand. This was exacerbated by an embryonic and fragmented distribution structure and a continuously migrating population, both from east to west and from rural to urban areas. Moreover, even when there was sufficient supply, its distribution was at best uneven and inefficient, at worst nonexistent.

Other innovations were happening as well. A young German immigrant named Levi Strauss moved from New York to San Francisco to open a dry-goods store selling his newly designed rugged cotton twill pants, or blue jeans, to gold miners and farmers. Dr. John Pemberton concocted a mixture called Coca-Cola and sold it in a pharmacy in Atlanta as a tonic.

New ideas were sprouting up overseas, too. In 1856 Thomas Burberry launched a company in Hampshire, England, that would debut on the world stage in 1914 when the British War Office commissioned it to redesign the classic military officer's coat. After World War I, the trench coat caught on as a fashion item, and would become the icon of the Burberry brand for decades to come.

It was also during this time—which is considered, not coincidentally, the beginning of America's rise to global economic dominance—that two retail distribution models were conceived that would replace the then-dominant general store: the department store and the mail-order catalog.

Sears and Montgomery Ward in Wave I

Following a brief stint in the watch business, Richard Sears partnered with Alvah Roebuck in 1886 to form the classic American retailer Sears, Roebuck and Co. By 1895 it was heavily into the mail-order business, primarily targeting farmers and small-town residents, who made up the majority of the population during that period, and who had limited access to stores. It would grow bigger and succeed longer than Montgomery Ward, founded by Aaron Ward in 1872 and known affectionately for decades as "Monkey Ward's." Ward's would eventually succumb to the marketplace challenges of Wave II, as we will discuss later.

These catalogs demonstrated a brilliant distribution strategy: placing their "store" and all their products directly in the homes of all those farmers and people scattered across the country in small towns. These were people who needed things and had no other place to get them. In the truest sense of the old adage "location, location, location," these catalogs were in the consumer's face, in his living room, faster and more frequently than people's monthly

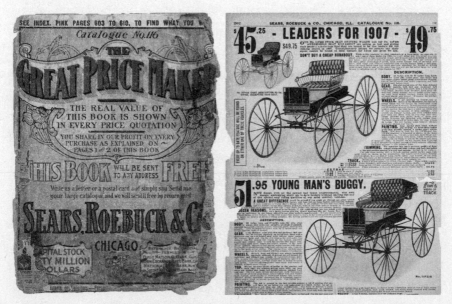

Figure 1.1   Sears Catalog pages, circa 1880.

Courtesy of Sears Holdings

treks from the farm to the general store in a town many miles away. Indeed, these companies' vision of bringing their value to the consumer was one of retailing's early and competitively innovative distribution strategies.

The Sears catalog would eventually grow to more than five hundred pages, offering everything from the cradle you rocked your babies in to the coffin you were buried in. You could even buy a readymade home with everything in it.

Today, of course, the Internet is the new catalog; however, it is not a replacement for the "old," but one of many additional distribution platforms: mobile electronic devices, kiosks, vending machines, airport stores, door-to-door selling, in-home selling events and ubiquitous stores on virtually every corner, to name a few. We live in an age of consumers having total accessibility. Therefore, retail success can no longer be just about "location, location, location."

In the early 1920s, as the population began migrating from farms to small towns, Sears and Montgomery Ward, continuing their distribution strategy of following the consumer, began opening stores in those towns. Now they had a multichannel distribution strategy, with both catalogs and stores, as well as the unique competitive advantage of offering high-quality essentials for fair and credible prices. They thus positioned themselves as the go-to stores for the growing middle class, a niche not competed for by the department stores that were growing rapidly in big cities.

The Department Stores: "Build It and They Will Come"

In 1846, an Irish-American entrepreneur named Alexander Turney Stewart opened a soft-goods store called the Marble Palace that sold European goods. Later, it would evolve into Stewart's Department Store, selling apparel, accessories, carpets, glass and china, toys and sports equipment.

In 1856, Marshall Field & Company was launched in Chicago. In 1858, Macy's was founded in New York City, followed by B. Altman, Lord & Taylor, McCreary's and Abraham & Straus. John Wanamaker opened the first Wanamaker's in Philadelphia in 1877. Zion's Cooperative Mercantile Institution (ZCMI) was opened in Salt Lake City in 1869 and became the first incorporated department store in 1870. Hudson's opened in Detroit in 1881, and Dayton's in 1902 in Minneapolis.

These and many others, most of which grew out of small general stores at the same time that their small towns became cities, would become the most dominant retail segment until well into Wave II (generally defined as 1950–2000).

These Wave I department stores were called "cathedrals" and "palaces of consumption" at the time. They became daylong outing destinations for families, at first because of their breadth of offerings, and later because of the additional sponsored entertainment, children's events, fashion shows, restaurants and more. Many of these palaces were also architecturally beautiful, using new building materials, glass technology and new heating, among other innovations.

In 1891, French entrepreneurs Joseph Tron and Joseph Léautaud opened the first "El Palacio de Hierro," or "Iron Palace," department store, selling European imported fabrics, soap and other "luxury items" in Mexico City's now-historic Zócalo Square.

In the late 1890s Kendals (now House of Fraser) and Harrods opened their first stores in Manchester and London. In Paris, two cousins, Théophile Bader

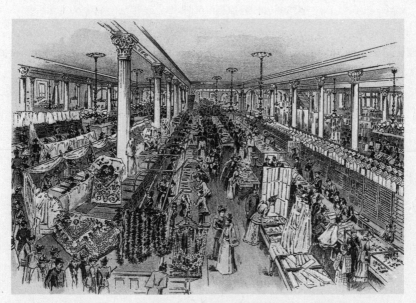

Figure 1.2   A. T. Stewart department store, mid-1850s.

Courtesy of Corbis Images

and Alphonse Kahn, opened a fashion store at the corner of rue La Fayette and the Chaussée d'Antin. Over the next decade and a half they would buy up surrounding buildings and expand Galeries Lafayette's product offerings to include home goods, gifts, toys and more.

Burgeoning retail industries began springing up in Asia, the Middle East and other parts of the world, many of which still are still dominated by the Wave I model. However, in those places the Wave II through IV evolution will occur much more quickly than it did in the United States and Europe.

Indeed, the line from the movie *Field of Dreams,* usually misquoted as "If you build it, they will come," perfectly describes the juxtaposition between the department-store distribution strategy and Sears' and Ward's original distribution model of following, and bringing their value *to,* the consumer.

We need look no further than what department stores became in Wave III, big stores loaded with so much merchandise that they were a daunting challenge for consumers. The contrast illuminates how the scarcity of competition and growing demand in Wave I provided these stores with enough pricing power, and therefore profit margins, to be able to afford all the compelling amenities that made them not just stores, but entertainment destinations.

The shifting balance between supply and demand, and how it drives changes in retail distribution models and in what it takes to be successful, is fundamental to our thesis, as we follow retail's evolution through Waves II, III and IV. Just as the early catalogs and department stores were innovative new distribution models responding to the supply-and-demand equation of the time and to real consumer needs, so too were their successors.

Ramping Up to Wave II

Despite the Great Depression, the period of Wave I from the early 1900s through World War II was one of positive economic growth, thanks to industrialization. The huge expansion of highways and railroads—indeed, of all transportation and communications—marked the birth of a modern distribution infrastructure, all centered on the growing population and its migration to the cities and suburbs.

Fueled by the growing use of innovative processes, assembly-line manufacturing and electricity, the supply side of the economy (products and services) could finally try to catch up to consumer demand. There was tremendous growth in housing, new household appliances and, of course, automobiles. All this growth would survive the severe downturn of the Great Depression and would presage the truly explosive growth after World War II and during Wave II.

Meanwhile, the retail industry continued its inexorable march on to Wave II. In 1902, James Cash Penney launched JCPenney, which would be incorporated in 1913. Despite initially offering only soft goods, and without catalog distribution, JCPenney quickly became a fierce competitor of both Sears and Montgomery Ward, with all three rapidly opening stores in small towns and suburbs, chasing after the growing American middle class. JCPenney, like its predecessors, offered high-quality basic products for a good value. This value model was exactly what enabled all three competitors to continue growing even through the Depression.

Following World War II and the subsequent explosive economic growth, Sears expanded upon its distribution strategy, following the migration of consumers to the suburbs, where it built and anchored the first regional malls, leading the way for rivals like JCPenney, Macy's, McRae's and Dillard's, all of which would also eventually anchor the rapidly expanding number of suburban shopping malls. And, to further solidify its domination of this niche, Sears vertically integrated and began to develop its own private brands (such as DieHard batteries, Kenmore appliances and Craftsmen Tools) and localize distribution, long before those concepts entered general practice.

This is the juncture, late in Wave I, when Sears began surging past its primary competitor, Montgomery Ward, which refused to enter the malls, considering them too costly. This would prove to be a fatal misstep and the beginning of Ward's long slide downward.

Sears' proactive response to the changing world around it allowed a long and powerful rise. By the early 1970s, it was one of the eight largest corporations, and one of the most powerful brands, in the world, with revenue surpassing that of the next four retailers combined. Indeed, it was more dominant, and had greater momentum, than Walmart does today.

The Downward Slide

But ultimately, like Montgomery Ward, Sears failed to see, understand and respond to the changing economic, consumer and competitive environments outside its own four walls. Sears took a great risk and reinvented its business model, but failed to strengthen it.

Ironically, latecomer JCPenney *did* evolve its business model, essentially adopting Sears' strategic advantages, such as private branding and distribution.

Sears and Montgomery Ward represent just two of many retailers whose business models and consumer value propositions were innovative and relevant to the consumer and economic environment at the time of their inception. They also evolved their competitive advantages, growing to occupy relatively dominant positions in the marketplace. However, they would ultimately represent the many chains that, after achieving such success, failed, for myriad reasons, to continue adjusting to the ever-changing economic and consumer conditions around them.

Wave I Key Market Characteristics

- **Production/Retail Driven**: Pricing power resided with manufacturers and retailers due to a dearth of competitors, a minimum and uneven level of products and services and a fragmented or nonexistent distribution infrastructure. Therefore, consumers had to accept what was available to them.

- **Production Chasing Demand**: Producers and distributors, including retailers, were all growing and expanding to chase and capture business from shifting consumer markets. With some exceptions, notably in the larger cities, supply would continue to underserve demand, primarily due to the growth of the population, including immigrants, and the migration of the citizenry from east to west and north to south, and from rural areas to small towns and cities, all challenging an embryonic, fragmented and inefficient distribution infrastructure.

- **Single-Product Specific Brands versus Cross-Category Brands**: Lack of cohesive marketing and communications infrastructure, as well as a scarcity of producers, resulted in both a limited availability of brands and their confinement to single-product categories.

- **Fragmented, Isolated Markets**: Geographically dispersed, largely rural and small-town markets, many isolated and unconnected by transportation and/or communications; therefore the distribution of goods and services, including to retailers, was at best slow, random and inefficient.

- **Fragmented Marketing**: Due to the dispersed and isolated market structure, and the lack of a national communications and media infrastructure, advertising and marketing of any type were sporadic, local, infrequent and inefficient.

Dominant Retail Models

- Freestanding department stores in cities ("palaces of consumption"), expanding later in Wave I to anchor the emerging shopping malls
- The Sears and Montgomery Ward mail-order catalogs (as responsive distribution to rural and small towns), which eventually led to their opening stores in small towns in the early 1920s
- Sears constructed and anchored the first malls, to be followed by department stores and JCPenney (founded in 1902) as additional anchors as they all raced toward Wave II and the mid-twentieth century

CHAPTER 2

WAVE II

DEMAND CREATION IN
A MARKETING-DRIVEN ECONOMY

Capitalism Unbound

There was explosive growth across all industries in the United States post–World War II and through the late 1970s, including retailing and all other consumer-facing industries, encouraged by the massive building of the nation's communications, transportation, distribution and marketing infrastructures.

By most accounts the war was the final and key factor in pulling the economy out of the Great Depression, thanks to the sheer magnitude of the effort in gearing up for global battle, both in dollars and manpower. Essentially, this effort reflated the economy. By 1945, the United States represented about 45 percent of worldwide GDP, way up from its historic norm of 25 to 28 percent. (Sadly, of course, this was also heightened by the economic devastation of much of the rest of the world.)

More important, the increased government and private investment in research and development required to accelerate industrialization and feed the war effort led to many innovations and advancements that benefited the postwar commercial economy. Advances in nuclear energy grew out of the war's Manhattan Project. Innovations in the aerospace industry were enormous: In 1958, the first commercial jet crossed the Atlantic. Radar and FM networks were war inventions. The synthetic fiber nylon, though invented in 1939 as a silk replacement in women's stockings, was used exclusively for military applications like parachutes, airplane cords and ropes during World War II. The rapid expansion in fiber-production capacity would later revolutionize the global textile industry. Cellophane film was used as a protective coating for undersea telephone, radar cables and medicine tablets during the war before becoming the leading consumer product packaging material in the 1950s and 1960s. The ability to mass-produce wonder drug penicillin was ramped up during World War II.

From Pent-Up Demand to "The American Dream"

Of course, all this innovation and growth could not have happened without an equally precipitous surge in demand. American consumers emerging from the Great Depression and World War II had an enormous, pent-up desire for a better quality of life. They aspired beyond just basic necessities to products, services and surroundings that would satisfy their dreams. In fact, it was during this fertile period that the term "American Dream" was coined. The goal of having a family, a home, a car, a steady job with benefits, a college education and all other things wonderful would be realized for millions of Americans. The new suburbia and planned communities were exemplified by Levittown in New York in the 1950s, providing tenth-of-an-acre-sized slices of paradise, many of which were financed by liberal access to GI Bill loans, to new homeowners.

Leave It to Beaver, Ozzie and Harriet, The Ed Sullivan Show and many other popular TV shows of the time fulfilled the Rockwellian ideal of tranquil families watching television together in their living rooms.

Yet if you looked outside those cozy living rooms into the undercurrents of American life, you could see the emergence of social, political and cultural trends that would have a major long-term impact on America as it marched toward the twenty-first century. Second-wave feminism, the counterculture and its resonance at Woodstock and the recognition of teens as a viable and independent cultural and economic force were among the trends changing the country. The invention of birth-control pills would usher in women's freedom and independence. The civil rights movement would be as big a step for mankind as was landing on the moon. The communist panic and the Korean

War of the 1950s would be followed by the Vietnam War and the political and social upheavals surrounding it in the 1960s. The Cold War would see a near triggering of a nuclear holocaust as the United States declared a blockade of Cuba, setting the stage for the first direct face-off with the nuclear-armed Soviet Union. The era would culminate in President Richard Nixon's resignation in 1974.

These transformative events, though enormous in their impact, failed to disrupt or even slow the pursuit of the American Dream.

Wave II in the United States brought not only unprecedented economic growth but also a huge jump in Americans' standard of living. It was a virtuous cycle of plentiful jobs providing discretionary income and therefore demand, which in turn drove the need for more production, driving the need for more jobs, driving more demand and more spending and so forth. Life was good. Life—at least on the surface—was simple. The message to the American people was clear: Work hard, be good and your dream will come true.

The Dream Begets Mass Markets and a Massive New Distribution Infrastructure

Another key factor that made the dream possible was the development of massive marketing and distribution systems. As more and more consumers chased the dream, they were forming enormous new blocs of purchasing power. Conversely, equally large product and service marketers were developing new and innovative ways to market and distribute to these consumers. Two phrases were coined to accurately describe the new market dynamics in this booming economic period: "mass markets" and "mass marketing." After all, if living the good life was the American consumer's dream, mass markets and their infinite potential for sales and profits were the capitalist's dream.

In order to serve the enormous and growing marketplace, businesses needed a vast national distribution infrastructure. This infrastructure had to be both physical, for the distribution of products and services, and strategic, for the distribution of communications, marketing and advertising. Wave II witnessed explosive growth in highway, air, rail and sea transportation, as well as the creation of multiple channels of retail distribution. And, for mass marketers, this was the golden age of advertising and national brand creation,

Figure 2.1   Tide advertisement, 1946.

Courtesy of Procter & Gamble

facilitated by the emergence of big media: nationwide access to television and the formation of the national broadcasting channels; the national consumer print media, including specialty niche magazines; catalogs; and billboards and direct-marketing mediums.

From a retail perspective, the Federal-Aid Highway Act of 1956 was a huge catalyst for all that followed. It played a key role in population migration (from rural to urban and then to suburban) and in increased mobility. It helped establish our dominant automotive industry, new retail models and the physical distribution of goods. The irony was that the original intent behind the construction of the massive US interstate highway system, a huge matrix of 45,572 miles of road, was national security. Fortunately, as it turned out, the United States never had to use it for evacuations or to mobilize troops to defend its borders against attack. However, its timing was perfect to pave the way for the explosive growth of suburbia, quickly followed by an accelerated expansion of shopping centers and large regional malls. Before World War II, there were about eight such centers. By 1970, there were four thousand.

This vast matrix of highways, shopping centers and malls, combined with automobiles and cheap gas to get to them, also accelerated the growth of national and regional retail chains. Most expansive were the two original national chain department stores, Sears and JCPenney, which realtors incentivized with attractive lease arrangements to anchor the malls, as consumer-drawing traffic builders. These malls were also to become home to many of the newly minted apparel specialty chains, the innovative branded retail model launched in the 1960s, exemplified by such pioneers as Merry-Go-Round, Esprit and Gap, and to traditional department stores like Marshall Field's, I. Magnin and Macy's, previously located in downtown areas.

Also during this period, Sam Walton had a vision that small-town America needed basic products of great value for low prices. Thus Walmart was launched. Its rural target was different from Kmart's positioning in suburban shopping centers. Growing out of the S. S. Kresge five-and-dime stores founded in 1899, Kmart was the first discounter, launched in 1962 in suburban Detroit. Target Stores was introduced in 1962 by its parent, Dayton-Hudson. It was positioned as a more upscale discounter, carrying products and brands at a price-point level just above Walmart's and Kmart's. Later, of course, it became known as standing for "cheap chic." Kohl's was also born in 1962 to cater to the boundless appetite of an expanding middle class. Later in Wave II, the big-box retailers (the so-called category killers) such as Toys "R" Us, Circuit City and Home Depot were introduced.

Both the value/discount stores and big-box category killers were massive distribution machines. Indeed, the category killers intended to do just what their name suggests—eliminate all competitors by carrying everything in one product category (such as toys, electronics, sporting or home goods) at volume-driven low prices.

The category killers and branded-apparel specialty chains, all specializing in single-product categories, along with the new discounters delivering basic, more commoditized goods, began together to win over a large share of traditionally loyal department-store customers. Their lower cost structures allowed more competitive pricing, which, combined with specialized products and services, gave these new retail models a great advantage.

So, while the department stores had the distinction of being palaces of consumption and highly enjoyable shopping experiences during Wave I, they were now facing two major strategic challenges that would begin to erode their market share: price competition from the emerging low-cost competitors; and merchandising competition from the specialists, all of which were taking share in their focused niches from the complex array of the department stores' offerings. As Wave II evolved, the pressure to reduce their operating costs began forcing the department stores to cut back on product categories, particularly those they were losing to the specialists (such as electronics, appliances and toys). Cost-cutting also reduced many amenities, services and entertainment—the very things that had made department stores compelling destinations in Wave I.

JCPenney, Sears and Montgomery Ward were especially challenged by the discounters and category killers because their own value propositions were also founded on offering basic products for great value. Their customers, therefore, were the easiest prey for the new models. While all three originally targeted smaller, underserved middle-class towns and suburbs, JCPenney and Sears continued their expansion into the malls and shopping centers of Wave II, while Ward made the strategically fatal decision not to do so. It would begin to fail in the late 1970s, and it would eventually close what was left of its retail and catalog operations in 2001.

Though Sears spearheaded and built many of the early centers and malls, rising to its preeminent position as the largest retailer in the world by the mid-1970s, it ignored the new competitors, discounters and specialists alike, that were chipping share away from every category of its business. It did not remain responsive to the changing consumer environment. Consequently, Sears continued to operate with a relatively high cost structure, failed to shed categories in which it had lost competitive advantage and began its slow descent in the early 1980s.

JCPenney expanded both its locations, into the centers and malls, and its product offerings, adding furniture, electronics and sporting goods. Essentially it converted itself into a full-service department store, albeit still serving the middle market. Unlike Sears, JCPenney responded to the market pressures, and later in Waves II and III it shed many of the categories being picked off by the category killers, specialty chains and discounters. However, it would go through a particularly rough patch when it tried to second-guess its customers' desire for value in late 2011.

As a result of the launching of these innovative new retail models, a growing economy, increased mobility, nationwide population shifts and massive new marketing and distribution systems, the latter part of Wave II would also mark the beginning of the traditional department-store sector's steady decline, which would continue into Wave IV.

Wave II as we have defined it will likely be viewed historically as the period of "nationalization" in the United States: the interconnecting of a huge national matrix of communications, transportation, distribution and marketing, all facilitating the creation, marketing and distribution of national product and service brands and national retail chains.

The Beginning of Competitive Congestion

As we've seen so far, the American Dream for consumers also became the American Dream for producers, suppliers, marketers and retailers—until it wasn't.

As more competitors emerged across all consumer-facing industries during the end of Wave II into early Wave III, and as existing companies grew larger, markets became increasingly saturated during the early 1980s. This saturation affected retail, automobiles, airlines, consumer package goods, services, travel, leisure, entertainment—virtually the entire economy. The competitive congestion began to drive disequilibrium in supply and demand and a shift in power from producers to consumers. Simply put, because of increasing supply and more efficient distribution, consumers gained greater access and improved selection. They began forcing competitors to innovate, add more value and differentiate, giving rise to such retail brands as Borders, Bed Bath & Beyond, Ann Taylor and Liz Claiborne, among many others. The market had matured to the point at which consumers needed more dream-compelling reasons to purchase one competitor's offering rather than another's.

Whereas in production-driven Wave I producers couldn't make or distribute products and services fast enough to satisfy demand, now they had to figure out how to *create* demand—how to compel consumers to choose them. "If you build it, they will come" was giving way to the new consumer chorus: "Give me a compelling reason to come to your store or to buy your brand."

Accordingly, power in the marketplace was shifting from the supply side to the demand side. It was transferred from producers, service providers and retailers to consumers.

This major paradigm shift for all consumer-facing industries from a production-driven to a marketing-driven economy meant that marketing became the primary strategic driver across the entire marketplace. It also spawned whole new businesses in the advertising, media and communications industries.

Known as the golden age of advertising, and glorified in the popular television show *Mad Men,* Wave II was arguably the most commercially creative era in American history. If consumers demanded compelling reasons to buy brands, they would get them in spades.

A Golden Age: The Rise of Innovation, Branding and Advertising

The American Dream was kept aloft by the dual forces of consumer desire for new, more and better, and consumer-facing industries' ingenuity in creating new, more and better products and services.

However, the real engine driving this growth, and the engine necessary to create demand for one's product or service, was marketing—more specifically, branding and advertising.

You could see product promotion on the three big television networks (ABC, NBC and CBS) and in magazines like *Time, Sports Illustrated, Life, Look, Collier's, Saturday Evening Post, Glamour, Cosmopolitan* and others. Deeper into Wave II (during the 1970s and '80s), segmented marketing targeting focused demographic groups was born, supported by special-interest magazines like *Ebony, Rolling Stone, Mad, Jet, Mother Jones, National Lampoon* and others.

Big brands were expanding nationwide, and new brands were sprouting almost daily from leading consumer product companies such as Procter & Gamble, R. J. Reynolds, Coca-Cola, Levi Strauss & Co., General Motors, Ford, Timex, Playtex, Anheuser-Busch, General Mills, Gap and hundreds more.

Finally, this era marked the emergence of the biggest engines of all: the now-iconic advertising agencies, big and small, that are credited with creating the cleverest, funniest, sincerest and most compelling messages to consumers in America's history. DDB, BBDO, Ogilvy & Mather, J. Walter Thompson, Leo Burnett, Grey Advertising, McCann Erickson, Ted Bates & Co., Wells Rich Greene and Kenyon & Eckhardt were but a few of the giants of that era. Together they turned out such legendary spokespersons, ads and slogans as the Marlboro Man, "Nothing gets between me and my Calvins," "I'd walk a mile for a Camel," "Hey Mabel, Black Label," "Fall into the Gap," "It's the real thing," "Plop, plop, fizz, fizz," "Ring Around the Collar" and "Flick my Bic," among others.

In retailing, Gap began its meteoric rise from a little shop in San Francisco selling Levi's Jeans to the largest private-label branded-apparel retailer in the world. Others, such as Esprit, have diminished in their American presence but remain strong international brands. A third group, including Merry-Go-Round (one of the first specialists), is no longer in business at all.

Interestingly, the success or failure of these early specialists was all a result of how they operationally executed what will be described later in this book as our three strategic principles of superior value-chain control, preemptive distribution and an irresistible consumer experience. At their inception, it's unlikely they would have defined their models on those principles, or they might have articulated them differently. However, with or without their understanding, the specialty business models were, and still are to a very large extent, the quintessential example of our thesis.

Ralph Lauren: A Wave II Visionary

From among the iconic national brands being launched almost daily, and the existing brands being built to enormous scales, a true branding visionary emerged during the 1960s. Ralph Lauren was born Ralph Lifshitz in 1939 in the Bronx, a few years before another Bronx-born brand genius, Calvin Klein. Lifshitz changed his surname to Lauren at the age of sixteen, the first of many steps he would take to create the life he aspired to. After a couple of years at a local college studying business, Lauren got a job selling clothing at Brooks Brothers. In 1967, he began selling his own necktie designs to major department stores. Most brands during Wave I and most of Wave II were single-product category brands, such as Levi's Jeans, Coca-Cola, Tide detergent, and Lucky Strike cigarettes. All these great brands spent millions of dollars on marketing, advertising and publicity, pushing their single-product message about the product's actual benefits into consumers' minds.

Ralph Lauren's Polo brand, on the other hand, did not emanate from a product. It grew out of his vision of a Gatsby-like world where he and his brand would play a dominant role. As seen in his advertising, and even in his head-quarters on Manhattan's Madison Avenue, the entire imagery of his brand powerfully communicates that lifestyle. Lauren's brand emanated from his dream of an elegant and sophisticated world in which hundreds of elegant and sophisticated men, women and children are all using hundreds of elegant and sophisticated products, all branded Ralph Lauren. He was fond of saying, "I don't design clothes, I design dreams." Rather than slapping his name on a bunch of different products, he attached his name to a lifestyle, which repre-sented the dream he wanted to share with his customers.

The Wave II shift from single-product brands to lifestyle brands rein-forced the power of the perceived or emotional benefits that a brand could offer consumers, which would eventually supplant tangible product benefits such as fit, price and performance. Ralph Lauren was the first to use the power of dreams to create demand for a brand, compelling consumers away from the single-product-driven competition.

For example, when you hear or read the brand name Levi's, you think of blue jeans. When you hear or read the brand name Ralph Lauren or Polo, it conjures up images in your mind, almost like a movie that you dream of be-ing in. And since his brand's inception more than fifty years ago, the pictures used in his advertising have done their job—coaxing countless consumers to enter the Ralph Lauren lifestyle and buy it all, from Polo pants to Polo paint. Conversely, Levi's created blue jeans and put them into pictures (ads) that they spent millions of dollars on, for about a hundred years, indelibly burning into the minds of consumers that the Levi's brand stands for blue jeans.

Thus, the lifestyle branding model launched by Ralph Lauren in Wave II was superior in two respects to that of the single-product-category brands like Levi's Jeans: first, a lifestyle permits the brand to offer multiple products pro-vided they fit the brand's particular lifestyle positioning (from pants to paint, yet both within the same imagery); and second, a lifestyle permits the brand to create products for all consumer segments, from men to women and children, provided they fit the brand's lifestyle imagery.

Despite numerous attempts over many years of attaching its brand to sportswear, jackets and other products in order to reposition the brand as a lifestyle, Levi's remains a blue-jeans brand, even with its chain of retail stores that sell other casual-wear items.

Marvin Traub's Bloomingdale's:
A Retail Game-Changer

If Ralph Lauren was a lifestyle brand visionary, the late Marvin Traub, CEO of Bloomingdale's during Wave II, was his equal on the retail side. In fact, it was Marvin who gave Ralph his start by allowing the "lifestyle" presentation of Ralph's line in what was mostly likely the first shop-in-shop in the department-store industry.

Bloomingdale's broke new ground in elevating the shopping experience, initiating a strategy of creating a continuous series of themed events during the 1980s, many of them based on the cultures of countries around the world. "A Mediterranean Odyssey," one of many such themes kicked off by black-tie parties attended by local and national luminaries, featured indigenous products, fashions and artifacts from the various Mediterranean countries. Some of these promotions lasted a month or longer and transformed the Fifty-ninth Street store in Manhattan into a kind of experiential bazaar.

It was this kind game-changing vision by Marvin Traub that gave credence to the advertising slogan: "Bloomingdale's: Like No Other Store in the World."

The Bridge to Wave III

Another interesting take on Wave II, one that business leaders of the time would likely agree on, is that it was a time when conducting business was actually easy relative to later years, because there was lots of white space and opportunity for real, organic growth. While competition was heavy, markets were not oversaturated to the extent they would be in Wave III, when the battle for market share in a slow-to-no-growth economy would become ferocious. Indeed, in Wave II, the ad guys on Madison Avenue could enjoy a three-martini lunch with clients and still make their numbers. In Wave III, they would be lucky to squeeze in a sandwich at their desks while working ten-hour days just to keep up with the competition.

In closing the chapter on Wave II, we reemphasize the forces that drove this period of enormous and unprecedented growth. It would not have been possible without mass marketing, advertising, communications, distribution and all that uniquely American brand building and demand creation.

Wave II Key Market Characteristics

- **Marketing Driven**: As the overabundance of Wave II grew beyond the bare needs of consumers, producers and retailers were forced to create demand and to create compelling reasons for consumers to shop at their stores and/or buy their brands.
- **Demand Creation**: The economy, and with it retailing, shifted from being production-driven and chasing demand in Wave I to marketing-driven and demand-creating in Wave II.
- **Lifestyle Branding**: Similarly, there was explosive growth in brands across all industries. Such competitive congestion also required brands to become more compelling, to lure consumers away from competitors. Lifestyle brands, the first of which was launched by Ralph Lauren, would therefore begin to gain an advantage over the less-compelling single-product or single-category brands.
- **Mass Markets**: As the population migrated to the fast-growing cities and suburbs, and as communications, distribution and marketing infrastructures expanded to serve these huge blocs of purchasing power, the term "mass markets" was coined.
- **Mass Marketing**: The launch of television and the national broadcast and print media spawned a similarly explosive growth in advertising and other forms of communications, giving birth to the apt description "mass marketing" in Wave II.

Dominant Retail Models

- Major expansion of traditional and national chain department stores, specialty chains and discounters across the country

- Sears and JCPenney as anchors to strip centers and regional malls
- Launch and accelerated growth of apparel specialty retailing chains to fill in rest of mall
- Launch and growth of Kmart, Walmart and Target
- Launch of big-box category-killer retailers such as Toys "R" Us, Home Depot, Bed Bath & Beyond and Circuit City
- Launch of specialty catalog sector—Lands' End, Lillian Vernon, etc.—precursors of e-commerce
- Demise of downtown shopping areas

CHAPTER 3

WAVE III

APPROACHING TOTAL CONSUMER POWER

On the Edge of Transformation

Wave III, which began in the early 1980s and lasted until around 2010, marked the penultimate phase of one of the most important economic shifts in history—called "an enormous global power shift from producers to consumers, from those who make, to those who buy," by Professor Rosabeth Moss Kanter of the Harvard Business School.[1] The forcefulness of that statement points to a new consumer and marketplace paradigm. The power shift described by Kanter was driven by easier, smarter, cheaper and quicker access to an increasing abundance of goods, services and information.

More and Cheaper Access

According to the International Council of Shopping Centers (ICSC), the share of total retail space accounted for by the shopping-center industry has grown every year for the last three decades, despite four recessions. There were 7.5 billion square feet of shopping-center space in 2013, more than double the 3.3 billion in 1980. This figure has grown more than twice as fast as the average 1 percent rate of population growth during the same period. There are now more than 20 square feet of shopping-center space for every man, woman and child in the United States. To put that into a global context, the United

Kingdom is a runner-up with 3 square feet per capita. That's pretty staggering, especially considering that these numbers measure only the roughly 32,000 largest shopping centers of more than 50,000 square feet, or 33 percent of the total gross leasable space. If the other 67 percent of small shopping centers and freestanding retail space were taken into account, total square footage in the United States would be about 22 billion, or an incredible 68 square feet per capita.[2]

One of the factors driving much of this Wave III expansion in retail space was the emergence and expansion of discounters like Walmart, of big-box stores and wholesale discount clubs like Costco and Sam's Club and of category killers like Home Depot, Lowe's, Barnes & Noble, Best Buy, Linens 'n Things, Toys "R" Us, Blockbuster Video and others. There was also accelerated expansion in many other categories, such as fast-food purveyors Starbucks and Dunkin' Donuts and dollar stores like Family Dollar and Dollar General.

In terms of "cheaper access," Wave III was also the period during which globalization was becoming a reality, particularly as industries in the United States and other developed countries began sourcing the manufacturing of their products to low-cost developing countries, particularly to China. In fact, by the end of Wave III, more than 95 percent of all textiles and apparel sold in the United States was made in the various low-cost-manufacturing countries and regions (China, Vietnam, Bangladesh, Indonesia, Latin and South America and others). This resulted in a massive reduction in costs and prices across the marketplace. For example, the average cost for manufacturing a T-shirt in 1989 was $4.90, but by 2005 it had dropped to under $2.50. The cost of manufacturing a pair of denim jeans dropped from over $16.60 in 1990 to under $8.00 in 2013.[3]

The Behemoth of Bentonville

We would be remiss if in our discussion of Wave III we failed to address the impact that Walmart's expansion had on the meteoric growth of retail selling space and the surge in abundance of goods on the American retailing landscape. Despite his far-reaching vision, Sam Walton probably could not have foreseen what Walmart would become to the retail world. Walmart's growth, particularly in the United States, was achieved by expanding and scaling its everyday-low-price model in the 1980s by opening huge, inexpensively con-structed stores in rural areas throughout the South and Southwest, where land was cheap. By 1990 it had become the most profitable retailer in the United States.

In the 1990s, Walmart began to evolve from a regional retailer to a truly national one, entering every market it profitably could, with Walmarts, Sam's Clubs and Supercenters building larger and larger stores containing ever-increasing quantities of product. From 1990 to 2010 Walmart caused a retooling in just about every consumer product market, from apparel to food. Compa-nies hoping to do business with the retailer would do everything in their power to take cost, waste and inefficiencies out of their products and processes.

By 2010, essentially the end of Wave III, the Bentonville, Arkansas–based retailer's sales had exceeded $400 billion (more than double the total annual sales of Target, Macy's, TJX, Kohl's, JCPenney, Gap and Limited *com-bined*), a number that has since grown to almost $480 billion, which works out to $1.3 billion every day and makes Walmart the world's largest retailer and the biggest company in the Fortune 500. In addition to more than 4,000 doors in the United States, the company had 2,700 units in China, Brazil, Canada, Mexico and many other countries around the globe. With 1.9 mil-lion employees, Walmart had grown to be the retail industry's single-largest employer and employed more people than anyone in the country except the US government.

Local economies where a Walmart opens feel "the Walmart effect," a term that has come to mean the economic impact felt by local businesses when a large firm such as Walmart opens in the area. The Walmart effect usually manifests itself as smaller retail firms losing market share, trying to restructure their costs and eventually disappearing. Many local businesses oppose the introduction of Walmarts into their areas for this reason. How-ever, given the company's superior distribution, it was a driving force in cre-ating cheaper and easier access. It also raised the bar for the definition of operational excellence.

However, one competitive sector, the dollar stores, not only would sur-vive Walmart's onslaught but would also copy some of its best practices and position a differentiated retail model that would begin to steal a big portion of Walmart's market share by the end of Wave III. The dollar-store model primarily consisted of a multitude of smaller stores located in neighborhoods closer to where their core consumers lived, thus providing more convenient and fuel-saving accessibility for lower-income customers. The dollar-store model also accommodated the more frequent "paycheck to paycheck," smaller-transaction-size shopping favored by cash-strapped consumers, particularly during the Great Recession.

The Rise of Outlet Malls and Off-Pricers

Another retail model that hit its stride in Wave III was the outlet store. Outlet stores called factory stores date back to the 1930s, but the first multistore outlet mall, opened by the Vanity Fair lingerie company, known as VF Corporation today, opened in Reading, Pennsylvania, in 1974. Belz Enterprises opened the first enclosed factory outlet mall in 1979, in a suburb of Memphis, Tennessee. Outlets grew along with the increase in the general public's awareness of and desire for designer labels and the increased importance of value. More in-season merchandise would be available in outlet stores. Throughout the 1980s and '90s, both outdoor and enclosed outlet malls experienced rapid growth, growing from about 50 malls in 1980 to 183 by 1990. By the end of Wave III, that number would grow to more than 225.[4] Most of the malls were built "off the beaten path" so that their discounted prices wouldn't negatively affect their full-priced business at regional malls and downtown shopping areas. Even today, busloads of tourists and residents travel from cities to spend the day at outlet malls like Woodbury Commons in Upstate New York, the San Marcos outlet center outside Austin, Texas, and others. Some brands, like London Fog, Van Heusen and Calvin Klein, have essentially built their businesses on the outlet channel. Despite the heavy promotions at conventional retail channels, the outlets—with their extreme values, surprise finds and entertainment features—remain a tremendously popular retail option.

Off-price stores like Marshalls, Ross Stores, Burlington Coat Factory and others were also founded at different points in Wave III, and grew along with the insatiable American appetite for value and designer brands. These stores tended to sell distressed, overstock or out-of-season merchandise that department and specialty stores were no longer interested in but that consumers were only too eager to snap up.

Cheap Money

Fueling the retail expansion during Wave III was a massive increase in liquidity in the financial markets, much of which was used to support marginally performing stores that would otherwise have closed. Retailers' rationale for keeping these underperforming stores open was that despite their lower profitability, they still contributed minimally, while their closure would have been a net reduction to growth. Furthermore, as consumer spending continued to rise, retailers reasoned that the promise of future sales would offset the current lower returns from underperforming stores.

Along with this industry-wide use of excess liquidity to maintain poorly performing stores in pursuit of increasing share of a slow-growing and highly competitive market, retailers also used access to easy financing to open stores with lower returns on capital. In some cases—the Steve & Barry's apparel chain is the most pronounced example—entire business models were created on the basis of attractive financing arrangements that more than covered low or nonexistent operating profits.

Figure 3.1   Retail saturation. The US retail market is overdeveloped relative to other markets.

Source: Cushman & Wakefield; KSA research and analysis

And, of course, all these rapidly growing shopping centers and the stores within them were not empty. They were full of products and services, which also indicated that supply-side growth had outpaced demand and population growth.

Today, one need only scan through any of the major print or broadcast media, or eyeball the seemingly infinite stream of new brands in the stores and malls, to get a sense of how much the overload of "stuff" has outpaced demand. A few anecdotal facts also support the idea of an imbalance. In 1980, there were about six major blue-jean brands. Today, there are at least eight hundred. There were about fifty major apparel brands in 1980, and our projections are that there are more than four thousand today. In 1947, there were roughly twenty automobile brands in the world; today, according to Kelley Blue Book, there are eighty-five. And while worldwide production capacity for automobiles is 90 million, there is demand for only 60 million, according to the International Organization of Motor Vehicle Manufacturers. Tide detergent was a single branded product in Wave II; today, there are almost forty Tide sub-brands, including Ultra Tide, Tide To Go, Tide Boost, Tide Free and, in what many consider one of the biggest packaging innovations in the twenty-first century, Tide Pods single-load packs.

While such explosive growth in brands across all industries was obviously intended to capture a share of additional market segments, this expansion would not have been possible without globalization and the reallocation of resources worldwide, combined with new technologies and greatly increased productivity (the ability to make more for less). These dynamics facilitated the more efficient and effective distribution of the ever-increasing number of brands and services.

Quicker and Easier Access

Accelerating the growth of retail space and the number of product and service brands to fill that space was the onset of new technologies and their more sophisticated implementation, providing a multiplicity of new, more rapid and more responsive distribution platforms. Internet retailing was launched (with countless sites, including the behemoth eBay), which led to the onset of mobile and social commerce. TV retailing took off, most notably with HSN and QVC.

Specialty direct-mail brands like J. Crew, Talbots, Lands' End and L.L.Bean were a Wave III phenomenon, and enjoyed rapid sales growth as consumers sought convenience and the enjoyable shopping experiences that these catalogs, many of which looked like beautiful lifestyle magazines, offered. And door-to-door sales, pop-up stores, and in-home and event marketing all continued to grow. Hundreds of new branded specialty chains were born, along with new consumer product brands and services of all types, and expansive sub-branding and licensing of brands across all consumer industries. Differentiated specialty grocery stores like Whole Foods, Trader Joe's, Sprouts, Mrs. Green's and others began to feed the demand for differentiated food products like healthy, gourmet, local and prepared meals. Moreover, aided by new information technologies, consumer-facing businesses could instantaneously identify where and when demand existed and track sales as they happened. The new distribution technologies also enabled businesses to immediately respond and deliver to those demands. The fastest-growing retail model in Wave III was the small, independently owned boutiques in neighborhoods close to their consumers. Large retailers adopted the strategy of spinning off smaller neighborhood-store formats to provide their consumers quicker and easier access.

Smarter Access

The expansion of information and communications media in Wave III, particularly the explosive growth of the Internet, was unprecedented, giving consumers instant access to virtually all the information and knowledge they would ever need with the tap of a key.

Although electronic computers had been around since the 1950s, when UNIVAC and IBM first began selling huge digital processing units to governments and business, personal use of computers didn't really start until the late sixties. Hewlett-Packard, Compaq and Apple were among the first producers of desktop workstations. In 1982, the Internet Protocol Suite (TCP/IP) was standardized and first used by government and academia. In the late eighties, commercial ISPs that would forever change commerce, culture and society were launched.

JCPenney was one of the earliest retailers to use technology in its back end, transmitting orders to vendors through Electronic Data Interchange, or

EDI, and requesting that all its suppliers get up to speed, so to speak, on this nascent technology. The use of computer-aided design and manufacturing was also gaining momentum, and allowed brands to communicate with their domestic and off-shore manufacturers more quickly and accurately, resulting in a slow but steady shortening of lead times and collapse in the supply chain.

Technology was changing communication as well. In 1981, IBM launched PROFS, its mainframe-based mail system that would eventually become Lotus Notes. Though still a very rudimentary and cumbersome system compared to today's email, it revolutionized the way many organizations and individuals communicated with each other.

By 2010, there were an estimated 200 million websites and counting, a number that is now closer to a billion.[5] There were hundreds of TV channels, compared to only a handful in the early years of Wave II, and myriad trade and consumer print media, most serving arcane niches. Mobile electronic devices, still in their infancy, were on the verge of explosive expansion.

Consider this fact: Between 1999 and 2002, the amount of information communicated in the form of print, film, magnetic and optical storage was equivalent to 37,000 Libraries of Congress (each of which holds 22 million books). That amount of information is equivalent to a thirty-foot-high stack of books for each of the world's more than 7 billion people. Yet between 2002 and 2013, it is estimated to have grown more than tenfold.[6]

On a pragmatic level, as Wave III drew to a close, shoppers would soon be able in a matter of seconds to search and compare prices, quality and the performance or style of a particular item or service, which not only made them more intelligent shoppers but also eliminated hours of physical effort and transportation costs. While shopping in a given store, consumers were now able to compare the price on a product with the prices on the same product in all other stores in the area on their smartphones and tablets. There is a technology called Meality that scans shoppers' body dimensions for apparel and then prints out a report advising which brands in a given mall will best fit that shopper. Retailers also began to use data on consumers collected from loyalty program participation, geo-fencing, apps for cross-selling other products, apps for scanning UPC or QR codes that trigger videos of the product story of other information and other burgeoning technologies to assist consumers and retailers.

Consumer Power on Steroids

Simply put, in Wave III consumers began to have unbridled and instantaneous access to an unlimited selection of anything and everything they wanted, anywhere. Thousands of equally compelling retailers, products, brands or services were available at their fingertips, across the street or delivered to their front door. And these products and services were getting newer and less expensive every day.

Because of this growing power over the marketplace, consumer behavior began to change. Retailers either had to fulfill consumers' deepest desires or watch them walk out the door to a competitor across the street or tap into a search engine to gain access to any one of thousands of equally compelling products or services. And the revolution was just beginning.

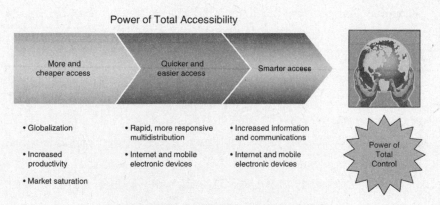

Figure 3.2   Power of total accessibility

Wave III Key Market Characteristics

- **Consumer-Driven**: Enormous global power shift from producers to consumers, from those who make to those who buy, due to more access to product.
- **Growth in Supply Begins to Outpace Demand**: Total square footage of retail selling space doubles, growing more than twice as fast as the US population.

- **Quicker and Easier Access**: Rapid growth in direct-mail (catalog), e-commerce and TV retailing, and a major push in use of technology to increase back-end efficiency.
- **Cheap Money**: Retail expansion was fueled by an increase in financial market liquidity.
- **Brand Proliferation**: Increase in the number of consumer product suppliers and brands. The number of blue-jean brands grew from six in 1980 to eight hundred in 2010. Tide detergent was a single product in Wave II; today there are around forty Tide sub-brands.

Dominant Retail Models

- **Mass Merchants:** Walmart expands nationally, reaches $400 billion in sales by 2010, dwarfing other retailers. Costco and Target also expand significantly
- **Dollar Stores:** Family Dollar, Dollar General and others offering incredible value dramatically grow their footprints
- **Category Killers**: Home Depot, Best Buy, Linens 'n Things, Toys "R" Us and Bed Bath and Beyond begin to dominate in home, electronics and toys, causing department stores to shed many of those categories and focus on apparel
- **Specialty Catalogs:** Lands' End, Eddie Bauer, J. Crew and Talbots all expand
- **Outlet Stores and Off-Pricers:** TJX, Ross, etc., gain momentum, mirroring American consumers' growing demand for designer and lifestyle brands and value
- **Differentiated Grocery:** Whole Foods, Trader Joe's, The Fresh Market, Sprouts and others all start to gain substantial share

CHAPTER 4

WAVE IV

TECHNOLOGY EXPLODES:
THE JOBSIAN AND BEZOSIAN ERA

During the early part of Wave III, the Internet and all the new technology innovations seemed to be evolving at an orderly and digestible pace. Then, in the early 2000s, there were signs that this stable evolution was about to tip into a full-blown revolution. Indeed, by mid-decade, it was as if Silicon Valley woke up and realized that the "next big thing" was in retailing. The explosion of technology, empowering both consumers and retailers, ushered in a new wave in consumer commerce.

The telltale signs: Amazon accelerates its Pacman-like expansion into multiple retail and distribution platforms (eschewing profits for scale, to "get big fast," according to Jeff Bezos' "Day One" mantra), including a huge investment in and early bet on cloud technologies to support its growth; Apple accelerates its retail-store expansion, reaching critical mass and becoming the Starbucks-like "third place" for computer lovers (and the most productive retailer in history, anywhere); eBay wakes up to the Amazon phenomenon and totally repositions its original auction model to become a disrupter in its own right by acquiring GSI Commerce, which it would rename eBay Enterprise, and by rapidly expanding its PayPal business and other technologies to connect with the consumer more quickly, easily and experientially; Google begins to transform the way retailers market to consumers; and the social networking site Facebook debuts, with visions of e-commerce dancing in founder Mark Zuckerberg's head. These are just a few of the major players behind the earliest rumblings.

Then, late in the decade, the lid blew, and the most profound transformation in the history of retail was on the technological equivalent of steroids. And the single most powerful accelerant that ignited this revolution, and paved the way for the limitless creation of empowering tools for consumers and the industries that serve them, was the smartphone.

Originally launched in 1993 by IBM and Bell South, but not really ready for prime time until the electrifying introduction of the first Apple iPhone in 2007, the smartphone's onset was a watershed moment in Wave IV, and has had a profound impact on driving the New Rules of Retail forward ever since.

Had the smartphone not been invented, computers and the Internet would have been limited as tools of consumption, similar to that of the stationary telephone or TV. Regarding e-commerce, the Internet alone would be nothing more than a giant, sophisticated catalog, with the store, so to speak, digitally distributed to your PC, perhaps even in several locations. But a smartphone in the hands of consumers gives them entrée, not only to all retail stores and all of commerce but also to, well . . . the entire world: unlimited and instantaneous access wherever they are, whenever they want it, however they want it and how often they want it. The invention of the smartphone was a game-changer that moved the Internet from a PC-centric system to a mobile-centric one.

Of even greater significance was the fact that the smartphone opened the floodgates to the creation of more applications, or apps, than the human mind can even imagine today. There are currently more than two million, with more being launched every day.

It's as though the consumer were the storied Clark Kent, the mild-mannered newspaper reporter, until he entered the phone booth and changed into Superman. Except in this case, it was the smartphone booth. And the smartphone turned the consumer into a superconsumer.

Wave IV also represents the third and most significant commercial phase of the Internet and technology. The first phase, early in Wave III, was about unlocking incredible efficiencies and speed at the back end of the supply chain, which also opened the path to globalization. The second phase was its use to deliver information and the advent of e-commerce in the 1990s. And now, in its third phase—what we are calling the "Jobsian and Bezosian Era"—we are witnessing the powerful convergence of the "art and science" of retailing at the front end of the supply chain, using the power of the Internet and new marketplace technologies to connect, watch, track and engage consumers with compelling experiences in the new high-tech, high-touch world of retailing.

If consumers in Wave III had the power of unlimited and instantaneous access, and thus control over the marketplace, in Wave IV they are omnipotent. To respond and cater to this superconsumer, retailers are using this wave of technology to adopt new strategies and business models. And those who do not, or cannot do so, will eventually disappear.

Smartphone Apps: Just the Beginning

We are in an era in which, every day, more power is accruing to the consumer. By the time this revised book is published and released, there will be a multitude of new consumer- and retail-empowering technologies.

A snapshot of a shopping day with a couple we'll call John and Sarah only begins to describe the one-to-one, personalized connectivity between retailer and consumer that not only is possible in Wave IV but will become commonplace as new technologies take this connection to ever-higher levels.

These technologies are possible because John and Sarah have given permission to a select group of retailers, brands, products, services, information and entertainment media to connect with them. They have done this through their lifestyle's behavioral patterns, which have been identified and recorded at browsing or transactional points of contact, allowing both online and retail stores and other entities to create a more personalized, higher-touch, superior experiential connection with them. This is the Big Data collection and analytics that permit Amazon or Macy's, for example, to know what a young working mom in an upscale suburb of Chicago buys, where she eats, what movies she likes to watch, her music preferences, favorite charities and other information.

A (Shopping) Day in the Life

While finishing breakfast on a Saturday morning, John does a mobile search for custom-fitted pants and discovers Bonobos, Etsy and eBay. He also sees that the Bonobos brand is sold in his local Nordstrom store and decides to head right over, thinking maybe he'll pick up a couple of shirts as well. On his way, he gets a text from The North Face via its geo-fencing app, which knows John is within a certain distance from its store (which he permitted them to do, since he is a frequent and loyal customer), telling him a new backpack has just arrived that is perfect for his hiking treks. Since The North Face is on his way to Nordstrom, he decides to check it out. As he enters the North Face, the store's location-based tracking system tells the manager that John has arrived. Since they have his purchase history and understand his preferences, once he has considered the new backpack, they can begin to suggest other items they know he might like.

While experiencing the power of technology used by The North Face to more effectively engage him and make the sale, John also experiences how the technology empowered him. It becomes his curator, selecting and permitting only those things he enjoys. This connection is just one example of how Wave IV technology represents a new "science" of retailing, which is also converging with the experiential engagement and connectivity—what we are calling the "art" of retailing.

John's shopping experience at the North Face store is also enhanced by streaming videos on LED screens of people skiing, hiking and mountain climbing, along with the attendant sounds of nature and action. Coffee is served, and knowledgeable associates discuss the history of the new backpack, its detailing and how it's customized for serious climbers like John. All these elements constitute the art, or "high touch," of the retail experience.

On to Nordstrom, where John, with not too much time left before his lunch date with Sarah, enters a fit-scanning booth in the mall, where, fully clothed, he gets scanned in ten seconds and is issued a report that lists all the pant brands and sizes in Nordstrom that would best fit him. He texts his Nordstrom personal sales associate, who, by the time he enters the store, has a selection of pants waiting for him to try on. His time running short, John asks to have the pants delivered so he can try them on at home. He promises to return those he doesn't want and will pay online for the pair he keeps. Running to lunch, John passes a Best Buy and remembers a flat screen TV that was recommended to him by Amazon. He quickly runs in, goes to the TV department of the store, and scans the barcode of the television in question. The showrooming app on his smartphone tells him about five other stores where he can find the TV cheaper. The Best Buy associate sees what he is doing and tells him they will match whatever the lowest price is. He engages John in a very brief and friendly discussion and tells John he will personally deliver the TV to his home for evening viewing. The Best Buy associate employed The Yacobian Group's Blue Day technology and Big Data process, which manages both the efficiency and effectiveness of sales associates' interactions with customers, enhancing the overall shopping experience which in turn yields increased sales and profits.

Sarah has an interesting and productive morning as well. While leaving the house, she keys in a code on her smartphone that orders her favorite large latte and a cranberry muffin for pickup in ten minutes at the Starbucks on her way to the mall. The app on her phone alerts the Starbucks barista that Sarah has arrived to pick up her order and automatically charges her through a digital wallet. Not having to wait in line, she had time to stop in her local drugstore to pick up a couple of items she had been alerted about via an online circular, with ads that were personalized for her.

Upon leaving the drugstore, she receives a text from her sister in London, who, while shopping in the Burberry flagship on Regent Street, found a handbag that she thought had "Sarah's name all over it." Sure enough, Sarah finds the bag using her Burberry mobile app. She "tries it on" virtually, using the augmented-reality feature of the Burberry mobile site, and orders it for pickup in the store at the nearby mall.

With about an hour to go before she needs to meet John for lunch, Sarah heads to the mall. Passing through Nordstrom, she spots a beautiful scarf by a designer she has never heard of. She scans the barcode with her smartphone, which takes her to a YouTube video featuring a narrative by the designer describing the scarf's pattern and fabric, where it was made and the story behind its inspiration. Sarah is also able to link in several of her Facebook friends, who all "like" the scarf. After taking a photo of herself in the store wearing the scarf and posting it on Pinterest, she buys it, asks the Nordstrom sales associate to email her the receipt, and continues on through the mall.

After picking up the Burberry bag, Sarah stops at Macy's to check out a new collection of authentic global cooking tools. The next day is John's birthday, and she wants to make him his favorite dinner. She then attends an INC fashion show, which one of her colleagues at work had texted her about earlier in the day along with three outfit ideas she had for her, knowing Sarah's preferences.

So, standing in front of a virtual fashion mirror, Sarah downloads (using hand gestures) the colleague's recommendations so that the outfits appear on Sarah's body, allowing her to see how they would look and fit in real life. On her way out she realizes she needs some lipstick and body lotion, so she stops by Macy's touchscreen interactive beauty kiosk to get some suggestions without wasting time with an associate. Sarah buys an outfit, some beauty products and a couple of items for which coupons appeared on her smartphone as she arrived at the store. She checks out in a matter of minutes with a biometric scanner, since cash registers are barely used anymore in Macy's. On her way out of the mall, she passes the Tory Burch store and remembers her sister's birthday. At this point, totally out of time, Sarah uses the store's front window, which is actually a touchscreen, to order a pair of sandals, and has them sent, along with a gift receipt, to her sister's home outside London. Of course, before shipping the sandals, the store will check its database to make sure Sarah has ordered the correct size and color for her sister, based on her sister's prior purchases and preferences, and will notify Sarah by text if she should adjust her order.

After lunch, before heading to their next appointments, John and Sarah spend time on John's tablet, where they visit their grocery store remotely, using an online system of webcams and robots that travel across the store's produce and meat sections, allowing them to select the pieces of fruit, vegetables and meat they will have delivered that day, along with the regular delivery of staples they buy on a subscription basis from a low-cost warehouse distributor.

That evening, while their children are doing their homework and playing learning games on their tablet devices, Sarah watches a streaming video on the HDTV in the couple's kitchen, learning how to make John's favorite Thai dish with the new utensils and kitchen tools she purchased at Macy's earlier that day.

While she does that, John is in the next room, listening to the voice emanating from his personalized global communications center, an audio stream of information that he has permitted in the evenings. He has been driving a BMW for two years. The voice reminds him of the mileage he has accumulated and then informs him there are two great models he might like to check out.

Porsche has also been permitted into his space, and it describes its newest models. The messages are totally informational, with no hype. Later, however, as he's watching a documentary on his favorite sport, car racing, John taps the pause button to permit a three-minute "infotainment" segment, a hyped-up, Hollywood-level piece, dramatizing the performance of the new 911, all with special effects and music and in HD.

The Wave IV consumer's entire working, social and leisure life will be punctuated with these sorts of customized and controlled, or permitted, communications. In this new communications model, which has replaced traditional advertising, businesses will be permitted to enter the consumer's life, or space, only with either factual, informative/educational or entertaining messages. However, all these messages will be customized to the individual's needs, wants and lifestyle. And all will be delivered when, how, where and for the duration permitted by the consumer.

In addition to its revolutionary effect on retailing, this customization will also have an enormous impact on the media industry. Like everything else going forward, the content and programming of print, broadcast or online content must have their own intrinsic value for the consumers who permit the medium into their lives. Consumers will determine its value and will pay a fair price for that value.

The good news for all marketers in this projected future is that they will be able to communicate directly and precisely with their existing and targeted consumers more efficiently, more effectively and with very quantifiable measures of return on investment.

These innovations are happening elsewhere in the world as well. In South Korea, Tesco constructed a virtual grocery store on the walls of the subway stations so that commuters could get off the train, scan the barcodes with their smartphones of the groceries they want and get delivery to their front doors within an hour. Marks & Spencer's recently opened store in the Netherlands features an "e-boutique" containing three huge screens and corresponding racks of clothing, which it calls a "virtual rail," that seamlessly integrates digital and physical products. Shoppers can place orders for free delivery to the store through in-store order points or with tablet-equipped sales associates. They can also shop via their own mobile phones.

These examples of the convergence of the "art and science" of retailing are indeed fundamentally transforming retail. High-tech and even higher-touch are not only creating indelible neurological connections with consumers, they are also driving pure e-commerce to open physical stores.

Technology Works Both Ways

So far we have emphasized technology and its superempowerment of consumers. However, retailers, brands and virtually all consumer-facing industries are becoming equally empowered. This third iteration of technology is providing more sophisticated tools that will essentially redesign the value chain, to create seamlessly integrated, more efficient and rapidly responsive value chains on multiple distribution platforms, both online and off (the integrated and interchangeable "omni-channel.")

Technology will be embedded in every process, from Big Data gathering and analytics (facilitated by the new consumer-tracking technologies that will be permitted by the Wave IV consumer) to the creation of personalized products and experiences, to the shrinking of product development cycles, increasing speed to market, pricing optimization and more efficient distribution- and inventory-tracking models. And, most importantly, the new technologies must facilitate getting brand messages to the consumer, first and faster than the hundreds of equally compelling competitive offerings, and being wherever, whenever, how and how often the consumer wants it.

These technologies will also tell the retailer where and who the consumer is and how he or she is feeling. There is now a heat-mapping technology that retailers can use to track and analyze traffic patterns in their brick-and-mortar stores. One specialty retailer said it was "like Google Analytics . . . but for a physical store." Facial-recognition technology can be used to identify high-value consumers when they enter a store or mall. It can also be used to read their shopping "body language," to determine whether they've got time to browse or are in a hurry and in need of immediate help.

Globalization and the One-World Consumer

Consumers are now global, and therefore present an enormous opportunity for US-based consumer-facing industries to expand internationally. Just as the Wave IV technology advancements have created the superconsumer, so they have also driven über-globalization, characterized by a one-world marketplace, and accordingly a one-world consumer, including those in the developed areas of emerging economies. The entire planet is integrating, digitally connecting 24/7, providing access for everyone to everything, instantaneously and all the time. So, in what could be described as this new "melting pot" called Earth, one-world consumers have common interests and desires wherever they may be. They are best defined by the millennial generation of young consumers around the world, who will replace the aging baby-boomer cohort as the dominant consumer segment in Wave IV. Forrester Research estimates that millennials will account for about 30 percent of all US retail sales by 2020.[1]

The Convergence of the Art and Science of Retailing

We use the phrase "the Jobsian and Bezosian Era" to represent the significance and powerful disruption that this convergence of art and science will have in Wave IV, driving retailers, brands and all consumer-facing industries to accelerate their transformation.

And although neither the late Steve Jobs, iconic CEO and Apple visionary, nor Jeff Bezos, founder and CEO of Amazon, was responsible for creating the art or science of retailing, they did embody their powerful convergence in Wave IV. Therefore, we felt it was appropriate to attach their names to this era we are just now entering.

It's also important to clarify that despite our choice of "Jobsian and Bezosian" to describe this era, amid the current and potentially overdone stories about Apple's and Amazon's incredibly brilliant and successful retail accomplishments, Wave IV is not just about them. It is also about what other retailers and brands can learn from how these two visionaries elevated the art and science of retailing, creating more engaging and compelling experiences for consumers. Indeed, these are two business models that exemplify the magnitude of transformation necessary for all retailers as well as the power of the emerging New Rules of Retail.

It's also instructional, when describing this era and Wave IV, to compare and contrast Jobs and Bezos. Although neither man's genius is in dispute, each created his legacy in a different way. Bezos graduated from Princeton with degrees in computer science and electrical engineering, and is less known for the art of retailing than for how he leveraged the science of the Internet itself to produce the juggernaut of all juggernauts: an entire global marketplace where anybody can set up shop, selling anything and everything to the world.

Figure 4.1   The art and science of retail

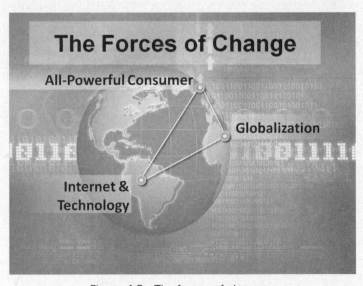

Figure 4.2   The forces of change—
consumer, globalization, and technology

Conversely, Jobs, who dropped out of Reed College in Portland, Oregon, after six months, is better known for his mastery of the art side of the convergence, understanding the technology well enough to know how far he could go in creating its magnificent design along with the ease and fun of its use for consumers.

The most fundamental and visionary principle that Bezos and Jobs had in common was their relentless focus on satisfying consumers, which Bezos continues to do. No decision would be made or strategy implemented by either of these giants unless there was a discernible, and significant, benefit for the customer.

Jobs enacted the final ingredient of his compelling, holistic experience when he launched the Apple Store, an artfully designed and consumer-friendly place for customers to learn about and purchase Apple products. Like the "third place" (after home and office) that Starbucks founder Howard Schultz envisioned for coffee lovers, Jobs created a "third place" for computer lovers.

Unlike Apple, Amazon has yet to complete its "art and science" convergence by opening stores, which would be a "third place" for Amazon customers. However, we predict that they will, as will other pure e-commerce players. Two key reasons for this are the synergies gained by operating on multidistribution (omni-channel) platforms and the ability to provide more of the art (high-touch experience) to consumers. According to Forrester Research, 70 to 80 percent of all future retail sales will still be made through brick-and-mortar retailers.

However, as of this writing, Amazon is still going full tilt on the science side of the convergence, realizing its Day One goal to "get big fast." And for Bezos, getting big is measured in sales, not profits (which, when generated, are simply invested in getting bigger faster). While Amazon is the biggest e-commerce player by far, pushing $74 billion in sales (compared to runner-up Staples at $11.8 billion and Walmart at $7.7 billion), it has not yet declared a final sales measure for what Bezos would define as "big." And among other pure e-commerce players such as eBay, whose e-commerce sales were $8 billion last year, no one even comes close as a threat to Amazon's size, scope and further scalability.

In fact, Amazon's business model will take decades for competitors to replicate (if they can even figure out how), and by then it will be too late. Amazon will likely be well into creating another revolution.

Wave IV: Beyond Apple and Amazon

As we enter Wave IV, we are witnessing at once the most exciting and the most challenging of times for retailers, brands and all consumer-facing industries.

It is the most exciting of times because the Internet and the explosion of new enabling technologies for both consumers and retailers, along with global expansion opportunities, *should* provide more efficient, effective and faster growth both domestically and globally.

However, it is the most challenging of times because Wave IV, as we go to press with this book, finds retailers and brands right smack in the middle of what some CEOs have called chaos, or to a lesser degree, the anxiety of technological overload and the disruption of almost all ways of conducting business. Some of the best and brightest business leaders struggle to find even the right questions to ask, much less understand how to use the overwhelming new technologies bombarding them almost daily. The industry is deeply challenged not only by the new concepts of omni-channel and Big Data but also by the much broader universe of hundreds of new technologies profoundly affecting and enhancing the way consumers shop and buy, as well as those technologies to be used by retailers to enhance the shopping and buying experience.

The good news, then, is that the magical digital world is almost upon us, promising untold levels of efficient and rapid growth, domestically and internationally. The bad news is that it will be enormously challenging for retailers to figure out how to turn that atmospheric magic into reality.

But figure it out they must. Smart brands are already addressing the challenge, and learning how to structure their businesses, organizations, leadership, and strategies, to survive.

Overcapacity Defies Gravity

The well-documented Wave III scenario of overcapacity—too much stuff in too many stores and websites—marches onward in Wave IV, defying the laws of Economics 101 and free-market competition, in which supply and demand always seek equilibrium. In fact, the full-blown effect of technology-driven globalization has further exacerbated the excess. While the United States envisioned the entire world as its oyster for organic growth opportunities, the world now views the United States as its land of opportunity and has increased its rate of attempted entry in Wave IV. There has been a continuous stream of foreign brands and retailers entering the United States, with each thinking it will be the "next big thing." However, once they get here, they can't figure out how to compete in the most intensely competitive marketplace in the world, with its enormously complex distribution, marketing and communications infrastructure. In the end, most fail.

However, in the aggregate, new retail space is expanding at a faster rate than old, underperforming space is being shed. This is occurring for a number of reasons, not the least of which is that it's often less costly to keep a store open than to suffer the financial penalties of closing it, particularly since real estate developers are often willing to incentivize retailers to stay.

One of the negative side effects of this relentlessly growing overcapacity is discounting, a practice that has been further exacerbated by the technological capabilities of Wave IV. Taking many forms, such as "Buy One, Get One," Gift with Purchase, couponing, Groupon-type deals, flash sales, loyalty programs and many more, discounting has reached epic intensity. It has at times been called "the race to the bottom," the ultimate implication being that businesses in general risk the devaluation of goods and services to the point of driving a true economic deflation. While most experts believe this will not happen, at the very least, it is squeezing margins to death and is driving the perception of value down, truly risking the credibility and integrity of many brands and retail nameplates. This share war in Wave IV finds competitors shifting from the use of discounting as a weapon of choice, for getting rid of excess or for marketing reasons, to a strategic weapon of desperate necessity. And, unfortunately, another irony of technology is that its best and brightest users will likely figure out many additional ways to discount, which will make differentiation even more critical.

On to the Wave IV Transformation

Wave IV began with the powerful dynamics of the technology revolution: the accelerated advances of mobile devices, the Internet and all contiguous technologies converging on the world of commerce and consumers. Indeed, every new innovation, launching on almost a daily basis, augments and intensifies the impact of technology. It is further empowering an already powerful consumer. It is empowering all consumer-facing industries. And it is driving globalization: access to everything for everybody, anywhere and all the time.

Therefore, major shifts are occurring across the consumer landscape in demographics, behavior and expectations. Accordingly, major structural and strategic shifts are emerging across the commercial and retail marketplace.

All these shifts will be explored in the next chapter, which will provide a necessary bridge to the New Rules of Retail, as well as the answers for survival and success in this transforming world.

CHAPTER 5

WAVE IV

THE TRANSFORMATION

Consumers Still Driving It All

Lest we forget, consumers, now global and more empowered, enhanced and enabled by technology than ever before, are still controlling and driving every aspect of commerce and its transformation. Therefore, it is imperative for consumer-facing industries to understand the emerging lifestyle trends and demographic shifts that will impact the implementation of the New Rules of Retail in transforming strategies and business models to succeed in Wave IV.

Macro-Demographic Shifts

While the following major demographic shifts relate primarily to the American marketplace, similar shifts may be occurring in the more developed parts of emerging countries as well. All will be discussed in more detail in future chapters.

Income Polarization

Beginning late in Wave III, polarization of the retail market began to intensify, with luxury brands and retailers thriving on one end and discounters and dollar stores, warehouse clubs, off-pricers and outlet stores gaining share on the other. Although this trend was interrupted and modified during the Great Recession, when sales of luxury brands plunged, it has continued into Wave IV. One of the drivers of this trend is the increasing power and influence of the top income groups. This shift has also led to what many are calling income inequality—a widening gap between the richest and poorest Americans.[1] Increasing immigration, a winner-take-all marketplace, a bigger education gap (with greater numbers of highly educated on the one hand and undereducated at the other), the wealth effect of rising stock-market values, which directly affects a disproportionately small number of upper-income consumers, and a decrease in manufacturing, middle-management and other typically middle-income jobs as companies replace people with technology and increasingly outsource functions to developing nations—all these are related to the trend of the rich getting richer and the rest stagnating or getting poorer. Since income and net worth are two of the primary variables affecting spending, this trend will have a huge impact on the attitudes and behavior of consumers going forward and will present numerous challenges and opportunities to the brands and retailers that cater to them.

Urban Migration

Almost 80 percent of the US population lives in cities, a number that is expected to continue growing as young people tend to prefer and gravitate toward the urban lifestyle. This will accelerate the deployment of physically smaller store strategies across all sectors, providing retailers and consumers quicker and easier access to one another. Examples include Walmart Neighborhood Market and Express stores, CityTarget, Petco Unleashed, dollar stores such as Family Dollar and Dollar General and others.

Population Shift

The population is growing older. The segment that has been labeled "millennial," defined by Pew Research as the generation that first reached adulthood around the year 2000, with a population of about 80 million, will be replacing the 75-million-member baby-boomer generation, born during the postwar baby-boom years between 1946 and 1964, as the dominant retail consumer group, estimated to account for 30 percent of all retail sales by the year 2020.[2] Both shifts will drive major strategic and structural changes throughout all consumer-facing industries.

The emergence of millennials as the new generation of global über-consumers will have the greatest impact on the transformation. Already, early in Wave IV, their influence is accelerating. Because they are totally tech savvy— literally born into it—they are demanding more elevated, contemporary and technology-driven experiences than older cohorts. They are forcing retailers to offer more high-tech and high-touch engagement, greater personalization, more accessible quality and more value-driven luxury. They are demanding more frequent introduction of new high-quality products and services and are applying their lifestyle values in all parts of their lives. Social networking, community involvement, cause-based retailing and the pursuit of sustainability are present in everything that this growing and powerful group does.

Another important demographic trend is the blurring of gender lines. Men are making more decisions in everyday shopping matters, and women are gaining power educationally (they now make up the majority of students pursuing masters and PhD degrees in the United States), financially, politically and in business. These trends will no doubt accelerate as millennials get older.

Racial and Ethnic Diversification

The United States is becoming more racially and ethnically diverse. The non-Hispanic white population is projected to decline from 63 percent to 44 percent of the total by 2050. Blacks will increase from 12 percent to 13 percent, Asians from 4 percent to 9 percent and Hispanics from 12 percent to 29 percent.[3]

These shifts will also drive major changes in products, services, brands and how these groups are engaged by all consumer-facing industries.

Lifestyle Trends and Shifts

With instantaneous and unlimited access to virtually anything they might be dreaming of, Wave IV consumers are capitalizing on their newfound power with full force. They are defining value for themselves differently.

As the United States outsourced much of its production across all industries to underdeveloped and emerging countries during the early part of Wave III, many economists declared that the ceding of the US production base transformed the economy from one of value creation to one of value consumption, further adding to consumer power. Consumption as a percentage of GDP (gross domestic product) rose from 62 percent during Wave II to more than 70 percent in Wave III, resulting in a fundamental shift in how consumers sought and defined happiness and satisfaction. Judging from numerous studies that have found there is no correlation between the accumulation of material things and greater happiness, one can conclude that consumers started to become sated with, and perhaps even turned off to, "stuff."

The same holds true in other developed countries. In Japan, for example, between the early 1960s and late 1980s there was a fivefold increase in real income and no increase in average self-reported "happiness."[4] And in the United States, according to a 2002 study by Ed Diener and Robert Biswas-Diener, once household income reaches $50,000 in current dollars, happiness levels plateau, even when compared to households with an income of over $90,000.[5]

Therefore, while increased wealth may lead to increased purchasing, it does not buy happiness or satisfaction. In fact, as another recent study reveals, additional material possessions rarely create any lasting joy for individuals. "Individuals adapt to material goods, and . . . material goods yield little joy for most individuals. . . . Material goods have little effect on well-being above a certain level of consumption . . . people's aspirations adapt to their possibilities and the income that people say they need to get along rises with income."[6]

It seems, then, that American psychologist Abraham Maslow's broadly defined term "self-actualization" now holds the key to consumers' happiness and well-being. This strongly suggests that once their basic needs are met, consumers are increasingly apt to spend more of their wealth on experiences rather than on things.[7]

Metrics in support of this major shift in consumer behavior from stuff to services (which includes experiences) and "self-actualization" can be seen on the accompanying chart. As consumers sought higher states of well-being, there were six major consumer lifestyle value shifts from Wave II to Wave IV, many of which were driven by the millennenial cohort:

1. **From Needing Stuff to Demanding Experiences**—the "thrill of the hunt" offered to brand-savvy bargain hunters at T.J.Maxx and Marshalls, and the Apple Store turning electronics shopping on its head

2. **From Conformity to Customization**—specialized, personalized and localized niche brands like Nike ID and Keurig single-serve coffee machines begin to gain share from large megabrands, the continued growth of special sizes in apparel and footwear and the rapid growth of 3-D printing

3. **From Plutocracy to Democracy**—accessible luxury for all: Missoni at Target, Vera Wang and Rock & Republic at Kohl's, Karl Lagerfeld at Macy's, Isabel and Ruben Toledo at Lane Bryant and the explosive growth of Michael Kors' "affordable luxury"

4. **From Wanting New to Demanding New *and* Now**—what's new today is cloned tomorrow, favoring fast-fashion brands like Zara and Forever 21 that create two new lines every week, the convenience of e-commerce, free delivery and neighborhood stores

5. **From Self to Community**—proliferation of social media, social shopping, community interests such as sustainability, global initiatives like

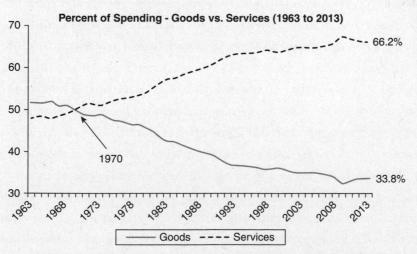

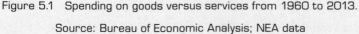

Figure 5.1   Spending on goods versus services from 1960 to 2013.

Source: Bureau of Economic Analysis; NEA data

human rights and safety; all are trends, no longer simply commercial promotional gimmicks

6. **From Technology for Work to Technology for Life**—technology enabling the blurring of lines between "life" and "work," people are working during their "off" hours and playing during their "work" hours, getting what they need to get done whenever and however they can, using technology to save time and money, enhance entertainment

From Needing Stuff to Demanding Experiences

With so many closets, kitchens and garages full of stuff, the appetite to keep buying more was falling dramatically. Yet a study at Cornell University measured the comparative satisfaction of material versus experiential purchases over time, and the results were startling. The level of satisfaction dropped dramatically for material purchases and increased for experiential purchases.[8]

Research overwhelmingly suggests that consumers in pursuit of happiness will be acquiring more experiences, even if they involve products. Examples are everywhere. A woman who wouldn't dream of plunking down even a hundred dollars on beauty products will burn through many times that amount while undergoing a makeover at the Clé de Peau counter at Neiman Marcus. Most ten-year-old girls would give anything for a trip to an American Girl store, not only so they can buy new clothes and accessories for their dolls, but also so they can have their doll's hair done in the store's opulent salon and then sit and have "tea" with her in the store's café. Besides being more enjoyable, experiences are co-created by provider and consumer, making their perceived value much higher than their price. The North Face provides the environment of an energetic, outdoor-lifestyle shopping experience. Lululemon became a cult favorite because it offered motivating yoga classes and other customer-centric events. The consumer, at the moment she is in the environment, is reacting and shaping that experience to herself, to make it complete. There's a buy-in, an emotional investment. The conceptual, personal and temporal (a one-time happening) uniqueness of the co-created experience elevates its value. Moreover, it compels the consumer to return more often because he or she anticipates the experience will be unique each time.

Conversely, every day consumers can look at their stuff and wonder whether the car sitting in the driveway or the pair of jeans now hanging in the back of the closet was really the best purchase they could have made.

Moreover, because of the temporal and individual nature of experience, the evaluation is also fleeting. It is almost impossible to systematically assess and compare whether the purchase of one experience was better than other options, particularly when the experience is predominantly part of the consumer's memory. Therefore, while products can be evaluated on the basis of physical and common criteria, co-created, unique experiences cannot, making the pursuit of them more anticipatory and exciting. Finally, and more significantly, consumers will pay more for an experience than they will for a material thing.

Yet another perspective on too much stuff comes from Barry Schwartz's book *The Paradox of Choice: Why More Is Less.*[9] He points out that "piles of stuff" in a store, while attempting to create the positive impression that there are plenty of options, actually have the opposite effect. Rather than making consumers happier with an abundance of choice, it frustrates and exhausts them before they even begin to shop. So not only is it an unpleasant experience, it's actually a turnoff. Well-edited retail brands, on the other hand, which know their consumers' likes and dislikes, provide the emotionally connecting experience in which less is more. A good example would be Trader Joe's, offering a more limited selection of each category than in traditional grocery stores, yet consistently surpassing its consumers' expectations. An oftheard remark is "Trader Joe's knows what I want!" Another example is Lane Bryant, a sportswear brand that caters to plus-size women. According to David Jaffee, CEO of Lane Bryant's parent company, Ascena Retail Group, the store's customers are fierce loyalists who feel that the company knows exactly what they want and advocates for them.[10]

Because of demand shifting toward experiences, the New Rules of Retail are being written by those who want to blur the distinction between a material purchase and an experiential purchase. For instance, consumers are no longer satisfied with buying pants or jeans, items they don't need any more of, off a shelf. Levi's has therefore opened a store in New York City's Meatpacking District where one can have a pair of personalized, perfectly fitting bespoke jeans custom-made by a master tailor out of one of the many bolts of shuttle-loom-woven selvedge denim they have in the store and trimmed with buttons selected by the customer. Or consider the specialty retailer Zumiez, where teen boys can hang out and play video games while having a customized skateboard made to their specifications. Consumers will spend much more time enjoying the experience and will pay much more for the product than they would have in a traditional store—or, in the best-case scenario for the retailer, the experience itself might compel them to buy "just one more." It's the difference between buying lingerie off a rack in a department store and buying the experience provided by a Victoria's Secret, or between buying Barbie dolls or teddy bears in a toy store and creating your own, complete with names and birthdays—essentially an entire life story—in the festive, fun-filled workshops of a Build-A-Bear store. It's the move from plain old sporting-goods stores to Cabela's, which offers free fly-fishing lessons, two-story mountains, waterfalls, trout ponds and an archery range. It's the difference between buying a can of Maxwell House coffee and the Starbucks experience.

The online flash sales on e-commerce sites RealReal and One Kings Lane and the huge selection and convenience of Zappos set the standard for a great digital shopping experience. The videos on Bobbi Brown's YouTube channel "I Love Makeup" collectively create an immersive world of beauty for fashion-conscious millennials.

Consumers are demanding a compelling experience even when shopping for stuff they need, like in the fresh, fun food emporium Whole Foods, a supermarket unlike any other. The future of retailing will be shaped by the growing propensity among consumers to move away from shopping in big stores, preferring instead the cozy experience and differentiated products in the growing number of independently owned neighborhood boutiques, like Junkman's Daughter in Atlanta, Georgia, which sells wigs, vintage apparel and costumes, all in a glittery, offbeat and wildly designed environment.

It's not just in the specialty retail brands or the independent mom-and-pop stores, though, that consumers expect an elevated experience. They expect every major retailer, from Walmart to Neiman Marcus, from Home Depot to Best Buy, from McDonald's to the Outback Steakhouse, to provide a pleasant experience. Disney repositioned all its stores to focus on elevating the shopping experience. From games to entertaining events to robust audiovisual presentations, it's all aimed at creating an emotional connection with the customer. Starbucks' highly publicized unraveling a few years ago was largely the result of its losing focus on experience, which was the core driver of its exponential growth, for the sake of cutting costs. It implemented an accelerated global growth strategy with fewer amenities and, realizing its mistake, moved quickly to regain its position by reinstating the experiential piece.

More and more traditional retailers are following suit. About Bloomingdale's store in Dubai, CEO Michael Gould told *Women's Wear Daily,* "It's all about selling the experience."[11]

It's also important to note that the experiences anticipated or expected by consumers will vary according to the retailer, brand or service. For example, it is most likely a utilitarian or rational experience that the consumer expects from Walmart or Dunkin' Donuts. Kohl's rapid growth was largely due to its total focus on making the shopping experience convenient, easy and quick for the time-starved mom. Thus the experience is very utilitarian, but in keeping with consumers' expectations.

Consumers also began to expect some level of emotional experience from *wholesale* consumer brands and services of all types, simply because they could. This is driving brands such as Patagonia, Kate Spade, Tommy Hilfiger, Apple, Microsoft and others to roll out their own stores so they can better provide these experiences. They get to their consumers directly and more quickly, and because they own and control the point of sale, they control the presentation and the whole brand experience, from imaging to music to events—essentially the brand's entire DNA. This is an enormous and sustainable competitive advantage compared to being jammed into a departmentalized retail environment, where the retailer will have cherry-picked items from the brand's line and presented them stuffed on racks and shelves in a hodgepodge of colors, shapes and designs.

The same holds true online. A few years ago Ben Fischman, the CEO of online retailer Rue La La, told attendees of a Macy's/Wharton Business School seminar: "The first mistake of e-commerce is that we believed it was all about convenience."[12] His goal was to make their site fun, engaging, informational, exciting—an experience.

To take that point further, one reason we believe online retailers such as Amazon, eBay and others will ultimately open brick-and-mortar, showroom-like stores is so that consumers can touch and feel merchandise (such as apparel, for which creating an experience online is very difficult) before they buy it. Unlike traditional stores, these showrooms would be fun and engaging learning centers, and would have screens next to displayed merchandise to order for home delivery or pickup. Furthermore, such live showrooms would provide the human interaction and real-time consumer research not well facilitated online. Finally, thanks to the huge databases of these online retailers, they would be able to customize and localize their offerings and experiences according to consumer preferences almost by neighborhood.

Finally, from the perspective of associates engaging customers as an integral part of the overall experience, a study conducted by Kurt Salmon finds that we have not even scratched the surface of providing a higher-"touch" environment at retail.

The study discovered that 45 to 60 percent of customers exited stores without having had any engagement with an associate or product. Among the typical retailers in the study, it was found that no customers had experienced "cross-selling" based on their personal purchase history and search preferences, and only 8 to 15 percent were actually offered cross-sell opportunities.[13]

Given the new technological capabilities and myriad shopping and tracking apps, making smartphones and retailers even smarter, the opportunities for "high touch," and even more of it, are endless. As we will explain in the next chapter, some of them weigh in more on the science or technology side, others more on the creative or "art" side.

Regardless, it's important to note that another result of all the technology-enabling tools is their enhancement of the shopping experience. Great experiences in Wave IV can be had in many new ways beyond just the tactical, sensory Wave III experiences such as the Abercrombie & Fitch "nightclubby environment" or Best Buy's adrenaline-rushing assault on the senses. As Blake Nordstrom, CEO of Nordstrom, pointed out, "For one consumer sitting at home at midnight shopping online, looking at the latest brands, well curated with personal suggestions and having everything delivered in the morning is a truly great experience. For others it is the store associate helping them in the store with personal attention and no obvious visible use of technology."[14]

As exemplified by Apple through the vision of Steve Jobs, an equally important component of the art, and therefore of the ultimate retail, experience, is the shopping environment itself. This aspect of retailing doesn't necessarily have anything to do with technology or science per se. For example, the less-is-more clean, crisp and cool architectural design of the Apple Stores, along with the rectangular recessed lighting, the cantilevered shelving and the particular materials used in the décor (including a rare blue-gray marble used for the tile floors available only from a particularly quarry in the mountains north of Florence, Italy), are all imperative for providing the experience. In fact, Apple was able to trademark the distinctive store layout and design.

So the scramble among many retailers to randomly select technological gizmos and gadgets just for the sake of doing so, in attempting to elevate the consumer experience, will end up being a one-off at best. As Jobs showed, there must be a strategic convergence of all elements of the business that ultimately benefits and delights the consumer.

And perhaps the strongest glue for fusing the art and science of the experience is the human touch offered by store associates or brand advocates. The Apple art/science convergence could not exist without its incredibly well-trained, eager, energetic and knowledgeable salespeople, whose job is not to sell, but to delight and find solutions for customers.

From Conformity to Customization

Consumers have moved away from desiring mass-marketed megabrands, meant to be a shared identity with fellow consumers. During Waves I and II, when there were fewer brands to select from, these national brands were considered cool and fashionable. Consumers felt they were part of the "in" crowd if they wore the same logo as their friends and peer groups. Consumers still want what's cool, but cool has taken on a more individual meaning according to one's own definition. Today, as new brands proliferate on a daily basis, targeting specific consumer niches, consumers are shunning the need to be included and are instead pursuing exclusivity and individuality. Another catalyst for this shift, of course, is easy access to information and knowledge about all products and services. Consumers now want something special, even customized, for their own particular desires, real or perceived.

In fact, brands like the Gap and Starbucks that initially grew very quickly in response to seemingly limitless markets discovered that ubiquity (a store on every corner) was a major factor in their decline and that they needed to reposition themselves to reduce overexposure. As consumers seek exclusivity, the brand that's available to anybody can quickly become uncool to everybody, which partly explains the rapid growth of e-commerce: small niche players can avoid the initial expense of opening brick-and-mortar stores but still appeal to a small, specialized group of customers across a wide geographic swath. Leading fashion-trend forecaster David Wolfe of the Doneger Group describes the new consumer landscape this way: "It's bye-bye mainstream and hello to thousands of tiny consumer tribes."[15]

These tiny niche tribes, in pursuit of special, exclusive value, are driving major changes in all consumer-facing businesses. The structure of the marketplace will be redefined as an infinite number of finite market segments ("communities") being served by an infinite number of finite brands, micro-marketed through mediums that specifically target those niches.

Many branded-apparel specialty retailers understand this consumer shift. Accordingly, they are spinning off segmented niche brands, growing their original brand by extending it into other product and consumer markets. Examples include J. Crew, the men's and women's casual-wear retailer, opening Crewcuts children's-wear stores and Madewell casual-apparel shops. Urban Outfitters, Free People and Anthropologie are all retail brands of Urban Outfitters, Inc. Each targets a different consumer segment, providing an eclectic mix of apparel and selected hard goods. Ascena Retail Group has five branded sportswear chains for different demographic niches: Catherine's and Lane Bryant for full-figured and plus-size women; Maurice's and Dress Barn for value-conscious working women; and Justice, the largest tween specialty chain in the United States. Chico's, the casual-wear chain for boomer women, acquired the White House | Black Market casual- and dress-wear stores for a younger consumer, and launched Soma, an intimate-apparel retail brand for fashion-conscious baby boomers. Home-furnishings master Pottery Barn acquired West Elm to appeal to a younger, more contemporary customer. Polo Ralph Lauren bought Club Monaco, a specialty-apparel affordable luxury brand with a modern sensibility appealing to a younger, more fashion-conscious consumer.

The shift toward exclusive niches also favors lifestyle brands such as Ralph Lauren, which is not linked to a single product or classification of products, or to one consumer gender segment. The brand can therefore launch into any consumer or product segment that is compatible with its brand positioning as an upscale, elegant and sophisticated style of living. The brands that were launched and heavily marketed as single-product megabrands, such as Nine West shoes, have found it extremely difficult, if not impossible, to launch their names in other product or consumer markets. Furthermore, consumers, with their closets overstuffed with all kinds of brands, will tend to try a brand that isn't being worn by everybody else, rather than choosing yet another one of the ubiquitous megabrands, which explains why there are now eight hundred brands of jeans.

Traditional department stores are also being forced to meet the expectations of the exclusivity-seeking consumer. They are forging exclusivity agreements with designers and national wholesale brands and accelerating their private branding programs. In a recent study, NPD, the leading retail industry source for consumer purchasing information, found that in 1975, 25 percent of all apparel consisted of private or exclusive brands. That number reached close to 50 percent in 2005. NPD predicts it will eventually reach 80 percent.[16] Macy's has exclusivity agreements with Tommy Hilfiger, Martha Stewart and others, as well as private brands INC, Alfani and more. It also has a localization program called "My Macy's," which distributes different line mixes to different stores based on geographically variant consumer preferences. Best Buy has a similar localization program. It's estimated that private and exclusive brands make up more than 50 percent of JCPenney's revenues, and that five of its private brands, including Arizona, Stafford and St. John's Bay, each provide more than a billion dollars in revenue per year. JCPenney's exclusives include Liz Claiborne, Sephora, MNG by Mango, Nicole Miller, Joe Fresh and many more. Moreover, Kohl's, Target and even Walmart continue to accelerate their private and exclusive branding strategies.

In grocery stores across the United States, the penetration of private brands has reached 19 percent of total sales, according to the Private Label Manufacturers Association (PLMA), and is continuing to accelerate. Recent studies found that close to 80 percent of consumers across all income strata said that store brands are as good, if not better, than national brands.[17] Such consumer preferences will continue to drive the growth of private branding. A good example is Whole Foods, where growth of private brands was four times the rate of national brands during the recession, and even now continues at more than three times faster. There is still a big gap on this front between the United States and Europe, where 60 percent of grocery-store brands are private. But consumer choices will close the gap in the United States.

The huge growth of small, independently owned retail boutiques can largely be attributed to consumers' pursuit of special products and services. The National Retail Federation recently conducted a study that found the fastest-growing retail sector across all consumer segments and price points is small stores.

Finally, there are many brands and retailers, both online and through catalogs and stores, that can provide actual custom-made products. One example is the Nike/Hurley/Converse combo stores, aptly named Salvation, that offer in-store product customization. Each consumer can select from a series of designs and color schemes to personalize shirts or shoes. While shoppers wait for their customized products, the store offers an experience: an environment where people can listen to music, lounge about with friends and just hang out. Vans provides a similar customization service online.

Another factor favoring smaller, segmented niche brands is that in slow-growing markets, brands reach maturity more quickly than in underserved, fast-growing markets such as in Wave II. Their life cycles are much shorter. They cannot grow infinitely; they must steal a limited share of market with one brand. Paradoxically, the more niche brands there are, the more they benefit, because they're all taking share from the megabrands. And consumers will make sure that this axiom continues indefinitely as their quest for "something special for me" continues to gain momentum.

From Plutocracy to Democracy

Armed with their newfound wealth and on their search for happiness, consumers have shifted from accepting the notion that only the wealthy deserve luxury to demanding "democracy"—affordable luxury for all classes. The run-up in the stock market in the past few years has resulted in a resurgence of the wealth effect, not only for the top 1 percent of traditional luxury customers, but also for a younger group of upwardly mobile consumers in tech and other professions. The creation of a new consumer segment, "luxury aspirants," drove the launch of many brands to cater to the up-market "yuppie" core of that segment. Brands such as Coach, Lacoste, Bloomingdale's, Cusp (a Neiman Marcus spin-off), Dooney & Bourke, Michael Kors, Tumi, Tory Burch, Bonobos and others have successfully captured the contemporary, young, almost-upscale consumer, called HENRY ("having enough, not rich yet"). Restoration Hardware, recently renamed RH so as not to limit its mission to just home décor, has disrupted the home-design market with its strategy of delivering high-end items like salvaged-wood farmhouse tables and aerodynamically designed chairs to the masses, and has been one of the most successful turnaround stories in retail in the past few years.

Further down-market, the democratization of luxury is being catered to by an explosion of designers creating brands for mainstream retailers, including Michael Graves, Jean Paul Gaultier and others at Target; Norma Kamali at Walmart; Nicole Miller at JCPenney; Marc Jacobs at Macy's; Stella McCartney at GapKids; and Monique Lhulier at David's Bridal. This revolution is the result of the same market forces driving the other shifts. Luxury-level designers and brands found it increasingly difficult to achieve adequate and profitable growth in overcompeted, slow-growing markets. Therefore, *diffusion*, in the form of sub-brands like those mentioned above, continues in all channels of distribution. Nowhere is this more obvious than in the explosion of growth in outlet stores and off-pricers, both of which are used to liquidate overstocks and excess inventory, allowing full-price stores to better preserve their pricing strategies.

Concurrently, on the demand side, consumers' expectations continue to rise to the level of the selection they are given, thereby perpetually raising the bar for the supply side. And this in turn will perpetuate the democratization of the marketplace.

Finally, as consumers have become more knowledgeable through access to greater amounts of information, they are better able to understand the true value of the products and services they are shopping for. Mobile electronic devices or online searches can compare prices in a matter of seconds. Therefore, consumers are much more closely scrutinizing price/value relationships. Consumers' blind acceptance of any price tag on a luxury item, just to be able to flaunt the name among their wealthy peer groups, is giving way to their demand for real value. This reassessment of value has led to selective quality trumping quantity and "bling." As Burt Tansky, former CEO of Neiman

Marcus, said: "Our wealthy customers used to buy a designer bag without even looking at the price tag. Today, they are comparing the bag to the price, and there is nobody who understands value better than our customers."[18]

From Wanting New to Demanding New *and* Now

New no longer trumps all. Consumers still want new, but they also expect to have it right here, right now. Innovation itself is not enough to win in a 24/7 world, where what's created today is cloned tomorrow. It's now necessary to create knockoffs of *yourself* every day of the week.

The reasons we desire new, fresh and frequent products and experiences everywhere are rooted, once again, in our desire for happiness. Recent studies have shown that when consumers go shopping and discover something new, the brain releases dopamine and serotonin (chemicals associated with feelings of well-being, happiness, and addiction). As Dr. David Lewis, the director of Mindlab International, has said: "Shopping experiences trigger brain activity that creates these 'euphoric moments.' But what is most interesting is that these 'euphoric moments' can be created by the frequency of new items in the stores and the expectation of finding something unexpected."[19] A *Wall Street Journal* article reported on a study of rats that found that "when a rat explored a new place, dopamine surged in its brain's reward center."[20] This would certainly be the equivalent of a consumer discovering a new store, mall, brand or even a new store assortment and layout.

Additionally, a research team from Emory University found that dripping Kool-Aid into the mouths of volunteers on a regular basis had little increase in brain activity, while those who were given random "dripping" had a heightened level of activity. This indicates that the anticipation of the reward, whether it is Kool-Aid or a new dress, is what gets consumers' dopamine pumping. Retailers are starting to use these neuroscientific insights to gain share by providing "new *and* now" value (along with experiences, of course).

A good example of the shift to new and now is Zara, the Spain-based apparel chain with more than two thousand stores around the world. Zara has proven that supply-chain innovation trumps product innovation, by delivering two new lines every week to each of its stores, meaning the line mix may be different for two different stores just a few blocks apart, based on the

consumer preferences of each. Zara's average core consumer's annual visita-
tion rate is seventeen, compared to a retail industry average of about four, simply because Zara fans are compelled to see the twice-weekly new lines. They
are also compelled to buy something if they like it, knowing it might not be
there the following week. H&M and Forever 21 are also a part of the "fast fashion" club, and others are racing to adopt this model.

Urban Outfitters, which operates the Anthropologie brand of home, lifestyle products and apparel, and Five Below, the hot new tween and teen dollar store (everything costs five dollars or less), are two specialty retailers that
have adjusted their strategy to accommodate consumers' desire for new and
now. Both ship new merchandise to their stores every few weeks, encouraging
customers to visit more frequently, seeking the dopamine surge that will accompany the discovery of fun new products.

The drive to new and now has also affected expectations about delivery
for all channels. Amazon Prime made free and two-day shipping standard for
the industry, causing the launch of eBay Now same-day delivery, Instacart and
other services.

From Self to Community

Finally, one of the more positive results of accessible abundance is that many
consumers are now able to achieve the pinnacle of Maslow's hierarchy of needs:
self-actualization. Their material desires are being satisfied and they are able
to move toward maximizing their human potential: to seek knowledge, peace
and aesthetic experiences, and to realize their true identity. Interestingly, since
reaching this stage means that one's basic needs have been met, this shift includes heightened interest in community over self. One major manifestation
of this shift, as well as one of its ongoing enablers, is the phenomenal growth
of electronic social networks. While these rapidly populating worldwide communities are the commercial targets of many retailers and consumer product
companies, they are finding that traditional marketing pushes fail. They must
be given permission to enter these communities, and they are not allowed to
sell in the classic way. Businesses must shift from talking *to,* or talking *at,*
to conversing *with* the consumer. So much has been written, discussed and
lectured about social commerce, or seeking a commercial path through social

media, that one's head spins trying to identify and understand the myriad ways in which this new science, so to speak, can converge with the art of retailing.

Retailers and brands are still seeking "social" acceptance, trying to figure out how to commercially engage their various "communities" without being scorned as hawking pariahs. But there is not even a sliver of doubt that if brands and retailers do not learn how to become cherished members of these social groups, they will be taking one big step toward oblivion. Conversely, for those who do converge social media with their art, or products and services, there will be tremendous growth. One major reason for this is that the most powerful medium for influencing purchasing decisions is word of mouth.

Finally, on social media, while its influence on purchasing behavior is beyond dispute, Facebook's attempts at expanding into an e-commerce marketplace (or "F-commerce," as it's been called) have so far been a struggle. Its first foray with 1–800-flowers.com in 2009 was a flop, after which several other retailers, including Gap, JCPenney and Nordstrom, pulled their Facebook programs. About social commerce, which saw itself as another Amazon-type retailing channel, Forrester Research's Sucharita Mulpuru said, "It was like trying to sell stuff to people while they're hanging out with their friends at the bar." So, though s-commerce, or social commerce, will likely not be the dominant engine going forward, mobile commerce will be.

Online retail clubs One Kings Lane, The RealReal and Net-A-Porter, as well as blogs like Cupcakes and Cashmere, Refinery29, Hypebeast and many others are communities within themselves, attracting millions of devoted followers. There are also plenty of ways to create a community environment offline and add brand authenticity, such as what many health and fitness stores (Gap's Athleta brand, for example) are doing: offering classes and links to trainers and local events, all of which makes members feel part of a broader community. Photo-sharing sites such as Instagram and Pinterest are at the forefront of a new wave of social networks that drive "social shopping" by showcasing beautiful images uploaded by designers, brands and consumers, thus spreading style ideas across the globe in a way that is unfettered by linguistic boundaries. Topshop, Burberry, Home Depot, Nordstrom, T.J.Maxx and many others have encouraged customers to post photos of their favorite products, winning new customers in the process. Teen brand Hollister (a division of Abercrombie & Fitch) realized very early on that teens are so connected that paid advertising is less effective than it was even as recently as a few years ago. The brand uses social commerce to connect with and engage customers, and to communicate new products, promotions and other events. It has ten million fans on Facebook and more than half a million followers on Twitter.

This shift toward self-actualization has an altruistic element to it as well. The consumption binge of the last quarter century reached epic proportions and then crashed early in the new millennium. This experience fed into the realization by consumers that self-actualization should take the form of "less is more," even among the wealthy. In correlation with the shift from plutocracy to democracy described above, ostentation has given way to understatement.

Furthermore, consumers are finding satisfaction in taking up causes, such as environmental advocacy and charity work. The remarkable strength of this trend is driving businesses to attach their commercial efforts to these same causes. Walmart is a great example of leading sustainability initiatives in the retail and consumer product industries: reducing the toxic emissions of their huge trucking fleet; selling only fluorescent lightbulbs; forcing its vendors to reduce the volume of their packaging; and much more. Walgreens recently opened what it believes to be the nation's first net-zero-energy retail store in the Chicago suburb of Evanston, Illinois, designed to produce energy equal to or greater than it consumes, with two wind turbines, nearly 850 solar panels and a geothermal HVAC system that reaches 550 feet into the ground. If successful, the company hopes to convert more of its eight thousand stores to this technology. Outdoor-gear and apparel retailer Patagonia partnered with two environmental nonprofit organizations to develop a "Vote for the Environment" campaign in the weeks before the 2012 elections. Customers were asked to share on Twitter what they loved about the environment. Patagonia then included images of their responses on in-store displays and on social media. Not only did the promotion engage Patagonia's customers, it helped register 110,000 new voters. The day after the devastating earthquake in Haiti in 2010, the high-end online fashion club Rue La La suspended its daily online sale and instead directed its members to the Red Cross website, suggesting they divert their planned Rue La La spending to the Haiti cause. The subsequent member accolades and increase in sales were enormous, which resulted in similar programs when subsequent disasters like the tsunami in the Philippines and others occurred. TOMS shoes and Warby Parker are two other brands that have become synonymous with giving back. Both donate a portion of sales in kind to people in need in developed and developing countries.

On the other hand, the giant Nestlé was blindsided by environmental activists using social media to attack them for their purchases of palm oil, which they use in Kit Kat candy bars. Protesters posted a negative video on YouTube, deluged Nestlé's Facebook page and peppered Twitter with claims that Nestlé is contributing to the destruction of Indonesia's rain forest, potentially exacerbating global warming and endangering orangutans.[21] The allegations stem from Nestlé's purchases of palm oil from an Indonesian company that Greenpeace International says has cleared rain forest to establish palm plantations. So, just as those who do the *right* environmental thing will attract and even convert consumers, those who don't are at great risk of losing business or even being publicly shamed, particularly by younger consumer cohorts. When a video of an Angora rabbit obviously in pain while being plucked for its fur by a company in China that supplies H&M went viral, the retailer very quickly adjusted its certification and sourcing strategy to make sure that no animals were harmed or tortured by companies it does business with. Other brands followed suit. The recent tragedies at factories in Bangladesh and elsewhere, born out of the relentless quest to reduce manufacturing costs, had many US and European consumers up in arms and threatening to stop buying goods made in those countries.

The winning businesses of the future will understand and respond to this major consumer shift. By turning their brands into compelling communities that generate ideas, causes and/or other altruistic concepts, as opposed to just selling stuff, they will succeed.

From Technology for Work to Technology for Life

Technology is enabling the blurring of lines between life and work, resulting in a huge shift in the way people are going about their lives. They are working during their off-hours, staying connected with colleagues and clients 24/7 and playing during their work hours, as symbolized by Ping-Pong tables in the Silicon Valley offices of tech firms, the basketball court at Under Armour and the dining rooms and television lounges at Google's New York offices. This will ultimately do away with the concept of working nine to five. Everyone will be working, playing, raising kids, doing charity work, running errands, relaxing, etc.—at all hours and days of the week. The concept of working a certain number of hours per week will give way to getting your work done—as well as everything else—whenever and however you can.

Technology is transforming the way we are spending our leisure hours as well. Internet TV and DVRs allow us to watch a show or movie when we want to, not when some network executive thinks we should. StubHub and TicketHub let us purchase tickets to concerts and other events on a moment's notice and download an electronic ticket rather than go to a box office or ticket agency. Similarly, online travel sites like Priceline, Expedia and Orbitz, where one can navigate through thousands of flights, hotels, activities and other options and plan a trip in minutes, have revolutionized the planning and affordability of both business and leisure travel. Major League Baseball's collaboration with eBay on Beacon, Disney's MagicBand electronic bracelets for its theme park visitors, electronic trackers for races and other athletic events, athletes at the opening ceremonies of the Olympic Games recording the whole event on their phones, blurring the lines between the stars of the show and the audience, people paying bills and managing their finances online, following current events on social media, communicating 24/7 with everyone in your life via text—all are examples of the impact of technology on our lives.

Fear of Missing Out (FOMO) and the Retail Experience

Much of the exploding use of technology by consumers, of course, is enabled by people's addiction to smartphones. This has also resulted, however, in a chronic condition called Fear of Missing Out, or FOMO, anxiety or worry that one might be missing an opportunity for social interaction, a novel experience or some other satisfying event. British psychologist Andrew Przybylski led a study that found that the less people felt autonomy, competence and connectedness in their daily lives, the more they felt FOMO. People high in FOMO were also heavy users of social networks, which provide constant opportunity to compare one's status with those of others, and to make sure that you are having as much fun and excitement as you perceive that others are having. Once a chronic ailment only among millennials, FOMO is quickly spreading to older folks as well. FOMO is so great that, according to reports, the smartphone has replaced the cigarette as the first thing people reach for after sex.

FOMO manifests itself in many ways. A young professional might be worried he'll miss an important email from the boss and jeopardize his career. A teen is fretful that another party is better than the one she's attending. Millions of people caught up on unwatched seasons of the television program *Breaking Bad* during the two weeks leading up to the concluding episode (resulting in record business for Netflix), just so they could experience the series finale in real time with millions of others.

The successful brands in the next phase of our industry's evolution will be those that create a compelling and neurologically connecting in-store, online and mobile customer experience. They'll use our obsession with our mobile devices to pull us into their 24/7 omni-channel world. And if those retailers are really smart, they'll capitalize on the FOMO pandemic to engage us, connect us to their brand and keep us buying their stuff. The brand promise, customized to each of us individually, becomes irresistible in that context.

Fast-fashion giant H&M opened its huge new store in New York's Times Square with none other than Lady Gaga cutting the ribbon. Thousands of customers lined up for as long as thirty hours before the store was set to open to get a glimpse of the superstar. Twenty customers were randomly selected to earn early access to the store and to shop with Gaga before the remaining shoppers were let in. The new store was open twenty-four hours on opening day, with a digital runway and countdown announcing hourly offers. The opening was blasted all over social media so people who were unable to come to New York for the event could enjoy it on a virtual basis.

Gaga's appearance did a tremendous amount to burnish brand awareness and cement brand loyalty among core consumers. H&M created an irresistible customer experience in the form of a one-off event, linked that event to its brand promise and then sat back while its customers trumpeted news of it to others.

Major Market Shifts and Growth Issues
Driving the New Rules

From a macro perspective, derived out of the foregoing marketplace dynamics of Wave IV, the transformation essentially expanded, elevated and empowered consumers even further, and created an equivalent yet challenging empowerment for retailers, brands and all consumer-facing industries.

Following is a diagram of major market shifts (consumer and strategic), which in turn have driven the major growth issues listed below the diagram. Both provide the driving forces of the New Rules of Retail, and will transform the retail marketplace into three successful sectors:

1. **Commoditization sector**—the low-cost producers, retailers and brands, selling primarily basic, commodity-like products
2. **Omni-Brand to Consumer sector**—fastest-growing segment of highly differentiated and experiential, optimally controlled value chains, and most proficient in "omni-channel" direct-to-consumer brands and retailers, including independents, small or large specialty chains, luxury brands and select multi-branded department stores
3. **Liquidation sector**—outlet and off-price retailers, opportunistic deals on high-end brands

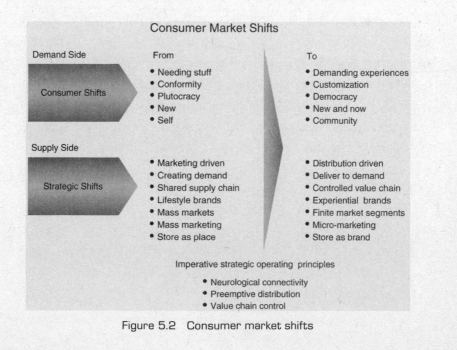

Figure 5.2 Consumer market shifts

We will expand on this prediction in later chapters. It is important to note here, though, that when we talk about retailers or brands throughout Wave IV, we are referring to both brick-and-mortar and digital stores.

Major Growth Issues

- How to gain quicker and easier access *to* consumers and how to provide quicker and easier access *for* consumers—first, faster and more often than hundreds of equally compelling competitors in an oversaturated marketplace?
- Once consumers are preemptively engaged, what is the differentiated and personalized value offering—including an experience—that will win the largest share of their wallet and will keep them coming back?
- How to identify and pursue international growth opportunities?
- How to transform the strategic and structural business model utilizing current and new technologies to address the three issues above?

This Is a New Era

All the new Wave IV technologies—the science and the art—and even some of the cool gadgets should not be viewed as random, one-off kinds of store enhancers. They should be understood as components of a strategically holistic new business model and an incredible new era in retailing, one in which the winners will converge science and art to create an experience so powerful that consumers will be compelled to make it a must-go destination, both offline and on.

The New Rules of Retail will tell you how to do that. Read on.

PART 2

THE NEW RULES OF RETAIL

CHAPTER 6

MAKING THE MIND CONNECTION

NEUROLOGICAL CONNECTIVITY

On January 9, 2007, on a big stage at the Macworld convention at the Moscone Center in San Francisco, Steve Jobs unveiled the first iPhone. With the already unprecedented cult following of Apple—and for that matter, of Jobs himself—this would be the first of many launches in Wave IV that would further fuel one of the most powerful brand-consumer connections ever.

This unveiling, of course, was merely the warm-up. Steve Jobs' grandly staged presentation would trigger an intense anticipation among Apple "addicts" that would be satisfied only by the actual sales release of the iPhone itself.

This would happen at 6 p.m. local time on June 29, 2007, as the doors opened at Apple Stores nationwide to welcome hundreds of cult followers anticipating their fix, so to speak. Some media sources at the time were dubbing the iPhone the "Jesus phone." In fact, in New York City the line started forming twelve hours before Apple's flagship store opened and ended up winding around two city blocks, or roughly a quarter mile, with more than a thousand avid cultists in it. Some had even camped out overnight. Obviously the Apple addicts had learned that if they wanted the new phone, they had better be present when that door opened, or be forced to wait for weeks.

Apple's connection with its consumers has gone way beyond the simply emotional. It has succeeded by actually connecting with their minds. We call this neurological connectivity.

Neurological Connectivity

We believe neurological connectivity is achieved when a retailer, brand or service creates a strong psychological and emotional response that operates on a subconscious level for the consumer in a way that is typically neither readily understood nor necessarily recognized by the consumer. As various research studies in the field of neuroscience have found, when people encounter an elevated experience, their brains release many chemicals. One in particular that has attracted a lot of attention is dopamine, which leads to feelings of euphoria, self-satisfaction and well-being, and which can also actually lead to addiction.

Consumer connectivity is no longer about merely the physical or practical connection of products or services with consumers. This, too, is simply a point of entry. Far more important is the *mind* connection, or neurological connectivity.

Simply stated, a brand or store has a neurological connection with its customers if those customers approach the store visit as they would a visit to the home of a good friend. The trip requires almost no perceivable effort because they know it is going to be a fun and enjoyable experience.

The consumer mind–connecting process created by Jobs for Apple is instructional for all consumer-facing businesses because of its holistic approach. Once connected, Apple and its cult of addicts are impervious to competitors.

Steve Jobs was almost obsessed with building this deep connection with consumers. His ability to translate science, technology and innovation into artistically designed, consumer-friendly products is now legendary. The unique Apple Stores served as the final link in the connection.

However, the business model did not stop there. Apple creates prelaunch excitement for its products through tantalizing announcements at Macworld, showcasing the product to hard-core fans months before launch and typically after subtle leaks have already aroused interest. Without revealing details of the product, Apple stimulates its fans' expectations, sometimes in shrewdly creative ways. (Who can forget the theft of the iPhone 4 prototype "accidentally" left behind at a San Francisco Bay–area bar in 2010 that Apple sued to get returned?)

The buzz begins building, first with dropped hints, then with escalating stagecraft, until the anticipation is palpable. As demand accelerates, Apple warns of scarcity, which further heightens demand and drives an enormous volume of preorders. All in all, before the product is even released, consumers' minds are filled with Apple, leaving no space for thoughts about competitive brands.

Finally, through both its integrated products and sophisticated retail stores, Apple further strengthens mind-share and connectivity by having the consumer co-create a whole series of fun, learning experiences at the store's Genius Bar with Apple's young, tech-savvy associates. Even the sleek, modern product box is designed to neurologically connect with consumers.

The supreme proof of the strength of Apple's neurological connectivity, however, is that it succeeds at satisfying all six of our major consumer value shifts in Wave IV (toward demand for experiences, customization, democracy, new *and* now, community and technology for life).

One widely held view that has been promoted is that Apple consumers exhibit the same neural patterns as the religiously fervent do when beholding a spiritual leader or icon. While we may not totally subscribe to this theory, we do know that for any consumer-facing business to even come close to replicating Apple's consumer connection, every part of the organization, across the value chain, must be maniacally—even religiously—focused on creating a superb customer experience and an Apple-like subconscious connection.

What Traditional Brand Strategies Miss

It is also vital to understand the distinction between neurological connectivity and how traditional brands connect. The concepts are overlapping—brands, of course, have always sought positive mental reactions from their consumers—but they are far from synonymous.

Zara, the apparel retail specialty chain, has developed its brand based on some highly specific and pragmatic consumer benefits that its customers can readily identify and describe. They would explain that Zara has fresh new assortments almost every week, that its prices are below those of competitors and that the store has a nice, broad range of products, including apparel, accessories, shoes and bags. And even though Zara built the brand with minimal advertising (0.3 percent of revenues versus 3 percent for most traditional brand advertisers and their competitors), it is widely known among its target consumers for its unique brand attributes.

However, what consumers will not articulate is that Zara has developed a neurological connection with them. In fact, the term does not exist in most consumers' vocabulary. It's also unlikely that Zara's management would refer to this great competitive advantage as a neurological connection. But in fact it is. It has created an experience, a feeling of excitement or euphoria that occurs around the regularly scheduled deliveries of new, select and limited-time merchandise. To put it simply, Zara has a brand with "a sense of tantalizing exclusivity."[1] This would not be the case if it employed traditional brand management, however competently.

In fact, the fundamental factor driving Zara's success has nothing to do with traditional brand management. It has to do with an entire value chain that is vertically integrated and highly collaborative, and with the fact that it has reduced its product development cycles to the point where new lines are released almost weekly. Moreover, the entire organization is focused on Zara's extraordinary experience. Neuroscientists have proven that the anticipation of rewards—or the potential of *not* getting what you want—will produce dopamine, which actively drives behavior. Consumers visit Zara seventeen times per year, compared to only three or four times for traditional retailers, because they are afraid of missing something new and exciting. The connection is so strong that customers are compelled to buy in fear of the item's being bought by someone else. Zara's whole business model is built around this goal.

Other fast-fashion brands such as H&M, Forever 21, Uniqlo and others have similar models and are likely connecting neurologically. These brands have captured a greater share of market and are growing faster than the traditional, slower-cycled and rigid branded-apparel specialty chains.

So-called flash sites such as RealReal, Gilt Groupe, One Kings Lane and Net-A-Porter are connecting with consumers in a similar way with their select, limited-time offerings that consumers anxiously await. These elements are part and parcel of the brand but transcend the traditional elements of brand positioning and equity, brand awareness, perceived quality, associations and conscious loyalty. Only now, as they have expanded with less exclusive and lower-value branded product, have they started to see their growth challenged.

Other great examples are the "thrill of the hunt" experiences enjoyed by shoppers at off-pricers and outlet stores as they search for designer brands with incredible discount deals. Warehouse club Costco places exclusive upscale brands such as Coach in an area that has to be sought out by customers, offering them a true "treasure hunt."

A Less Obvious Neuroconnector

Over the past five years, the Converse brand has achieved extraordinary success by identifying and aligning with many of our six major consumer shifts.

First of all, Converse realized that its classic Chuck Taylor sneaker created an experience for a variety of consumers that had never been fully exploited. For some, it reminded them of playing sports with friends; for others, it represented their first rock concert; and for still others, it symbolized their first teen rebellion against their parents. However, in all instances, these were safe memories to reignite with friends and parents—kind of cool and not too edgy.

The question was, how could Converse harness this goodwill to create more of these experiences in people's lives, and improve business in the process?

First it expanded its product development and built unique products that linked to different events in people's lives that enabled them to express their individuality with different variations of sneakers. So Converse created what at the time was referred to as "T-shirts for feet." This clever moniker came from Converse's realization that most consumers had growing piles of T-shirts representing meaningful events in their lives, and that for nostalgic reasons they would not discard them. Converse therefore developed a strategy based on the T-shirt analogy, capitalizing on consumers' desire to have footwear that was important in different life experiences, essentially personalizing the sneakers. Examples would be the John Varvatos sneaker or the "One Star" at Target. The culmination of the strategy can be found in the Converse stores, where customers can design their own shoes using the latest printing technology. This strategy also aligns directly with our consumer lifestyle shift from conformity to customization.

Obviously, these consumers aren't buying simply because they need another pair of sneakers. They want the experience, the memory. This kind of personalization, along with an accelerated cycle of new designs (aligning with the "new to new *and* now" shift), not only fueled rapid growth for Converse but also created an impervious neurological connection with its consumers.

Increasingly, brands and retailers are investing heavily to understand how best to create exceptional consumer experiences that can be measured and replicated as a part of their integrated business models. Google, Facebook, Motorola and Disney have all hired so-called neuromarketers to determine how consumers respond to different experiences.

Two other examples capture the importance that consumer package-goods companies place on trying to establish this connection.

The Hershey Company has spent a lot of time in grocery and other retail stores to get inside customers' heads. Former CEO David J. West was so sold on this kind of grocery-aisle consumer research that he told a conference of food analysts that the results would give Hershey a "competitive advantage in our category for years to come." Already, Hershey has psychological profiles on its array of customers. For these shoppers to splurge, almost everything has to be perfect—price, packaging, product display—or they'll zoom past without adding any Hershey's candy to their grocery carts. Although Hershey's ad spending has been steadily increasing for several years, topping $580 million in 2013, the company is also investing marketing dollars where consumers spend theirs: in the grocery and retail outlets where its candy is sold, in the aisles and at the registers and on research to understand and drive the in-store experience.[2]

Consider another example: For several years, Campbell's researchers studied microscopic changes in skin moisture, heart rate and other biometrics to see how consumers react to everything from pictures of bowls of soup to logo design. The *Wall Street Journal* reported that "this 'neuromarketing' approach is a fresh attempt by companies to better understand how consumers respond. . . . The Campbell's team figured it could boost sales by triggering more emotional responses in stores and prompting more people to focus on more soups."[3]

All these reports reinforce the power of this subconscious mind connection. And while we are still in the early stages of understanding how this process works, the evidence suggests that subtle neural processes are a powerful driver of our shopping behaviors.[4]

So how do we think the winning business model of neuroconnectivity works? The business model is designed to drive the entire experience of three things: the dopamine rush in anticipation of shopping, compelling the consumer to visit the store; the joy of the actual shopping experience itself; and the final satisfaction of consuming or using the product or service. This is the neurological connection with the consumer on all conscious and sub-conscious levels.

When successfully executed, these experiences are co-created by the consumer and the retailer, brand or service. The experience may be set up, or provided by, the Container Store, for example, but the consumer shapes or creates the experience to satisfy his personal desire at the very moment he is in the store. The setup is Container Store's highly trained associates (up to 235 hours of training, compared to seven or eight for traditional retailers), who act more as consultants than salespeople. They spend as much time as necessary to discuss with and advise each customer on his or her specific storage and organization needs. The co-created experience, therefore, is shaped by the customer's individual situation and the satisfaction of having a real expert solve his or her unique problem. This keeps the neurological experience indelible, unique and immeasurable.

And because the experience is co-created at one moment in time, a completely new and unique experience will happen the next time the consumer visits the Container Store, which adds to the force of the neurological connection. One might then suggest that this dynamic will increase the brain's reaction even upon merely hearing the name of the store. To be sure, one cannot attach a quantitative value to a neurological experience, since it will be different each time. It is for this reason that control of that experience is so critical.

We can borrow from the language of academia to elaborate on this point. According to the *MIT Sloan Management Review,* "Value creation is defined by the experience of a specific consumer, at a specific point in time and location, in the context of a specific event. The experience space is conceptually distinct from that of the product space, which is the conventional focus of innovation. In the experience space, the individual consumer is central, and an event triggers a co-creation experience. The events have a context in space and time, and the involvement of the individual influences that experience. The personal meaning derived from the co-creation experience is what determines the value to the individual."[5] In other words, like each time one visits a friend, each time one visits that retailer one has a uniquely enjoyable time that cannot be repeated outside that relationship.

So, although providing a wonderful new product or brand that has great functionality, awareness, value and emotional connectivity may get you to the retail "playoffs," to win the championship you must make a neurological connection.

Creating Connectivity

How, then, does one create neurological connectivity? The retailer, brand or service must align its brand positioning to deliver one or more of the six consumer value shifts (experiences, customization, democracy, new *and* now, community and technology), and then it must create the elements that will allow it to neurologically connect with the consumer. It's important to emphasize here that this process of creating the connection must be an integral part of one's business model—culturally, financially and relative to the entire value chain. This must not be viewed simply as a peripheral add-on to the business. If so, the process will fail.

In pursuit of neurological connectivity with consumers, the strategic planning process for all consumer-facing businesses, brands and retailers alike must be able to clearly and distinctly answer the following questions:

1. What is the unique, sustainable experience that I am creating or co-creating with my target consumer?
2. How is this experience being increasingly personalized for each unique consumer?
3. Do I need to create consumer access to my brand or stores at multiple price points? If so, how?
4. How do I increase the flow and rapidity of new product and experiences into every point of distribution?
5. Do I understand and connect with every community that is important to my target consumers, both online and off?
6. How can I utilize technology to create a better experience for the consumer?

Although creating the neurological connection is imperative, it must also be tightly and credibly aligned with the brand or retailer positioning, or DNA, in a way that consumers find believable, natural and compelling. Failure to do so is not only deleterious to the brand but can actually put the entire business at risk. The *MIT Sloan Management Review* also writes: "Changing a neutral experience into a positive one isn't easy, and there's no guarantee of success for companies that make the attempt. In the early 1990s, Tandy Corp. failed to get traction with its Incredible Universe superstores. The stores featured music, karaoke, laser shows and door prizes. The company carefully selected and trained employees and emulated Disney's approach to interactions between staff and customers. But after 17 superstores had been built, Tandy pulled the plug on these money-losing ventures. The fun elements weren't enough to make the stores profitable in the competitive consumer-electronics segment."[6]

One of the first examples of using technology for neurological connectivity was the army's use of virtual reality in its recruitment strategy. In Philadelphia, the army closed four of its traditional recruiting centers and opened a new Army Experience Center.[7] "Hands-on virtual reality experiences and simulations allow users to see, touch and learn firsthand what it means to be in the Army." As one seventeen-year-old remarked: "It's fun. It gives you the real experience. You can hang out and play games with your friends."[8] With more than fourteen thousand visitors in the first fifteen months, virtual reality's traffic-building power has already been proven. Whether it will help with gaining recruits long term is still in question. The larger message, however, is that given the widespread addiction to virtual-reality games on the web, its influence is likely to be immense.

More recently, countless retailers have begun to use technology to further connect neurologically with their consumers. At beauty superstore Sephora, customers can scan products to read ratings and reviews and watch how-to videos. Sales associates use a system developed with color authority Pantone called Color IQ to scan a customer's face to find the perfect shade of foundation. Then, using an iPad, the salesperson pulls up thousands of foundation products that can be filtered by shade, skin type and other variables to find just the right product. The promise of instant beauty is a hit: Sephora is the go-to retailer for millennials and a major disruptor in the beauty space.

Outdoor retailer Cabela's will soon be equipping its sales associates, or "Outfitters," with iPads that can give not only product information but also recommendations on where and how to use the products. For example, if you're planning to go fishing, the Outfitter can tell you which nearby lake to go to, what fish are biting and what gear to use to catch them—priceless information for a fisherman.

In what is probably one of the most delightful uses of technology for the neurological connection, Disney is transforming all of its more than 350 retail stores around the world to a new design that makes shopping there the "best 30 minutes of a child's day," according to Jim Fielding, the former president of Disney Stores. The store contains a Pixie Dust path, an interactive Magic Mirror and a theater where guests can select Disney content to view. Said Fielding: "It's truly the best 30 minutes of a family's day, because families create memories together . . . the store experience is truly magical, and we believe that we can create memorable, innovative, interactive experiences for guests of all ages."[9]

Social media is becoming an increasingly important way for brands to engage and neurologically connect with their consumers. Burberry customers upload photos of themselves wearing Burberry clothing to the brand's website, ArtoftheTrench.com. Club Monaco has a similar one called Culture Club. Consumer communities are also springing up around brands. There are hundreds of brand fan blog sites with names like "J. Crew Aficionada" and "Addicted to Target" with pages and pages of posts, photos, chats and other content about a particular store and its brands. Readers of these blogs are some of the most neurologically connected consumers on the planet, and these forums provide yet another way for them to indulge their addiction.

A Final Note on Neurological Connectivity

The New Rule of neurological connectivity and our foregoing description are intended to convey not only an imperative operating principle for success in Wave IV but also a means for retailers and brands to develop every aspect of their business models around the goal of achieving this powerful, competitively impervious and unique connection with their consumers.

We do not intend to convey that neurological connectivity is some deeply hidden, unknown process that drives the consumer, or that by studying the brain, businesses will be able to manipulate consumers into buying something they don't really want.

The study of the human brain and what drives behavior is still in its infancy. Our position is simply that we believe consumers buy something when they have an incentive to do so. Brands and retailers that are aware of the trends around consumer expectations are strongly advised to align their strategies accordingly. By doing so, we believe, they will indelibly bond with their consumers on a deep, almost unconscious level, and will sell to them not once, but over and over again. Stated another way: Failure to excel on the identified trends will put you in the commodity segment of the market, which, as we will discuss later, is a very challenging place to be.

It is also clear that smartphones have enabled consumers to check in with their favorite brands and retailers much more often than before. Likewise, brands and retailers are sending consumers personalized messages that they open and read like emails from friends. This is neurological connection.

The neurological connection precedes, but does not supplant, its essential partner, preemptive distribution, another of the three imperative strategic operating principles, or New Rules. In fact, as we just pointed out, the neurological connection is itself the most powerful preemptive distribution strategy, because once the connection is made, the brand is indelibly first and foremost in the consumer's mind, compelling them to get or go to that brand first, and to go back to it again, before they go anywhere else, including to a competitor.

In the next chapter, we will discuss how to capitalize on that victory.

CHAPTER 7

REDEFINING THE RULES
OF ENGAGEMENT

PREEMPTIVE DISTRIBUTION

Let's imagine that our two consumers from Chapter 4, John and Sarah, took a time machine back to New York City to spend a day shopping in the year 1970, during Wave II. They map out their day over breakfast, planning to go to Macy's, Lord & Taylor, Bloomingdale's and a couple of boutiques on the Upper East Side. They know they'll be lucky to have enough time to shop those stores given the traffic and pedestrian congestion in the city. And although they find the experience enjoyable once in the store, going from one store to another is a real effort. Furthermore, there is no guarantee they will find what they were looking for. And while they could have shopped through the Macy's and Saks catalogs without leaving their apartment, the catalogs would not have the newest merchandise or as wide a selection, plus the shipping costs and delivery time would prevent the immediate gratification of getting the product on the spot.

So off they go to the stores, and a long, exhausting shopping day.

Unlike in Wave IV, where Sarah has every store in the world in her pocket via smartphone and iPad, along with more apps than she can count, in Wave II she was bound by the limitations of what was physically and humanly possible. Wave IV consumers, on the other hand, are digitally and visually connected 24/7 to friends, family and socially networked communities. They even receive automated computerized reminders, suggestions and conversations. All this information is swirling around them, however, only because they've given "permission" to a select set of businesses. The physical world of shopping experienced by their predecessors in 1970 has been flipped on its head. Macy's and other big stores, including the future Amazon, all have satellite neighborhood stores, with personalized assortments and screens for ordering goods that are not in the store but that can be delivered the same day from elsewhere. The technologically enhanced experiences while in the store are awesome. And absolutely anything they want, wherever and whenever they desire, either online, through their mobile devices or in the physical store, can be ordered, purchased and checked out in nanoseconds and then delivered to their front door the same day or next, free of charge.

So, here we have John and Sarah right in the center of the commercial universe, so to speak, with the power of more, cheaper, quicker, easier and smarter access: with the tap of a key, a leisurely walk across the street, a hand gesture or whatever they dreamed about simply delivered without asking.

The consumer in Wave IV is the center of power. This is the consumer to whom brands and retailers must now go, on every distribution platform available, including digitally, through social networks, physically, sharing platforms with competitors, in airports, pop-up stores, kiosks, catalogs, etc. And, of course, we now have a one-world global consumer whom all of commerce must include in its strategies as one of the biggest growth opportunities.

And here's the kicker: Consumers are not just going to walk through your doors because your lights are on. As we so clearly described in previous chapters, there are more stores, products and websites than you can count, all of which have equally compelling offerings as yours. If you want to win their pocketbooks, you have got to figure out how to get to them first, faster and more often ahead of all your equally compelling competitors, or have such an awesome, neurologically connecting experience that they will go out of their way to come to you.

This is the Wave IV consumer and marketplace scenario. And the New Rule strategy here that is imperative for all consumer-facing industries to implement if they want to achieve success is what we call preemptive distribution.

Preemptive distribution addresses the overcompeted marketplace. It responds to the fact that consumers have hundreds of equally compelling choices, literally right at their fingertips, across the street or knocking on their front door. So it's understood that the competitor that gets to the consumer first, quicker and most often, preempting the hundreds of others, has a better chance of winning share. The strategy also requires distribution precisely where, when and how the consumer wishes to receive it. By definition, then, preemptive distribution requires an integrated matrix of all relevant distribution mediums, including distribution into faster-growing international markets.

This chapter will explore the many paths for gaining preemptive distribution. Some are already being implemented, and others will evolve as we proceed through Wave IV.

Let Us Count the Ways to Preemptive Distribution

1. From "Silos" to Integration to Preemption: Distribution in the faster-growing marketplaces of Waves I and II and in the early years of Wave III was fairly simple and straightforward. Retailers opened stores and consumers came shopping. The marketplace was not yet overcompeted. And even as competition accelerated in Waves II and III, along with an increase in distribution platforms, retailers and wholesalers alike operated their distribution strategies vertically, in "silos." For example, Sears' and JCPenney's catalog operations were organized and run separately from their store operations. Most wholesale brands, like Levi's Jeans, Tide soap and Coca-Cola, had not even begun to think about owning or controlling their distribution, nor was there the myriad of distribution platforms that have expanded into Wave IV, including TV, direct mail, catalogs, door-to-door selling, in-home marketing, event marketing, kiosks, airlines and trains, flea markets, street promotions, traveling van promotions and others. And no one had ever heard of the Internet until Wave III began to evolve.

Now in Wave IV, with increasing consumer demands and competition, further fueled by rapid technological advances, the ever-multiplying uses of the Internet and the continuing integration of global markets, the development of new distribution strategies is critical. Essentially, the winners will be managing an enormous matrix of distribution mediums, and they must all be seamlessly integrated into what is being called "omni-channel." Moreover, all the distribution platforms must be interchangeable so that the consumer can cross over easily from one to the other for different purposes: research, shopping, ordering, buying, picking up or returning, whether they are stationary or on the move. Furthermore, all consumer-facing businesses must determine which platforms are relevant to the value they are distributing, how they support a preemptive strategy, and whether they can be smoothly integrated into the matrix.

2. Laser Focused Ubiquity versus Total Ubiquity: Preemptive distribution does not equal ubiquitous distribution, nor does it mean every retailer must open more stores. It means that distribution must be laser focused, precisely aligned with where, when, how and how often the consumers want to receive the product or service. And today, through the new technologies of Wave IV, consumers have given "permission" to their select group of retailers, brands, products, services, information and entertainment sources to connect with them. This information is collected from the many contact and transactional points that businesses have with consumers. It is then built into Big Data bases, which can be analyzed to determine precisely where, when and with what offering the consumer is permitting engagement. This is a change that has enormous implications for the marketing, advertising and media industries—those businesses cannot just "push" their offerings onto consumers anymore. They must be invited, or at least given permission. And as advertising loses some of its credibility with increasingly savvy consumers, word of mouth is driving more sales. Marketers in consumer-facing industries can no longer talk at their targets. They must *engage* with them, often through their trusted friends and colleagues, and as explored earlier, they must figure out how to be welcomed into their social networks, such as Facebook, Instagram, Pinterest and others, and to get them to follow them on Twitter. This engagement tends to build communities around particular retailers; in marketing-speak, communities are the new segments. Consumers and their desires can no longer be accurately identified by being lumped together in big, demographically defined groups. The market can now be described as an almost infinite number of consumer segments, or thousands of tiny consumer "tribes" that are talking to one another.

All of this suggests too that the distribution platforms the brands or retailers use provide not only immediate access to consumers but also immediate access *for* consumers. So, technology and data analysis enable a preemptive distribution strategy to achieve laser-focused as opposed to total ubiquity.

Accordingly, this focused ubiquity also indicates that all consumer-facing businesses need not be on all distribution platforms. Some are simply not relevant for all business models. One measure of the viability of a given distribution platform is the degree to which it reinforces or enables the attainment of the six consumer value shifts. For example, why should the Net-A-Porter members-only club ever open a brick-and-mortar store? It already delivers on all six consumer desires: It provides a neurologically connecting experience (the consumer can't wait to key into the one-hour daily sale of discounted luxury goods); its sale for "members only" creates the perception of scarcity and special customization, as well as affordable luxury; it delivers on "new *and* now" by showcasing all new products every day; it creates a sense of urgency because the product will not be back; it's certainly a "community"; and finally, it's the use of technology beyond the workplace and into the consumer's life.

Amazon, on the other hand, with its huge databases of consumer knowledge (who and where they are and what they want), could easily justify a preemptive brick-and-mortar strategy, particularly for its fashion, beauty and footwear businesses, which would answer the customer's need for feel and fit required in those categories. In showroom-like stores Amazon could showcase only the products that the locals desire, as mined from its enormous database, and create a neuroexperience by using new, enhancing technology that allows consumers to customize outfits that can then be ordered online, in the store and delivered to their homes. Amazon knows all too well that consumers spend three to four times more when having both online and physical stores to shop in.

Warby Parker and Bonobos are two other brands that were launched as pure e-commerce businesses but that quickly discovered the importance of the neurologically connecting experience, as well as the increased revenue opportunity of the multichannel shopper, and immediately began opening stores. Subscription-based fashion commerce site JustFab, also realizing the importance of going omni-channel, has opened a store near Los Angeles in which customers are able to join the service and/or shop curated product displays with trend videos and in-store personal stylists offering advice on how to put together and wear different looks and featured trends. JustFab associates can check inventory instantly on iPads.

Somewhat counterintuitively, T.J.Maxx, of the TJX group of off-price stores, has launched a website that many experts believe will not replicate the "thrill of the hunt" luxury and designer discount-deal experience that plays out in its stores—which is what keeps its customer addicts coming back to the store over and over again for their neurological fix. The jury will be out for a while, but since it fulfills the six major consumer shifts in Wave IV expectations, TJX might, once again, be way ahead of the so-called experts regarding what's right for its value-conscious customers. The need to be constantly relevant and in front of the consumer will keep driving the best retailers to test new ideas. As for nonfocused ubiquity, many experts believe that a large part of Gap's and Starbucks' setbacks were due to their ubiquity (a store on every corner) and their cost-cutting to achieve scale, both of which ultimately resulted in a "sameness" and consumer boredom.

3. Neurological Preemption: Neurologically connected brands are the most powerful preemptors. They preempt the competition before the consumer even visits a website or goes to a store by triggering the dopamine rush. Ironically, one of the ultimate effects of achieving this connection may actually be a reduction in stores, thereby increasing productivity. If the connection is strong enough, as in Apple Stores or Starbucks shops, a customer will bypass a competing store that might be right across the street to get to his or her Starbucks or Apple "fix" a mile away.

4. Stores to Consumers: Preemptive distribution also means taking brick-and-mortar stores to the consumer, literally into the neighborhoods where they live. Beyond the independently owned small retailers, many large mall and freestanding big-box retailers are rolling out smaller freestanding stores placed in the consumers' neighborhoods, thus providing immediate, preemptive access. This also includes the dense and growing urban areas, in which 80 percent of the US population now lives.

Kohl's was arguably one of the first traditional department-store retailers to launch this strategy in the early 1990s. Identifying its core consumer as the time-starved working mom who did not have time to drive to and walk through a mall, Kohl's designed small, one-story, wide-aisled, quickly traversable stores with central checkouts and big parking lots. And they placed them in neighborhoods with lots of families.

Some experts have suggested that this preemptive distribution strategy is largely responsible for Kohl's explosive $10 billion growth during the 1990s, and that the majority of those revenues were stolen from JCPenney, because Kohl's core working-mom consumer had access right across the street to an equally compelling retail experience. JCPenney finally did acknowledge the loss of share due to Kohl's strategy, and subsequently developed and launched a smaller, freestanding, off-mall store strategy.

The small-store strategy is still being implemented today. Late in Wave III, Walmart launched Walmart Express, a small-store format averaging fifteen thousand square feet for urban and suburban neighborhoods, largely in response to the small dollar- and convenience-store retailers that accelerated their expansion into neighborhoods, stealing a huge share of Walmart's business as budget-constrained consumers opted to save on fuel costs, particularly during the Great Recession. Target has launched CityTarget, Petco has opened smaller Petco Unleashed formats in urban neighborhoods and Staples is testing two new "omni-channel stores" that, at twelve thousand square feet, are half the size of its typical stores. The stores contain only a fraction of the 150,000 items available on Staples.com, but they are staffed by tablet-toting associates, and contain web-connected kiosks from which customers can order products not on the store shelves. The company guarantees that orders placed online from the store, home or office will be ready in two hours.

To accommodate the spread of smaller stores and more local shopping, the development of "town centers" and shopping villages within neighborhoods is on the increase, while many of the underperforming regional malls are being shuttered or renovated to provide a better shopping experience: entertainment; restaurants; health and fitness centers; and so forth. The more rapidly growing, independently owned neighborhood boutiques, moreover, exemplify preemptive distribution, as well as a neurological connection to their very narrow consumer niches.

We predict that, ultimately, the continual pursuit of preemptive distribution will also drive the traditional department stores to spin off branded retail specialty chains carrying their growing private and/or exclusive brands, such as INC and Alfani stores for Macy's, Saks 10022-SHOE stores, Craftsman tool stores from Sears and others.

5. Bring It to Me, Just for Me, New and More Often: Delivering on consumer expectations also means that the products or services desired must be accessible on the distribution platform of choice, precisely when consumers want it, even if they are mobile. In fact, mobile e-commerce is on a rapid growth trajectory, and at some early point in Wave IV is expected to outpace the double-digit rates of stationary Internet growth, according to many experts.

A great example of a company embracing preemptive digital retailing, so to speak, and embedding one's brand into social communities is Disney. It is connected to millions of people each day through four hundred Disney-sponsored Facebook sites. Disney's strategy is to engage consumers in a dialogue and an exchange of information. Disney has points of interest for the consumer; accordingly, it can learn more about its consumers. Disney has clearly been "permitted" entry by the social communities.

Fandango, the online movie-ticket purchasing service, was one of the first entertainment collaborations with Facebook. When a consumer buys a movie ticket through Fandango, his or her Facebook friends are automatically notified and invited along. As Robert Iger, CEO of Disney, said: "This kind of 'word-of-mouth' among friends about a movie, or anything else for that matter, is worth seven times that of a recommendation from any other source. This new approach will destroy traditional media."[1]

Many retailers, including Kiehl's, Gap, Best Buy and Starbucks, are using geo-fencing, a virtual boundary using tracking sensors, to preemptively connect with their customers. Customers who opt in are sent promotional texts when they come within a certain radius of the brand's stores, billboards or other locations. Geo-fencing is what enables The North Face store to text our Wave IV consumer John, when he is within a two-mile radius of the store, that a new backpack has just arrived that is perfect for his hiking treks. A supermarket chain might use this technology to send a coupon for Special K to a customer entering the cereal aisle, for example.

Another superpreemptive strategy was employed by Procter & Gamble, which set up virtual stores in several European subway stations so that busy commuters can scan items like razors and soap that will then be delivered to their homes.

The future opportunities provided by this kind of mobile retailing and preemptive interconnectivity with consumers and/or their communities are enormous. Simply recommending purchases is quickly becoming the most basic use. The more advanced brands will be creating communities of their own in such a way that they will attract fans (that is, more loyal customers).

While e-commerce, mobile, catalog, direct-mail and other mobility-serving distribution platforms are obviously useful for taking the product or service to the consumer, they do not preclude some of the strategies emerging from the more traditional distribution platforms. The winners in these sectors are pursuing the customization and localization of their stores, product mixes, presentations and services, all according to consumer preferences in different regions, cities and even neighborhoods. The "My Macy's" program distributes localized line mixes. Wrangler, a jeans and casual-wear brand of VF Corporation, has the capability to deliver two different line mixes to two different doors of Walmart that may be across town from each other.

To successfully execute localization, the marketing end of the business must integrate qualitative and quantitative research; census, demographic and lifestyle data; sales tracking; loyalty cards; Internet sales; competitive intelligence; local management information; and even unsolicited comments, all from decentralized local stores and markets. All this information must also be continually fed into a highly centralized operations and distribution end of the business, to ensure that these large operations successfully distribute the decentralized, localized line mixes. Successful localization yields enormous increases in sales (up to 40 and 50 percent in some cases) and a reduction in inventory and markdowns.

Localization is not only about the merchandise. Former Saks CEO Steve Sadove maintains that localization has always been part of the Saks merchandising process: "I can't imagine anything more different from a flagship store in New York City than a small one in, for example, Raleigh, North Carolina. The brand matrix and style offering will be different. However, localization of marketing—having a different marketing plan for each store based on the demographics, lifestyle, age, values, etc., of the community is a new area for us."[2]

When done properly, customizing or localizing is very difficult for competitors to copy, and therefore provides a more sustainable competitive advantage. It encourages and rewards innovation and differentiation and ultimately builds a brand personality that connects in a neurological and emotional way with local consumers. Conversely, mass homogenization impedes innovation and rewards tightly disciplined operational efficiencies, ultimately eliminating strategic differentiation and the growth and profitability that accompany it.

A preemptive distribution strategy also benefits from shorter product/service cycles by distributing more new lines more often. In the apparel industry, this is the fast fashion that H&M, Uniqlo, Zara and Forever 21 are known for.

The exceptionally well-controlled and well-managed value chains of these brands are powerful examples of how process and system innovation can actually trump product innovation. It's easy to knock off a product, but not so easy to knock off a business model.

Even the traditional retailers and wholesalers are pushing their envelopes. Through better management and control of their value chains, also enabled by technology and globalization, they are reducing line cycles, thereby turning out more new lines more often.

6. Sharing Distribution with the "Enemy": A growing preemptive distribution strategy is identifying laser-focused pools of a brand or retailer's core consumers as shopping traffic in what might be considered competitors' stores. For example, Brooks Brothers, Topshop and Bonobos identified that a large segment of Nordstrom's consumer base consisted of consumers who also fit their own brand profiles. Thus, they collaborated with Nordstrom with shop-in-shops in many of the Nordstrom stores. Joe Fresh and Sephora have shops in JCPenney; Sunglass Hut and Louis Vuitton are in Macy's. It's a win-win synergy. Nordstrom captures new traffic from the customers coming to the store for the Brooks Brothers products. Likewise, Brooks Brothers gains new customers from those shopping Nordstrom without having to open another store.

Perhaps the biggest example of distribution platform sharing, and one in which the host platform is being called the "enemy" by some, is Amazon. Its distribution platform is capable of hosting, sharing, leasing space (or whatever one wants to call it) to every product, brand, retailer or service in the world that wishes to take advantage of its distribution superiority and cloud-computing capability. However, Amazon as host becomes Amazon as competitor when it becomes apparent that it is able to further build its Big Data base by capturing consumer information from the hosted sites, which can then be used by Amazon to gain an advantage. This also means the loss of control by a guest brand over its interaction with customers and their shopping behavior, and a negative impact on brand management. Furthermore, Amazon's cloud-computing capabilities are used by many businesses, giving it more access to competitive information. So, it's not as easy to see the same synergies as those cited above among the brick-and-mortar retail brands.

7. Global Preemption: Consumer-facing industries in the mature US marketplace can no longer ignore the necessity to gain a preemptive position in the developing countries that have much faster and sustainable growth rates. And it's not simply the need for growth that creates a sense of urgency. The world has become flat, to use a phrase coined by Thomas L. Friedman in his fascinating books on globalization, and interconnected in so many ways that if brands and retailers fail to gain a preemptive presence globally, they will find their home-based positions severely weakened. This is because consumers are globally mobile, literally and electronically, with similar interests and desires wherever they may be, and therefore must be distributed to preemptively, to secure a global presence. Thus, international expansion, then, is both an imperative and an opportunity.

Adding urgency to preemptive global expansion is the fact that the infrastructures in many countries are still relatively fluid. As they begin to mature, the opportunities will decline, and in some countries may simply disappear.

The challenges of expanding internationally are many and vary widely depending on the myriad political, economic, social, consumer and marketplace profiles of the host country. Equally complex issues exist for the business choosing to expand globally. Therefore, retailers and brands must first identify the global markets that best match the positioning of their brands with consumers in those markets and then develop the most effective business models for competing in each of those countries. So, while it's critical to start "thinking global," the phrase "act local" is just as important. For example, Walmart's forays into Germany and South Korea ended in retreat, due to its failure to align with cultural mores, local regulations and/or preferences in shopping behavior, products and more. Tesco's failed launch of its convenience food chain in the United States is another example of not acting locally—essentially not understanding the American consumer's shopping behavior and food preferences. Home Depot ended up closing its seven stores in China after realizing that the country lacked a do-it-yourself culture. Having learned from their mistakes, these companies have recalibrated and continue to pursue international markets.

There are two sectors that might be called first movers (or sector preemptors): luxury (Gucci, Armani, Prada, Calvin Klein, Ralph Lauren, LVMH brands such as Hermès and Louis Vuitton and many more) and high-volume hypermarkets (Carrefour, Walmart and Tesco).

Now, with the more technologically advanced and easier global distribution capabilities of Wave IV, as well as increasing wealth in many of the emerging countries, particularly China and India, the luxury and volume-priced brands and retailers are simply accelerating their expansion.

On the other end of the retail spectrum is the global preemptive distribution race in the volume-priced supermarket space, as competitors seek to establish primary positions in each region. In China, for example, Walmart, Tesco and Carrefour are all competing against local Chinese supermarkets to gain dominant share. In another sector, whereas Home Depot stumbled in China, it is thriving in Mexico, with sixty stores and growing. And all these big-box retailers are building infrastructure to support further expansion.

Obviously, as these retailers take major share early on in these rapidly growing countries, it will be increasingly difficult for new competitors to threaten their dominant positions when the markets begin to mature.

Target, long exclusive to the United States, is launching stores in Canada, Mexico and Latin America. Saks Fifth Avenue and Nordstrom are both expanding into Canada. Bloomingdale's opened a store in Dubai. And Macy's, with its international brand recognition, is considering its global options, eyeing China especially as a potential opportunity, as Neiman Marcus and Galeries Lafayette (one of Macy's direct competitors) begin their expansion there.

The biggest catalyst for global expansion is the emerging and rapidly growing middle classes in the developing countries. These markets represent enormous opportunity for many powerful mono-brand specialty retailers, such as Coach, J. Crew, Gap, American Eagle Outfitters, The North Face, Abercrombie

& Fitch, Iconix's Candie's stores and bebe. The fast-fashion branded specialty chains are also becoming worldwide hits, with an already established strong presence in most countries. Other brands, such as Lee, Wrangler, Levi's and Guess jeans and Nike footwear, are already dominant internationally and are rapidly expanding.

Among all the emerging markets, China is a primary target, with its middle class projected to reach 700 million people by 2020, according to market intelligence firm Euromonitor International.

Of Gap's $16 billion–plus in sales, Wall Street analysts estimate that more than 10 percent comes from its international business. Gap expects China to become the cornerstone of its global strategy. Former Gap Asia-Pacific head John Ermatinger clearly sees Gap preempting its competitors. He stated back in 2010: "There are a lot of brands in China, but in our space, there is not an American representation yet so Gap is looking forward to being that authentic purveyor of casual apparel."[3] The company expects to double its store count in China, from forty to eighty, before long. Coach has more than 120 stores in China, while other affordable luxury brands like Michael Kors, Tory Burch and UGG have only just begun their expansion into China.

Regardless of the degree to which any consumer-facing business is planning or actually implementing global expansion, the need to do so has never been more intense. With so many countries experiencing the highest sustainable rates of growth, there is an open field for those seeking early preemption of dominant share.

Nevertheless, every consumer business should have a planning matrix of target global markets prioritized by market attractiveness (that is, size, growth, competitive intensity, etc.) for their products and services, the potential mix of distribution options for that market (including all the latest digital platforms) and the investment required. Companies that succeed in executing these global priorities will thrive.

CHAPTER 8

THE IMPORTANCE OF
VALUE-CHAIN CONTROL

THE BOTTOM-LINE WINNERS

Just as Wave IV shoppers are happily reaping the benefits of unlimited and instantaneous access to whatever their hearts desire, including neurologically incredible experiences, and are delighted by all the Wave IV technologies and the magic of their mobile devices, the industry's retail and brand chiefs struggle to deliver these delights, and to deliver them preemptively. The only way a business can truly achieve the preemptive delivery of the neurological experience, essentially the first two New Rules of Retail, is by exerting maximum control over its value chain, either totally or collaboratively.

Nordstrom provides a good lens for examining the many new perspectives and moving parts required of the Wave IV value chain. Nordstrom's very enlightened leaders, as acknowledged by their peers in the retail industry, are nevertheless wrestling with the enormously complex challenge of harnessing and implementing the endless stream of new technologies to make consumers' dreams come true.

In the core business, Nordstrom is racing to implement the omni-channel strategy of integration and interchangeability, and reorganizing its operations, management and associates accordingly. Examples include the ability of consumers to order online and pick up in the store, or when shopping in the store, to order missing items online to be delivered to their homes; the optimization of existing shopping apps or creation of new ones; a website update or redesign to build a more responsive and connecting experience; new customer relationship management (CRM) systems to track and target personalized deals and build Big Data bases. Furthermore, Nordstrom continues to collaborate and create synergies with new brands and other retailers that fit within the Nordstrom stores, such as a series of themed, temporary shop-in-shops featuring carefully curated merchandise by designers like Prouenza Schouler, Rodarte and Merci. Last but not least, it continues to strengthen its private brands, while, of course, maintaining excellent in-store experience and superior service, which is the Nordstrom signature.

As if this weren't enough, Nordstrom must also address these same challenges for the Nordstrom Racks, its outlet chain, and ensure linkage and integration between those and the full-line stores, as well as with the HauteLook flash-sale site.

Lastly of course, it must face the issue of the enormous investment across the value chain required to make this transformation. Indeed, the stakes have never been higher.

Nordstrom is just one example. Across all consumer-facing industries, brands and retailers are struggling to turn this technology revolution into competitive advantage to win the Wave IV consumer. It is now a world in which the consumer can shop 24/7, how and where she wants to shop, across multiple platforms, selecting from a vast array of different price points, value propositions and brands, all enhanced or enabled by a variety of technologies and/or personalized services.

Thus Wave IV has reached a tipping point. The value chains of all businesses, as well as the requirements for managing them, are being totally redefined.

What Is the Value Chain?

It is important to make a distinction between how we define the terms "supply chain" and "value chain." Supply chain is typically defined as the back end of the business: the set of issues around the flow of goods or materials, the transportation network, logistics, distribution centers and the handling of the goods inside the distribution centers. However, we define the value chain more broadly, encompassing issues such as who creates the value, where it's created and where and how it's marketed, including its ultimate point of sale. In other words, it includes all the activities of the front end of the business as well.

The value chain is what we call a never-ending, fully integrated, virtuous cycle, starting with the consumer, pausing at point of consumption and then starting all over again (see Figure 8.1). There are three continuous and simultaneous steps in the process:

- **Definition:** Identifying and defining what consumers expect from, or even desire beyond expectations of, the brand. This is ongoing, using all research methodologies, including sales tracking, in-store interaction and testing. In essence, the real winners virtually live with their consumers 24/7. This process continually affirms the brand's core value, suggests improvements and guides new value creation and innovation. A clear point of competitive differentiation for the brand is articulated. If well executed, this process will yield a deep metaphor for what the true essence of the brand stands for and what the consumer is seeking.
- **Development:** Developing the value starts with using knowledge gained from research to conceptually plan for new and/or improved value (brands), then proceeding to actual value development, including the neurological experience. Also, in this cycle, the highly integrated, seamless and demand-driven back-end segment of the chain (as described later in the chapter) will provide continually innovative productivity strategies, while the integrated marketing or front end of the chain will continually innovate or strengthen the marketing strategies.
- **Delivery:** The final cycle in the virtuous loop is the preemptive, precise and perpetual distribution of the value, along with its neurological experience. It's also critical that the value (brand) creator have maximum control of this final cycle in the loop, and of its presentation and experience at the point of sale, which also includes line size, mix, frequency, flow of goods and as much of the operations as possible (sales and service).

Control of the value chain does not necessarily mean *owning* every function in the chain—otherwise known as total vertical integration. In fact, in

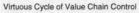

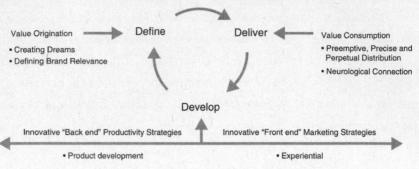

Figure 8.1 Virtuous cycle of value chain control

our commercially globalized world, you'd be hard-pressed to find many vertically integrated *or* owned value chains. In apparel, Spain-based Inditex comes
close by owning most of its production, and a few large Chinese apparel manufacturers own their retail distribution in China. But for the most part, globalization has driven the production operations of most industries to lower-cost
manufacturing in emerging countries.

However, while some functions in the value chain such as production or
distribution *will most likely* be shared or collaborated with third parties, the
entity that originates, owns and/or creates the brand (whether retailer, wholesaler or service provider) should exercise dominant decision-making control,
or at least be relentlessly pursuing it. Most importantly, it must control those
parts of the chain that directly connect with, or touch, the consumer. After
all, continuous innovation emanates from tracking and responding to consumers' ever-changing desires, so the dominant brand must control origi-
nation and development. It must also control marketing, which ensures the
continuing integrity of the brand and its consumers' expectations. It must
control distribution to gain preemptive access to consumers geographically
and strategically on all relevant distribution platforms. And finally, control
of the point of sale is perhaps most essential of all, as it allows the brand to
create the emotionally connecting experience we have found to be so critical.
Burberry, Victoria's Secret, Starbucks and Disney are examples of brands that
may share control, or collaborate in various functions of their value chains,
but that also exercise dominant control over all those functions that connect

with the consumer: creation, innovation, marketing, distribution and point of sale. By contrast, Lululemon hit a snag, so to speak, when it lost control over the value chain, and entire shipments of its best-selling luon yoga pants made with defective fabric hit its stores, causing a first-of-its-kind yoga pants recall as well as a media firestorm.

The following is our analysis of the key elements of value-chain control and the correlation between degree of control and the resulting success of various retail models.

Core Elements of Value-Chain Control

As we studied the various retail, branded wholesale and service models, similarities emerged in how they defined "control" and how their process was driven by four core elements. Our first discovery was that while some discussed controlling parts of their chains, others never used the word "control." And none, in fact, articulated a proactive strategy of totally controlling their value chains to achieve preemptive distribution and provide the optimum experience at the point of sale. Every one of those poised to be winning brands and retailers, however, was aggressively pursuing and implementing those strategies.

Ralph Lauren's declarations of controlling "destiny" have been, and still are, manifested by their buying back their many licensees (for control), continually increasing their retail business (now accounting for more than 50 percent of total revenues) and insisting that wholesale customers cede control of the presentation and operations in their designated store space. Eric Wiseman, CEO of VF Corporation (which includes The North Face, Vans, Timberland, Nautica and others), stated in the annual report, "We want to continue to present the brand in ways we can control."[1] The VF Corporation also continues to increase its retail business. Home Shopping Network CEO Mindy Grossman sprinkles the use of "control" throughout her numerous public presentations of "knowing what our consumers want, where, when and how they want it, so we've got to create and control the distribution and experience for her."[2] Here's how J. Crew CEO Mickey Drexler uses the word to express one of his primary business principles: "I don't ever want to be in a business where I don't control my distribution, period, end of sentence."[3]

And Macy's CEO Terry Lundgren may not specifically seek to control Macy's value chain, but the company is most certainly moving in that direction while it aggressively pursues growing its stable of highly successful (and "controlled") private and exclusive brands (estimated to be more than 30 percent of total revenues.) Kohl's, JCPenney and others are following suit.

As we perused what each of these CEOs said about the importance of control, we distilled several common objectives. Again, not surprisingly, we found their end game to be in sync with our thesis.

Control provides greater flexibility and enables rapid responses and adaptation to shifts in the marketplace, such as changes in consumer desires, the structure of the marketplace and competitive strategies and positioning. Tactically, control enables quick response to changes in required volume levels, inventory buildup and flow, to name a few key areas.

The key objective of value-chain control, as articulated in our thesis, is to create and control the preemptive distribution of a neurologically connecting experience all the way through to its consumption, including the all-important point of sale.

Another commonly expressed objective was to control the key components of the value chain that create the most value, and therefore are more vulnerable to competitors. In other words, they need control in order to leverage those parts that drive share gain, revenues and profitability. This corresponds to our thesis of controlling those elements in the value chain that directly connect with and/or serve the consumer. These are at the beginning of the chain to gain knowledge about the consumer (their behavior, wants and desires, and what they are dreaming of); the creation of that dream and its experience; and the final point of sale for optimum presentation of the dream and the experience.

Finally, the business needs the alignment of the entire organization, as well as external suppliers, to accomplish these objectives. This may seem obvious, but it was interesting that most of the leaders we spoke with referred to the challenge of balancing competing requirements. In many cases the tradeoffs did not necessarily optimize value-chain effectiveness. For example, Zappos would not manage costs at the expense of the customer experience, and Costco would not raise prices to offset its higher-than-average employee wages.

Likewise, Amazon realized that to meet its defined customer experience of rapid and reliable shipping, it would need to build excess capacity. Doing some simple math (actually, complex math), it realized that as product variety grows and demand becomes more variable, and as capacity utilization increases, lead times increase in a nonlinear fashion. In other words, without building excess capacity, Amazon would fail on its promise of timely delivery. Had Amazon not arrived at this insight—along with the two objectives cited above and the understanding of the need for value-chain control to accomplish all of it—then the investment in extra capacity would not have been justified.

After we had identified these objectives, our next challenge was to identify a coherent set of principles that would provide companies with the ability to successfully achieve them.

In managing the globalized value chain, there is a whole series of key elements that are critical and fundamental to the effectiveness of the organization. These elements include managing the complexity of lead times and volatile costs (transportation or commodity prices, to name two). For example, depending on where goods are sourced, the size of the order and its shipment can have an enormous impact on costs and the complexity of managing the chain.

Effective value-chain management has many other elements that are obviously critical: risk-management strategies; sustainability (or how to be "greener"); how to support different business models (that is, online value-chain requirements are quite different than those for brick-and-mortar retail stores); or simply how to manage costs. However, none of these suggests a comprehensive method or definition of how to measure value-chain control across the entire spectrum of different business models.

Furthermore, we must emphasize that in Wave IV, the requirements for the value chain have become so much more complex and extensive that *total* control is not an option. Each brand or retailer must determine what elements of the chain need to be totally controlled and how maximum control can be achieved through collaboration—and of course, with whom. Many potential partners may even be competitors. Collaborating with Amazon by placing your brand or retail store on its platform to gain preemptive distribution might amount to doing business with the enemy, or, as one CEO put it, "dancing with the devil." The question every retailer must ask is: What set of principles can we apply to achieve maximum value-chain control?

Our research led us to four common characteristics that we believe define value-chain control for all segments, whether the primary source of value is low-cost products or high fashion.

Regardless of the degree of control—from Zara on one end, with almost total vertical integration, to the Wrangler wholesale denim brand selling primarily through Walmart, on the other extreme—we determined that the successful companies all focused on four core elements that, when implemented, gave them greater control over their value chains. This required an integrated strategy, because these four elements, if implemented separately, might result in tactical or short-term advantages but would never result in maximum control. The execution must occur simultaneously. The elements, described in more detail below, are: (1) building technology into every part of the business; (2) increasing collaboration; (3) shrinking decision times; and (4) creating the demand-responsive, efficient value chain.

Building Technology into Every Part of the Business

In Wave IV, without integrating all the available technologies into every part of the value chain, from the back-end "creation" to the front-end "consumption," any level of value-chain control would be impossible. Given that there are innovations on almost a daily basis, it requires management vigilance to be screening and selecting those that are most relevant to one's business model. Suffice it to say that there are technologies for analyzing customers and potential customers, getting to know them on an almost intimate, personalized basis, tracking their shopping behavior and ultimately building Big Data bases to create product and experiences, to manage inventory levels, to increase the timely smooth flow of goods, to determine where, when, how and how often to distribute, to follow them into their communities and to connect with them at every touch point, and on and on. Finally, technology is required to create individually what each consumer is dreaming of, including a neurologically connecting experience, and to manage and control its preemptive distribution from creation to consumption.

Nordstrom CEO Blake Nordstrom commented on how his company incorporates, understands and implements technology to increase the integration and control of its value chain: "For us, IT [Information Technology] investments and upgrades used to run on their own cycle somewhat independent of the business needs or demands at the time and driven more by the technology calendar. The 'aha' moment for our executive team was when we all realized that technology was no longer the responsibility of the IT group, but was the responsibility of all of us and critical for all of us to manage together. From that day, how we have managed it has fundamentally changed."[4]

IBM Chairman and CEO Ginni Rometty described the impact of technology on retail this way: "Big data is so relevant now because there's not just one type of technology changing; there are a number of technology shifts and innovations happening now, and they are all converging at once." Referring to the shifts in mobile interactions, data advancements and social interactions, she said, "It's a new era."[5]

Rometty added that 2.5 billion gigabytes of data are created each day and 80 percent of all the world's data has been created in just the last two years.

Increasing Collaboration

Increasing collaboration, or leveraging human, intellectual and physical assets across the entire value chain can be achieved only by creating organizations that encourage collaboration. And collaboration must be with internal partners, consumers, vendors and customers.

Internal Collaborations

Wave I, Wave II and early Wave III value chains were organized around traditional functional silos. Production would manage and operate its business according to stated goals, with no understanding of, or dialogue with, the other silos—marketing, distribution, sales and so forth—each of which also operated according to its own goals. There was no integration or collaborative control, and the entire chain was driven by a forecasting model that "pushed" goods first into warehouses, then into stores, with the hope that their forecasts were right. In Wave IV, those businesses still operating with this model are hurtling toward extinction. An old phrase coined by one of those still-breathing dinosaurs is "Pile it high and hope it will fly."

The Wave IV winners are transforming their organizations into matrices of collaborative integration across all functions of the organization. Strategic planning, research, design, product development, operations, forecasting, production, logistics, distribution, marketing and often finance, HR and other staff functions operated with a holistic view: a clear understanding of both their brand's consumers and their function's contribution to delivering the ultimate brand promise. These chains are tightly controlled because all participants are operating under the same brand-to-consumer-driven objectives and strategies.

Most significantly, Wave IV requires that every organization understand and be capable of implementing multidistribution platforms, new technologies, multi-price-point offerings, new business models (e.g., flash-sale sites) and more.

For example, Gap reorganized its entire business essentially into four distinct branded businesses: Gap, Old Navy, Banana Republic and Piperlime. Each of the four will operate its own value chain and will drive its own internal collaborations. Most importantly, as a result of this reorganization, the old silo structure was blown away, and each brand now has an integrated and highly collaborative value chain, including the integration of e-commerce and physical stores.

Just as Nordstrom has accelerated the integration and interchangeability of its e-commerce and stores, so have Macy's and Saks Fifth Avenue. Burberry is another star example of progress on value-chain integration. By implementing this strategy, all its organizations have had to maximize their internal collaboration and streamline and increase control over their value chains. Another example of the effects of Wave IV driving value-chain integration: Walmart is calling its 4,800 US stores "distribution centers." It is also testing a new procedure through which it cuts costs and shortens delivery cycles by shipping products to Walmart Express and Neighborhood Markets from its Supercenters.

In fact, all major retailers are driving the collaborative integration and interchangeability of their e-commerce and physical-store value chains. Shopping, ordering, purchasing, picking up and returns are all functions that must be seamlessly interchangeable online and/or in stores. This also requires 360-degree inventory visibility and new organizational processes. And it is further driving new metrics governing the allocation of capital. For example, to achieve two-day delivery at peak demand, one must have redundancy in the chain, or use a third-party logistics (3PL) provider, to meet excess demand. All this integration is driving a whole new level of cross-organizational collaboration.

A final note: Nowhere across the value chain is internal collaboration more critical than in the integration and management of the multidistribution platforms now necessary to gain preemptive distribution. The winners will turn this complex matrix into a powerful synergy, allowing the consumer to be able to cross over easily from one to the other for different purposes, whether stationary or on the move.

Consumer Collaboration

The winners in retail today are obsessed with understanding what their ultimate consumers are dreaming of. They are continuously tracking and researching consumer responses to identify where new and different tactics are needed. Much of the best collaboration with consumers comes from the interaction at the point of sale, where the experience is happening and consumers can actually co-create new ideas along with the brand. For example, in Lululemon stores there is a chalkboard by the fitting rooms for consumers to jot down any feedback they might have after trying the clothes on. Then on a regular basis the store managers have a conference call with their design and production teams to share and discuss any action they should take on these consumer insights. Similarly, Staples asks every customer to complete a brief postpurchase survey with product and service-quality questions, and uses the results of these surveys to become more responsive to customer needs.

Vendors and Customer Collaborations

When it comes to externalizing the creation, marketing, distribution and ultimate selling of the brand, the most successful companies have intense, and in some cases exclusive, collaborations. Whole Foods employs full-time food foragers to continually identify and bring to market new products that are being developed by small producers, which are often more responsive to new consumer trends in the grocery sector. Whole Foods will even provide financing to producers needing capital to grow.[6] This exploration is also a continual source for private and/or exclusive products.

H&M, Forever 21 and Uniqlo, for example, where fast fashion (reduced, rapid-line cycles) is their primary competitive advantage and a major part of their customers' experience, make it a priority to ensure that their manufacturers understand that, and direct all their efforts toward supporting this advantage.

VF Corporation, with its diverse portfolio of brands, has a strategy called the "Third Way," a hybrid of complete supply-chain control and relationships with suppliers.

Marketing, advertising, packaging and communications vendors are also collaborative partners that communicate daily with their counterparts within the branded companies. This ensures that everyone is on the same page, literally and figuratively, in creating, developing and maintaining the brand's DNA and its presentation to the consumer.

Similarly, the close collaborative relationships between the department stores and their exclusive and private brand vendors are essential for controlling the timely flow of goods, presentation, environment and experience.

Shrinking Decision Times

The third element that we felt defined value-chain control was the ability to shrink decision times, or accelerate and optimize good decisions on how to execute against the target value proposition, across the chain. This is another hallmark of a highly collaborative organization. Shrinking decision times made possible the speed-to-market and fast-fashion models, which require both shorter product-development cycles and the agility to rapidly respond to marketplace shifts. And while the fast-fashion examples again come to mind, the concept is broader than merely getting new and fresh product to the market more often. It describes a culture that is consistently improving its responsiveness and organizational feedback loops to make better decisions. From an evolutionary perspective, organisms that are able to detect and respond to stimuli quicker have won out in natural selection.

This quicker response is directly correlated to the degree of control a business has over its value chain.

While this element is intrinsic in the fast-fashion business models, it is also present in their counterparts in the specialty branded retail sector (J. Crew, Chico's, Victoria's Secret and others), many of which have highly controlled value chains, thanks to their direct connection with consumers and suppliers. Their feedback loops are also quick, providing more responsive and quicker decision cycles. And the department stores are finding that the greater control they exercise over their private and exclusive brands, the more they can reduce cycle times, increase flexibility, maximize responsiveness to consumer changes, turn out more new lines more often and more easily localize their lines by store. This also increases differentiation and allows for greater pricing flexibility. Most important, its impact on productivity, the lifeblood of all retailing, is enormous.

Creating the Demand-Responsive, Efficient Value Chain

This fourth and final element, creating the demand-responsive, efficient value chain, minimizing inventory and ensuring the continual flow of goods, would not be possible without the synergy created by the first three: integrating technology, collaborative integration and rapid decision-making. The best companies we analyzed had core processes that could be defined as seamless, simultaneous, fast, flexible, responsive and cost efficient. The key elements that we identified included multiple value chains for different products, a built-in redundancy to manage significant demand variability and sustained investments in anything that increased speed and responsiveness. The successful business was driven by consumer demand—what consumers are actually buying, as opposed to what companies choose to push to comply with forecasting. The entire business is organized, managed and operated around a brand-to-consumer objective.

In this controlled, demand-responsive process, the product literally never sleeps. And in a wonderful ancillary benefit, this eliminates the old nemesis of too much inventory, which the old forecasting model inevitably resulted in. Instead, it provides more and smaller lots (responsive to consumers' demands for newness more often), speeds the flow of goods so they are not sitting idle (both in the warehouse and on the balance sheet) and enables rapid replenishment. It also decreases markdowns, increases productivity and, most importantly, keeps the consumer happily coming back to see what's new.

There are many technologies currently being developed to dramatically increase the efficiency and accuracy of the value chain, but one that is poised to have an immediate impact is radio frequency identification (RFID). Tiny chips (like those in the E-ZPass tags used to collect tolls on bridges and highways) that contain electronically stored information are printed onto a garment's tag or label or otherwise embedded in product or packaging and, when detected at short range by a "reader," enable the quick and accurate tabulation of what inventory is available and where, reducing out-of-stocks and increasing distribution accuracy. The combination of wanting to know where inventory sits, whether it can be shipped from the store to meet consumer demands and getting real-time feedback on what consumers have looked at or tried on is driving an increased adoption of the technology. Macy's, one of the earliest adopters of the technology, saw a 50 percent higher sales growth rate for products tagged with RFID. This technology alone will dramatically reshape the value chain and enable retailers to respond to demand shifts.

In the last ten years, leaders in the apparel industry using RFID shrank product-development times by more than 40 percent. For example, part of the resurgence of Gap has been due to its ability to respond more nimbly with shorter lead times to shifts in fashion cycles.

In the digital world, process breakthroughs are even more visible. Amazon altered an entire industry by redefining the process of book distribution through its Kindle. This also fundamentally changed consumers' expectations about both speed of access and price. The Kindle was simply a new spin-off of Amazon's entire enterprise, which was *the* original, game-changing retail model of online ordering and low-cost-shipping optimization.

Amazon also increased its response times and efficiency by building its distribution centers close to UPS shipping locations. This actually utilized all three principles described in this chapter and gained Amazon a huge competitive advantage over all other e-commerce sites.

A Cautionary Tale

One reservation often cited by retailers is that "We don't need to invest in these technologies or in getting more control over the value chain because we don't see how it will make money for us."

The story of the "3 Bs" may suggest otherwise. Borders, Blockbuster and Best Buy all faced small disruptive competitors that did not make any money. Blockbuster saw the economics of Netflix versus the potential profit of opening more stores and said that they did not need to respond to the threat, since Netflix "didn't make any money." Borders and Best Buy felt the same way about Amazon.

Of course, we know how this story ends. By the time the profit model became clear, there was no way for Borders and Blockbuster to survive, and Best Buy's market capitalization is a mere shadow of what it once was.

Nordstrom avoided this trap by studying Zappos early on. Despite the fact that Zappos was burning cash at an alarming rate, Nordstrom decided to aggressively invest in and upgrade its shoe department, one of the hallmarks of its heritage, knowing it could not rely on the negative cash flow to bring the upstart competitor down. It was wise to do so. With the acquisition of Zappos by Amazon, the competitor was not going away—but was here to stay at an almost unimaginable scale.

In summary, while control of the value chain does not necessarily guarantee perpetual success, as we saw with Gap, Starbucks and others, the inability to achieve it will almost certainly guarantee failure, and the winners in retail's share wars will most definitely have mastered it.

CHAPTER 9

WHAT IT ALL MEANS

TODAY, TOMORROW, THE FUTURE

The transformation is happening now. It's happening in real time and, for the more esoteric, in virtual time. It's happening today. It will accelerate tomorrow and continue infinitely into the future as the winning retail leaders pursue excellence in the implementation of our three New Rules by embracing and optimizing the use of technology and the Internet. They will be creating not only new business models and strategies to indelibly connect with ever-increasing consumer demands but also order out of the chaotic landscape wrought by the technology revolution.

As consumers around the world become what we envision as one-world consumers with similar characteristics, tastes and desires wherever they may be, the opportunities—and challenges—for brands and retailers are enormous.

We have identified and analyzed the converging dynamics of technology-empowered consumers, brands and retailers. And we have specifically pointed to examples of its impact on strategies and business models as well as the even greater imperative for the implementation of our New Rules in Wave IV.

Now it is time to explore what it all means, and to make some predictions about how the future of retailing will look.

From a macro perspective, all winning brands and retailers will be pursuing direct-to-consumer business models on multiple distribution platforms, meaning maximum control (ownership or highly collaborative) over all elements of the value chain from creation to consumption. This is imperative for the seamless, preemptive delivery of precisely what consumers desire (including a neurologically connecting experience), wherever, whenever and how often they desire it.

The New Retail Landscape

Going forward, brands and retailers will either embrace all these opportunities and challenges or, we believe, they will face extinction. Within this context, we predict three distinct retail segments will evolve and survive:

1. **Commoditization sector.** This is defined as the market space where large amounts of undifferentiated product will be sold, most often selling other companies' brands, but not without a continuing pursuit of their own private brands. Categories included in this segment will include electronics; consumer packaged goods; groceries, some apparel; health and beauty aids; and any other category mainly consists of basic high-volume goods. These categories make up the core of the revenues for Amazon, Walmart, Costco, dollar stores like Dollar General and Family Dollar and Target, to name the big ones. This segment will find that price is the weapon of necessity, combined with the new distribution paradigm we have outlined. The future battlefield in this segment will be analogous to a kind of World War III as these retailers fight for market share. Retailers that are either subscale or unable to invest in the technologies that are required to win in these wars will disappear.

2. **Omni-Brand to Consumer sector.** This is the space of highly differentiated and dominant brands that have achieved a high level of superiority in implementing the New Rules and that best align with the six major consumer lifestyle shifts and desires occurring today (experiences, customization, democracy, new *and* now, community, technology for life).

   We purposely do not use the word "retail," because the name on the door or the website must be differentiated and dominant enough to be a "brand" in the minds of consumers, whether it is selling other brands or whether all its products bear the name on the door.

An omni-brand can be as small and independent as Scoop (apparel store) or Eataly (gourmet Italian food store and eatery) in New York City, selling multiple brands, or as big as Apple, Gap or Louis Vuitton, selling only their namesake branded products. "Omni-Brand to Consumer" means they operate on all possible distribution platforms with such superiority that they competitively preempt the competition either by reaching the consumer first or by compelling the consumer to make the brand his primary destination (usually with a superior neuroexperience). The model also implies a nearly vertically integrated, highly controlled (or brand-dominated) value chain. For instance, Piperlime, a Gap brand and one of the hottest and rapidly growing brands in the apparel, accessory and footwear category, sells major designer and nationally branded products. However, Piperlime is the dominant destination brand for the consumer and therefore has primary control even over some of the powerful brands it sells, such as Chloe or Rachel Roy.

Other examples include many of the apparel specialty chains such as J.Crew, Uniqlo, Forever 21, Victoria's Secret and many more. Whole Foods is a growing, dominant omni-brand in the grocery sector. Newly emerging pure e-commerce brands such as Warby Parker (eyewear) and Indochino (customized suits) are opening physical stores and becoming omni-brands.

We also believe Burberry, Nordstrom, Bloomingdale's, Neiman Marcus in the traditional luxury sector and Macy's and Belk in the traditional department store sector are all evolving into the Omni-Brand to Consumer model.

Finally, we believe that this segment will experience the highest level of growth into Wave IV.

3. **Liquidation sector.** This is the segment that has been and continues to be dominated by the TJX Corporation and Ross Stores in the so-called off-price sector. In fact, TJX is the fastest-growing retailer in the world as of this writing, expanding rapidly across the globe, forecasting its business to reach $40 billion by 2020, up from $27 billion at the end of 2013. Other retailers growing in this space include Ollie's, 99cents, Grocery Outlet and the interesting thrift store Savers.

While the outlet-store model cannot literally be called a liquidation model, indirectly it also competes in this space. The model,
along with the shopping centers that house them, is growing at a blistering pace. In fact, major retailers that are launching into this space
are eschewing full-line stores in favor of outlets. Nordstrom, Saks,
Bloomingdale's, Chico's, Coach and many more are either already
gaining most of their revenues from outlet stores or project they will
do so in the future.

Success in this segment will require providing great value *and*
a great experience—such as the "treasure hunt" at TJX—as well as
unique product.

While major brands and retailers may be largely anchored in, and realize
most of their revenues from, one of these three segments, they may very well
operate in more than one. However, regardless of which of the three sectors a
retailer predominately does business in, to successfully compete it must figure out how to apply our three New Rules to its particular business model,
whether it be Walmart or Amazon in the Commoditization sector, Apple or
Burberry in the Omni-Brand to Consumer sector or T.J.Maxx or Nordstrom
Rack stores in the Liquidation sector. While the implementation of neurologically connecting experiences, preemptive distribution and value-chain control will be different for each sector, indeed for every brand or retailer, they are
strategically imperative for success.

The Collapse of the Traditional
Retail/Wholesale Business Model

You already know our Wave IV mantra—*the consumer is central, and holds all
the cards of commerce.* We described how this centrality evolved from a time
when retailers and brands *were* central, and not widely distributed, so that
consumers had to seek them out. Back then, it was also more efficient and effective for products and services to join together in one location (the store) and
to provide the consumer with the widest-possible selection of merchandise.
This aggregation model also expanded into mall and shopping-center structures. During this period, since the retail store was the compelling draw for

consumers and knew better than the wholesalers what its consumers wanted, it was more efficient and effective for the retailer to edit, purchase and present the wholesalers' goods.

That scenario no longer exists, and the jointly shared retail/wholesale relationship is both inefficient and ineffective, for several reasons.

For one thing, it makes control of the value chain much more challenging for both retailers and wholesalers. In turn, this severely challenges the ability of either one to execute preemptive distribution or achieve neurological connectivity. It's not impossible, but it's much more difficult.

For those creating the products and brands, the primary challenge is being able to control, influence or create the selling environment. The selling environment, of course, is where the brand must neurologically connect with the consumer, deploying the entire imagery and DNA of the brand. The traditional model affords those brand creators only limited access to consumers and the subtle shifts in their behaviors, desires and aspirations. Thus the brand will not be totally responsive in making the continual refinements and improvements necessary to stay connected to the consumer. If all the store interactions around the consumer are lost to the channel partner, this most valuable consumer feedback does not become part of the brand's development cycle.

The complexities of implementing a new consumer experience through preexisting distribution networks that must also address multiple demands from many other brands and products across multiple categories are immense. The decisions wholesalers must make about how much to invest in their channel partners (retailers), as opposed to their end customers, are also vexing. Which channel partners should they focus on? How do they develop a relationship that allows them more control over their brand and how it's mixed, presented and serviced throughout the store? How can they communicate with and be responsive to their end consumers, now that they are highly mobile and difficult to reach? All this makes for a slower, more cumbersome, less agile organization, resulting in a huge disconnect between brand and consumer.

For traditional retailers, the same challenges exist, as they focus on establishing their own neurological connection between customers and their store brand (e.g., Macy's, Nordstrom and others), as well as preemptively gaining access to consumers ahead of their competitors. Saddled with their traditional brick-and-mortar model, in a world where consumers no longer have to leave the house, how do they transform themselves to better connect with consumers to gain the market share they need to survive? What is it that their store brand stands for and how do their current product selection and in-store experience reflect this? How quickly can they respond to new, more agile competitors like e-commerce retailers and the Omni-Brand to Consumer retailers, some of which carry the same wholesale brands they do? And how do they integrate and operate their own omni-channel (the Internet and multidistribution platforms) and all the new technological enablers?

From a tactical perspective, it's complicated. How long is the planning process and how big is the investment to develop a new format, highlight a particular experience or experiment with new product/consumer segments as well as new distribution platforms?

The decline of the traditional retail/wholesale model can also be tracked by its financial performance over the past twenty years. By the measure of continuous share loss alone, this performance strongly suggests the trend will continue toward ultimate collapse.

Traditional department stores lost more than 50 percent of their market share between 1990 and 2013. There were also several notable bankruptcies during that period, among them Alexander's, B. Altman, The Broadway, Ohrbach's, Halle Brothers, McCrory's, Woodward & Lothrop, Mervyn's, Gottschalks and many more. Between 1997 and 2013, sales through the traditional sector fell by around 5 percent per year, transferring those $13 billion of sales to the specialty retail stores.

In the apparel sector, it was even worse. As we discussed, since its inception in the 1960s, the apparel-specialty-chain model grew faster and gained more share each year than all other retail sectors. Having surpassed department stores, which in 1987 held the number-one share at more than 30 percent, the apparel retail specialists owned close to 35 percent by the early 2000s. Department stores' share of apparel has dropped below 18 percent and continues to fall, along with the number of major department stores, which is down from about fifty-nine in 1989 to fewer than ten in 2013.[1]

Perhaps the most compelling example is what happened in the teen apparel market. From the late 1990s until the beginning of the recession, there was an explosion of teen apparel retailers, and the rate of growth for dollars spent on teen apparel grew at an incredible 14 percent per year. The growth of specialty retailers like American Eagle, Aeropostale, Zumiez, Tilly's, The Buckle and Abercrombie & Fitch all gained substantial share from the department stores over this period. The growth came from their ability to effectively create highly engaging, unique environments for their target consumers, which department stores could not match because of their lumbering business model. The ability of the specialty retailers to execute these strategies, of course, sprang from their tightly controlled value chains.

Inside the traditional department stores, one of the key strategic thrusts from 2005 to 2013 has been to take more control of the value chain by attaining exclusive distribution of wholesale brands and creating privately owned brands—precisely why we predict that private and exclusive brands will eventually reach 80 percent of apparel sales.

This realization is also driving the investments of many of the traditional wholesale brands. Ralph Lauren has committed to expand its direct-to-consumer retail business that is now close to 50 percent of revenues. VF Corporation, one of the largest makers of denim (Wrangler, Lee, Seven For All Mankind) and the owner of The North Face, Vans, Reef and others, understands the imperative of controlling its preemptive connection to and with its consumers, compared to goods being cherry-picked and stacked on a shelf in a traditional store. That's why it is aggressively pursuing expansion of the retail segment of its business and, in fact, will not acquire new brands that do not have a retail component. With the Wrangler brand, which is the second-largest seller of denim in Walmart (after Walmart's Faded Glory private brand), VF determined its retail potential through test stores and subsequently launched a freestanding Wrangler retail expansion.

As both traditional retailers and wholesalers, then, accelerate their efforts to build their own brands and distinct connections with their consumers while selling within the same space, conflicts are bound to increase. The traditional partnership at the point of sale to sell to the same consumer becomes a more divided effort, with each partner pursuing its own brand objectives. And, in doing so, they not only dilute their respective messages, they severely weaken the most vital part of the chain: the part that connects with the ultimate consumer.

How will this tug-of-war play out?

An early visionary who successfully wrestled with these issues was Paul Charron. He was appointed CEO of Liz Claiborne in 1995 and chairman a year later. After stabilizing the declining business, he proceeded to profitably grow it to be the fourth largest in its sector. The reality of managing this unprecedented growth revealed Charron's view of how the retail/wholesale relationship should ultimately evolve. And as Liz Claiborne Inc. grew into a portfolio of both retail and wholesale brands, the complexity of running both business models clarified its status as a "collapsing relationship." One of Charron's key challenges was how to maintain the organizational flexibility, creativity and management of a portfolio of brands; specifically, how to be excellent as both a wholesaler and retailer. In a world with an infinite number of finite market segments, Charron was arguably the first to realize the power of a portfolio strategy to be able to preemptively target and distribute to an infinite number of opportunistic segments. Further, under Charron, Liz Claiborne leveraged its huge back-end operating platform to scale and gain productivity synergies to service the highly complex and segmented front end (brand marketing) of the business, a pioneering strategy. It also leveraged intelligence from one segment against opportunities in related but different segments. Regarding this breakthrough model, Charron said, "It's a great concept. But, if you can't control it, it can become a nightmare."[2]

Indeed, subsequent to Charron's retirement in 2006, and under new management, the portfolio strategy began to unravel after a failed attempt to refocus on the weakened Liz Claiborne flagship brand, the sell-off of many of the brands that had been acquired to build the portfolio synergy and operational deficiencies, all exacerbated by an economy slipping into recession.

Collapse through Conversion

Even as we predict the collapse of the traditional model, we believe the enlightened and strategically savvy retailers and wholesalers that understand this conundrum will manage its collapse together and convert the old models into one of the three new sectors, as we have described them. Those that do not will disappear.

We believe the old models will take several paths, and all of them ultimately have to do with having as much control over their individual value chains as possible.

The wholesale brands will pursue, and the retailers will relinquish, control of the brand's product, service, presentation and ultimately sales within the store and online. There will likely be a new kind of financial arrangement, perhaps leasing, with some top- or bottom-line sharing.

For instance, Macy's, as a destination brand in its own right, will cede space ownership and control to traditional wholesale brands (Ralph Lauren, for example) and even other retail brands, as they already have done with Sunglass Hut. JCPenney is doing something similar with Mango, Sephora and Joe Fresh.

European and Japanese models have historically been organized around a consignment model. Consider Selfridges, essentially a collection of brands operating their businesses as boutiques within the Selfridges brand.

In other retail and wholesale sectors, operating control manifests itself in many different ways.

For example, the Wrangler brand may never operate a Wrangler store per se, in space it would lease within Walmart. But because the Wrangler brand is more knowledgeable than Walmart about its core consumers (what they want, where, when and how often, including different product preferences of consumers shopping different Walmart stores), and because Wrangler's superior supply-chain process is so rapid and responsive, Walmart currently permits Wrangler to manage and control its line mix and size, frequency, replenishment and presentation. We believe that this trend will intensify.

In fact, Wrangler's management of its space provides additional nonfinancial value to the partnership by creating a synergy that strengthens Wrangler's long-term position with Walmart.

Of course, this strong partnership did not preclude or impede Wrangler's rolling out its own freestanding branded stores into its core consumers' neighborhoods, exercising the principle of preemptive distribution even to the exclusion of its strategic retail partner.

Also, and similar to Wrangler, P&G's legendary research and marketing prowess gives it unparalleled knowledge about its consumers; its supply-chain logistics and distribution skills are also superior. All this (along with slotting fees where appropriate) qualifies its brands for control over mix, size, frequency, replenishment and presentation within its retail partners' stores.

P&G frequently opens pop-up stores to provide a brand experience: in a New York pop-up, customers could have their hair washed and conditioned with Pantene, get a makeover from Olay and Cover Girl and shop through a kitchen and laundry area where Tide, Bounce, Dawn and Downy are on display.

One of the most interesting preemptive distribution strategies is P&G's partnership with Amazon, allowing the Internet giant to build its distribution centers inside the P&G facilities to provide rapid and more efficient distribution of its most commodity-like brands. This is another great example of how to identify and utilize multidistribution platforms. It also exemplifies the concept of collaborative control: controlling those experiences that are critical and outsourcing those that are not.

We even asked ourselves, now that P&G owns the Gillette brands, why it can't either open barbershops or be allocated space within other retailers' stores for an experiential shaving or grooming area?

Wholesale brands will continue to launch and/or expand their direct-to-consumer retail businesses on multidistribution platforms, newly defined by us as the Omni-Brand to Consumer segment. These platforms include e-commerce, TV and cobranding with different branded product categories, but with similar consumer positioning for synergy. We believe these brands' retail businesses could eventually reach 80 percent of their total revenues.

It's important to keep in mind that, for traditional wholesale brands, a direct-to-consumer retail distribution strategy (Omni-Brand to Consumer) does not mean they will relinquish their retail "partnership" business. They will simply control those relationships.

Traditional retail brands (e.g., Macy's, JCPenney, Kohl's, Target, Walmart and others) will continue their aggressive pursuit of private and/or exclusive brands. We believe their share of total revenues could reach 80 percent as well. In addition to differentiation, having control of these brands affords greater responsiveness, flexibility, reduced cycle time and an ability to turn out more new lines, more often. They can better localize according to consumer tastes, and they control the better part of two profit margins, providing greater pricing flexibility.

Supermarkets offer a great illustration of how this trend is starting to play out. Trader Joe's is probably the best example of the creation of unique private brands that make up most of their selection and are an integral part of the neuroexperience. Moreover, they have configured the layout of their smaller stores to enhance the fun and intimacy of the shopping experience. These leading strategies in the grocery sector are forcing all food chains and supermarkets to follow suit. O Organics is another example. Owned by Safeway, O Organics (a private-label brand) has gradually been replacing the niche and fringe brands offering organic products. In fact, the private-label product of Safeway is crowding out the branded products, like Earthbound and Wallaby yogurts, across the board. In the future, the new private and/or exclusive brands will not be positioned as cheaper and almost as good as the branded products. They will be *as* good or better, and positioned and priced accordingly.

The traditional retailers will also seek higher productivity through leasing space (or other financial arrangements) to other retail brands whose consumer positioning is compatible, and whose presence would create a synergy. The traditional retail brands will adopt and/or expand on a strategy of rolling out smaller neighborhood stores, preemptively gaining access to more consumers and better enabling them to make the consumer connection by localizing their offerings (e.g., Walmart, Bloomingdale's and others). They will also leverage the power of their growing private and/or exclusive brands by rolling out smaller specialty retail chains (Omni-Brand to Consumer models), again increasing control over their value chains to create great experiences.

These retailers will continue to explore new distribution platforms of opportunity, such as pop-up stores (Kate Spade, Target and others), in-home marketing and event marketing, as well as innovative concepts such as mobile marketing and other preemptive distribution strategies.

Retailers Will Become Enclosed
Mini-Malls for Increased Productivity

Retail-space productivity (sales per square foot) is arguably one of the most important metrics for retailers to quickly assess the strength and growth rate of their business. As organic growth in the industry has steadily declined, driving retailers to increase market share, one such strategy is to focus on increasing productivity in underperforming space.

Unfortunately, we know that in the current slow-to-no-growth market, traditional strategies have become merely the price of entry. Simply restocking underperforming space with similar product, therefore, however new or better it might be, is not likely to result in either increased traffic or improved productivity.

So the new strategy involves management's defining its real estate as a mall owner would. Management seeks to lease space to other retailers, brands and/or services that will increase both traffic and productivity.

For example, while the department stores will continue to strengthen and control their nameplate brand and their private or exclusive brands, they will lease space and the control of it (operations and presentation) to compatible outside designer and national brands across various consumer products industries (e.g., Sephora's dedicated space in JCPenney, Peet's Coffee & Tea within Raley's grocery stores, Sunglass Hut and LVMH within Macy's). Selfridges department store in London has leased most of its space for many year to brands such as Vivienne Westwood, John Rocha, Dolce and Gabbana and, more recently, DCL (Dermatologic Cosmetic Laboratories), Skin and the Blink Brow Bar. This model doubles as part of a brand's preemptive distribution strategy, accessing additional and new distribution platforms.

The benefits are great for both the retailer and the joined compatible business. The newly joined business gets immediate, low-capital-invested growth in multiple locations, thereby reaching new customers geographically. It also benefits from the traffic generated by the host retailer. Likewise, the host retailer benefits from the destination traffic of the joined business. Finally, the combined businesses enhance the shopping experience and therefore mutually strengthen their consumer connections.

Taken to its logical endpoint over time, the collapse and/or conversion of the traditional departmentalized retailing model greatly consolidate the playing field. Thousands of currently weak, marginalized or commoditized wholesale brands will be eliminated, and the opportunity for creating new wholesale brands will be greatly diminished.

The first attempt by a major department store to convert its model into an enclosed mini-mall was JCPenney. As we described in the prologue, the attempt, though a dismal failure, demonstrated that then-new-CEO Ron Johnson was in fact a visionary. His goal was to create a Selfridges-like bazaar of great, neurologically connecting and preemptive experiences, and "streets" of exciting branded boutiques (collaboratively controlled). However, while his vision was aligned with our prediction, his implementation was fatally flawed, and it ended in disaster.

We believe that our prediction is still valid for all the foregoing logic. And we believe it is the only model that traditional department stores must pursue for succeeding in the future, if not for their mere survival. In fact, we speculate that Macy's will continue to evolve toward this model. While it may not proactively articulate this strategy, it is very successfully creating exciting experiences, adding great new exclusive and private branded shops and is on the leading edge of successfully converging the omni-channel, a seamlessly integrated and interchangeable multidistribution platform. All these initiatives have been possible because of management's strategic vision and superior operating capabilities to achieve it.

Finally, this transformed retail/wholesale model will have space only for those wholesale power brands with global recognition (Coca-Cola, Tide, Ralph Lauren, Louis Vuitton and other designer-status brands) or brands whose level of innovation remains high in growth categories such as technology (Apple), action sports (Under Armour or Nike) or consumer package goods (P&G brands).

To emphasize this point, as Trader Joe's has demonstrated, even power brands as nationally entrenched as Peter Pan peanut butter are vulnerable to retailers owning the experience and creating their own brands.

At the end of the day, the collapse and convergence of the traditional retail/wholesale business model also eliminate even the function of the words "retail" and "wholesale." In the eyes of the consumer, the products of those retailers and wholesalers that successfully transform their businesses will all simply be brands. Therefore their retailers and wholesalers would more appropriately be defined as brand managers.

The Death of "B" and "C" Malls and Shopping Centers

Correspondingly, as the traditional model collapses, and as e-commerce grows a larger share of all retail sales, smaller stores and the Omni-Brand to

Consumer sector will be the predominantly successful models. Therefore, we predict the closing of second- and third-tier "B" and "C" regional malls and shopping centers, while the "A" malls will need to be converted into entertainment destinations to survive.

Half of All Retailers and Brands Will Disappear

We covered the accelerated pursuit among all retailers of private and/or exclusive brands above primarily to demonstrate that this strategy will provide them greater control over their value chains, allowing them to become small, enclosed mini-malls. And we touched on the fact that many wholesale brands will be squeezed out of these new models, if not fail altogether.

We also declared that only those retailers and wholesalers that transformed their models to adhere to our three operating principles, the New Rules, would survive.

For both these reasons, we predict that 50 percent of all current brands and retailers will disappear.

We cited the growing percentage of private and exclusive brands in the major department- and discount-store sectors, and our projection that it would reach about 80 percent across retailing. In Europe, 60 percent of the supermarket shelf space is already occupied by private brands, and 50 percent of Walmart goods are already private brands.

In the future, retailing will be about narrowing assortments and reducing vendors and wholesale brands to drive greater control, productivity and profitability. Supervalu, Kroger and other major supermarket chains have been systematically eliminating brands and products from their shelves.[3] The consumer package goods industry, best exemplified by P&G, has always had a "conflictive collaboration" between its powerhouse brands and retailers' private-label goods. Recently, Walmart removed Glad and Hefty brands from its shelves, retaining only one brand, Ziploc. Industry observers expect similar decisions to play out across other categories as the behemoth of Bentonville accelerates its effort to simplify brand assortment and focus its support on its Great Value private brand. While the exact selection of products available in Walmart will ebb and flow, the trend is clear. Conversely, P&G, as mentioned before, is testing its own branded, stand-alone stores.

Both the narrowing of lines and the building of private brands are accelerating in other industries as well, such as drugstores Walgreens and CVS. In fact, CVS, in its SKU (stock-keeping unit)-cutting strategy, pulled Energizer batteries from the shelves in a bid to simplify choices for consumers, and it has eliminated many national brands in favor of its private label. Home Depot and Lowe's are beginning to follow suit.

Some experts believe that this emphasis on productivity optimization will reduce overall SKU count by more than 15 percent. Kevin Sterneckert, retail research director for AMR Research, believes that retailers are "far from done on the optimization and SKU-reduction fronts."[4]

As for the retail failures we predicted, there have been several over the past few years, among them Borders, the Bombay Company, Sharper Image, Fortunoff, Blockbuster, Filene's Basement, Syms, Loehmann's and more. We expect the failures to continue, not because of the recession, but because a growing number of them will not be able to transform their models and positioning to provide the elevated experiences we've been defining.

Major challenges are mounting at Kmart, Sears, JCPenney, Kohl's and the few regional department stores left. We believe these giant nameplates are at great risk, as they continue to muddle along in the middle market with no discernible strategic position or competitive advantage—neither special nor cheap. JCPenney tried to pull itself away from that no-man's-land but failed. Macy's seems to be successfully doing so, as does regional player Belk. However, this group of retailers stuck in a "paradigm past," particularly Sears and Kmart, will soon be struggling for survival. Their models simply do not currently fit into any of our three predicted retail segments in Wave IV.

The Gap is downsizing its brand in the United States and will likely continue to do so. Many small independent retailers that miss the transformation will fail. We hasten to add, however, that they have the greatest opportunity to outdo big retailers, thanks to their community presence and control over their environment. For various reasons—the need to control one's supply chain, to increase productivity and profitability, to narrow, downsize and accelerate private branding for differentiation and niche positioning—we conclude that there will be an enormous number of retailers and brands that will not survive into Wave IV—50 percent, in our estimation.

The Death or Diminishment of Megabrands

For reasons other than those causing the disappearance of 50 percent of brands and retailers as predicted above, we further predict that iconic brands like Tide, Chevrolet, Sony, Coca-Cola, Wheaties, Cheerios, Skippy, Calvin Klein and others are going to suffer a precipitous decline in relevance, sales and share of market; they may even potentially disappear altogether with the "50 percent" discussed in the foregoing section.

While this prediction may seem counterintuitive or even preposterous to most, we believe this will be a result of the increasing power of accessibility and selectivity of the Wave IV consumer and the continually increasing and excessive stream of new products, services, brands, retailers and e-commerce, with no equivalent offsetting of the excess. And, as acknowledged throughout this book, Wave IV consumers are further empowered by technology and digital commerce, which has enhanced quicker, easier and smarter access and has even empowered them with the ability to dictate pricing.

Those brands and retailers that do not understand how to adapt or transform their models to capture this more technologically enabled and empowered consumer will eventually disappear. Even those that do get it, and that change accordingly, will at best be grandfathered into niche markets, diminished in value and share.

To put this prediction into historical context, most of the current megabrands were launched in the marketing-driven Wave II years, when innovation, mass marketing and a very well-defined and narrowly tiered distribution structure targeted equally defined and structured consumer segments. Customers' relationships with brands and shopping behavior were easy to anticipate, understand and respond to. And during this period, while market saturation was beginning to form, it had not yet reached its Wave III and IV levels.

So, this more balanced supply-and-demand ratio fueled the epic expansion and scale of megabrands in a less complex and congested marketplace. Indeed, this was the era in which all the aforementioned brands, and hundreds more across all industries, defined the prefix "mega." "Mass markets" and "mass marketing" were the buzzwords, and it became known as the golden age of advertising. It was also the period when megabrands occupied the first-, second- and/or third-ranked positions in their respective industries, along with dominant share of market.

Then the so-called mass markets became massively congested markets. The rather traditionally competitive marketplace turned into a more complex market, requiring more sophisticated and complex marketing for gaining share and growth.

To use P&G as an example: There was one Tide detergent in the middle of Wave II. Then more competition prompted brand extension strategies. So it launched New Tide. Then there was Tide with Bleach. Then there was Tide to Go. And it continued through today's count of around 40 different Tide brand extensions, including Tide Pods.

More competitors, more copycats of P&G's best practices and the proliferation of private brands all contributed to the dizzying array of hundreds of equally compelling branded and private-label detergents jockeying for position on overstuffed supermarket shelves.

Thus, differentiation got fuzzier and fuzzier amid the chaos of unlimited choice. Accordingly, the effectiveness of the old-school P&G strategy of innovating and/or extending the brand into ever more niches, supported by millions of dollars of national advertising, began to wane.

Tide is but one example in one industry. Yet simultaneous scenarios were, and are still, playing out across all consumer-facing industries. Another example: There was one major Nike sneaker in 1972, the waffle-soled "moon shoe." Today there are more than seventy. Dannon had six yogurt flavors, compared to more than a hundred today.

Therefore, the "share war" battles intensified among all brands and retailers in pursuit of competitive advantage. This was exacerbated by the necessity to market the real or perceived differentiation among the thousands of equally compelling competitors, which were growing at breakneck speed.

Adding fuel to the competitive complexity in Wave IV is digital commerce. The good news is that it provides an incredibly powerful new channel of distribution for brands and retailers. Perversely, however, it also brings with it more online stores and stuff. Worse, the barriers to entry for new branded websites are very low, thus providing every wannabe entrepreneur the ability to be open for business overnight.

Furthermore, along with the Internet come mobile commerce, new apps on a daily basis and an array of shopping-enabling technologies to connect with consumers wherever, whenever, however and how often they want to be connected, and continuously providing the lowest-possible price.

Globalization also connects more consumers with more brands and stores, as international brands enter the United States and as US brands expand globally. Ubiquitous distribution, then, is an apt description.

Consumers Will Drive the Death or Diminishment

So far, we've been largely describing the supply side and how brands and retailers have had to keep raising their performance levels to survive in this new hypercompetitive, overcongested world.

However, all those characteristics have been, and still are, driven by the consumer on the demand side. And it is consumers who will drive the extinction, or at least the diminishment of the megabrands. To be more specific, it will be the millennials who will be doing most of the driving. And they are driving the marketplace into a total reassessment of value and values.

Their postwar grandparents lived in the more simplified, uncongested marketplace and coveted the megabrands and traditional retailers. And even the millennials' baby-boomer parents, in their early prime, carried a dimming torch for those brands in the waning, marketing-driven Waves II and III. A snapshot of their definition of value and values generally looked like quantity over quality, addiction to discounts (even for their beloved brands, luxury included), more "stuff," "McMansions" and status over experiences and lifestyle pursuits.

Conversely, the millennials, who are slated to account for more than 30 percent of retail sales by 2020, have almost diametrically opposite values. They seek quality over quantity and value shopping experiences both online and off, and that includes personalizing their desire for exclusivity and special brands rather than ubiquitous brands. They are more understated, and they pursue social networking and individual lifestyles.

Millennials are propelling the full-on transformative effect of overcapacity, globalization, the Internet and other consumer- and market-enabling technologies that will threaten the very lives of the megabrands and traditional retailers.

This scenario suggests a future marketplace with an infinite number of finite (limited) brands and retailers micromarketing to an infinite number of finite consumer niches that are more like small, social communities than cohorts. And brands and retailers will need permission and invitations into these communities, rather than simply talking *to* or *at* them. This also aligns with our prediction early in this chapter that the Omni-Brand to Consumer model would have the highest level of growth going forward.

In fact, if one can imagine the extreme, each consumer may very well have his or her own special exclusive brand for every aspect of his or her life. Take it a step further—no, try a leap ahead—and imagine the ability to literally self-customize everything in your life, including food, cars, beverages, clothes, home products and more. Three-D printing has come out of the garage and is advancing faster than you can say "Beam me up, Scotty."

The millennials, then, will hasten the demise or diminishment of megabrands, because they have total quicker, smarter and easier access to everything in the world, and because their set of values, along with how they perceive the value of things, does not favor megabrands or retailers.

Discounting Is Exacerbating the Threat

If this prediction weren't dire enough, the megabrands and retailers may end up committing a perverse form of suicide. As the daily tsunami of more stuff and stores continues, all of it starts to look, perform or taste alike—blurred, fuzzy and indistinct. In this environment, price discounting becomes not only a weapon of choice but one of necessity, also exacerbated by the great disruptor, Amazon.

Discounting, the race to the bottom, coupon and sale addiction—all are part of the equation that will kill the megabrands. Over time, these practices erode value, either in reality by taking quality (costs) out of the brand, or simply through compromising consumers' perception of the brand, thereby tarnishing brands' and retailers' integrity and image. Nobody wins in price wars, and one cannot cost-cut one's way to top- and bottom-line growth. Ultimately one cuts to the bone, with nothing left to cut. And it ends badly. This is not sustainable for either megabrands or retailers.

Tide recently announced plans to launch a new bargain version, adding to all its previous brand extensions, citing that 41 percent of households bought value brands rather than premium brands, which accounted for 29 percent of sales. P&G stated that the value segment is the only growth niche left in the detergent category.[5]

Outlet stores seem to be one of the only growth segments remaining in the luxury-apparel sector as well. The Coach brand realizes 60 percent of its total revenues from its outlet stores. Nordstrom and Saks have more outlet stores than full-line stores, and are planning to open even more outlets in the future. Bloomingdale's is accelerating its outlet-store program. Ralph Lauren, while brilliantly successful in slicing and dicing the brand into various niche segments, gains a big part of its revenue through its outlet stores. Michael Kors, Vera Wang, Nicole Miller, Karl Lagerfeld and many other designer brands have launched sub-brands into mainstream and discount stores to capture more growth.

And, as cited earlier, the fastest-growing retail sector is the off-price model, primarily used by TJX companies. Private brands have also moved beyond competing just on price to higher-quality and more sophisticated packaging and marketing. One survey conducted by the International Research Institute (IRI) found that 70 percent of millennial women believe store brands have excellent quality.[6]

These are all forms of discounting or insidiously devaluing the brands, and it's happening with the mainstream brands as well, across almost every industry.

Our message to megabrands and retailers, therefore, is that they must change their strategy from infinitely growing their mass brand to a strategy of infinite growth into finite niches—think "universes of one." Secondly, they must clearly align our New Rules with the new values and perception of value of the Wave IV consumers as well as their pursuit of the six lifestyle desires (experiences, customization, democracy, new *and* now, community, technology for life). And, even though these massive Wave II brands might then be diminished in size and share of market, they will still be alive, and likely more profitable and poised for growth.

Globalization and the One-World Consumer

It's interesting that the 150-year history of retailing evolved in a sequential manner in the United States, whereas Waves I, II and III are occurring almost simultaneously in many of the developing countries around the world, catapulting them into the same space the United States inhabits today. This suggests that the transformation of developing countries from production-driven economies into marketing- and consumer-driven economies is nearly complete.

Even as these countries continue to benefit from their low-cost production capabilities, they are simultaneously ramping up their marketing and consumption economies, which represents an opportunity for US brands to expand globally. However, since the world is now "flat," with global markets accessible to all, developing countries would be blind not to recognize that the US marketplace also offers their brands a great expansion opportunity.

As an article in the *Economist* pointed out: "The world's creative energy is shifting to the developing countries, which are becoming innovators in their own right rather than just talented imitators. . . . Even more striking is the emerging world's growing ability to make established products for dramatically lower costs: no-frills $3000 cars and $300 laptops may not seem as exciting as a new iPad but they promise to change far more people's lives. The sort of advance—dubbed 'frugal innovation' by some—is not just a matter of exploiting cheap labor (though cheap labor helps). It is a matter of redesigning products and processes to cut out unnecessary costs."[7]

Moreover, as these countries continue to grow, they will be developing their own brands, particularly for their mass markets. Big, globally recognized US brands may thus lose at least some of their luster over time. The *Economist* also pointed out that the winners in these markets will not be big (global) brands, but Chinese or Indian brands. Black & Decker, America's biggest toolmaker, is almost invisible in India and China, the world's two biggest construction sites.

Soon enough, then, there will be a twofold and globally disruptive dynamic occurring among the developing countries. First is the acquisition of US (and other) marketplace assets (brands and retailers), and with it the power of a totally controlled (actually owned) value chain. We believe

China will accelerate its asset acquisitions in the United States. Second will be the continuing development of their own markets, including innovation and creation of their own brands and retail businesses. Former investment banker Felix Rohatyn told the *Wall Street Journal:* "Control will go with capital."[8] And today, of course, China controls a massive amount of the world's capital.

Finally, since innovation is best executed by those who control the value from creation through distribution and interaction with the consumer, we believe there will also be new brands innovated in the developing countries to be marketed in the United States.

One historic example is Japan's contribution to innovation in the automobile industry, which turned the US market on its head. Japan not only created smaller fuel-efficient cars while the United States stuck to gas-guzzlers during the OPEC oil crisis and skyrocketing gas prices during the 1970s, but it also innovated quality-control standards and processes that produced cars that were initially far superior to American-made automobiles. Certainly the same potential for the developing countries exists across multiple retail and consumer businesses in the United States. Many companies, such as P&G, General Motors, Ford, Estée Lauder, Coach, Nike and many others, already see this challenge and have built a clear global competency in all elements of the value chain. Investing in a flexible value chain not only supports the complex and highly segmented markets in the United States, but also enables them to meet the unique demands of the new and developing markets.

Other companies might choose to become "masters of frugal innovation" for the developing world, innovating affordable new products and services specifically for those countries. For example, Unilever has opened its concept center in Shanghai to conduct day-to-day research on the Chinese consumer. Procter & Gamble is doing the same. Perhaps the current poster child is Nokia, producing inexpensive phones for almost every income stratum in Asia.

There remains one possible area of US competitive advantage that could be exportable: "experience" innovation, or our superiority in marketing and creating experiential branding and the shopping experience. What we have been discussing as an imperative for US brands will soon become even more crucial in the developing world. Indeed, survival into Wave IV requires a global presence one way or another.

Although this may seem like a dire scenario for the United States, we do not believe all our great brands and/or retailers will either be acquired by developing countries or replaced by competing foreign brands. In fact, we believe just as strongly that another of our predictions will more than offset this scenario. Because we are a nation of entrepreneurs, and with consumers desiring ever more customization, localization, niche brands and so forth, we predict the continual emergence of an infinite number of finite markets, served by an infinite number of finite or niche brands and/or services, distributed on an infinite number of distribution platforms. And because of their smaller size, resulting in tighter and more responsive value chains, much of the development and production of those brands and services will be domestic.

The Growth of Permission-Based Marketing

Just as retail, wholesale and service business models are being driven by consumers in saturated markets, these same dynamics are driving an equally fundamental transformation in the communications, advertising and media industries.

This matters because marketing occupies a critical part of the value chain. Without its effective implementation, the achievement of the neurological connection will be impeded. Also, preemptive distribution is enhanced when it is effectively led by communications and advertising.

So, along with consumer behavioral shifts, technological advances continue to expand an infinite number of distribution platforms for communications, products and services that can literally follow and access individual consumers 24/7. Unfortunately for marketers, the same technological innovations have allowed the consumer not only to block what they do not want entering their "space," but also to invite or grant permission to precisely what they do welcome.

What this means is that communication about products or services is no longer controlled by the company. The power of social network sites, blogs and other electronic platforms is that they more than counterbalance the traditionally well-orchestrated marketing messages from the consumer-products businesses. For instance, Pampers' launch of Dry Max diapers a few years ago was substantially hindered by online critics; an article in the *Financial Times* referred to the diaper and the online contagion by saying, "The criticism . . . spread like a rash."[9]

Hence there will be a fundamental transformation of the media and advertising industries to finitely target both content and distribution, where they can measure quality and cost of contact. In addition to the overabundance of stores, stuff and everything else over the past twenty years, there has also been a deluge of communication of all types, including advertising, accommodated by the equally enormous deluge of media and communications platforms including the Internet and social media.

With almost a billion websites emitting enough information to fill seventeen Libraries of Congress every three years, hundreds of TV channels (compared to a handful in Wave II), enough magazine titles to accommodate every niche interest and many, many more communications platforms, all chasing after every single consumer and bombarding them with noise, consumers have finally said, "No more."

The collective switches of the marketplace went from "on" to "off" several years ago. Traditional media and the advertising world are just now scrambling to convert their antiquated approaches into models that seek an invitation into consumers' lives.

As in retailing, short of a total overhaul, consumers will continue to turn off when confronted by advertising content and media overload. This is one of the major challenges currently confronting the online social networks, particularly Facebook. It has yet to determine how to commercialize the network as members feel intruded upon by marketers. Accordingly, marketers are trying to figure out how to be welcomed and "permitted" into the space. Remember, it is the consumer who switches your lights on in the morning and who can switch them off for good anytime, for any reason.

Viewership, readership and listenership have shifted, and continue to shift, from TV, magazines, newspapers and radio to the Internet and mobile. This is where consumers can find most content free or almost free, and where they can pull out what they choose, rather than having ads and information pushed at them. It's also interactive in real time, producing immediate gratification. As a consequence, all the ratings measures of the traditional media, along with all their top and bottom lines, plummeted in the 2000s, and continue downward today.

Traditional media and advertising, like traditional retailing, are transforming themselves to be responsive to the very same consumer shifts that are transforming all consumer-facing industries. The top brands have already shifted ad spending to new media (web banner ads, blogs, digital newscasts and newsfeeds and social networking). They're adopting burgeoning tech platforms that help integrate brand messages across all social media platforms, including Facebook, Twitter, Pinterest and Tumblr. Many have YouTube channels showing videos and commercials that are among some of the best in marketing. Those brands that do not make these strategy changes will disappear. Many already have.

P&G anticipated the shift years ago. As early as 2004, its global marketing officer, James Stengel, told Forbes.com: "The mass-marketing model is dead. This (word of mouth) is the future."[10]

Putting its money where its mouth was, P&G launched the Tremor Division, consisting of 280,000 teenagers who, for nothing more than a few coupons and product samples, spread the word (and samples), endorsing the products at school, at parties and sleepovers and digitally. At the time, moreover, only a third of Tremor's activities were devoted to P&G products. Most of the information spreading was for other national brands such as AOL, Coca-Cola, Kraft Foods and Toyota, for which P&G charged hefty fees.

P&G was ahead of the curve. Statistics show that advertising is no longer the main influence on a consumer purchase. Consumers are now learning about products via friends or other trusted peers online, by visiting other buyers' blogs or forum discussions and by reading buyer comments. Fashion bloggers are getting front-row seats at designer shows. Word of mouth has now become the primary driver across all consumer-facing industries. The consumer is truly in the driver's seat.

What's Next?

So what is the future going to hold for advertising, marketing and media? How are they going to transform their models to survive and serve the twenty-first-century consumer?

David Kirkpatrick, a senior editor and columnist for *Fortune* magazine, referring to the book *The Future of Competition: Co-Creating Unique Value with Customers,* not only reinforced our thesis regarding retailing's transformation but also provided a new framework for us to theorize about the future of media and advertising. He said we're entering a "bottom-up-economy," in which consumers will migrate to businesses that allow them to be participants in the process of creating what they want. Future consumers are going to be wired, but only to what they choose to be wired to. Consumers will construct their own life model, essentially a file of all those things they like or want—products, services, brands, books, magazines, entertainment, etc. They will key in those things that will be permitted entry into their space. Conversely, there will be an explicit list of what they will not permit, as well as instructions as to when and how they want to be reached. All consumer businesses will have access to that file.[11]

The good news for all marketers in this projected future is that they will be able to communicate directly and precisely with their existing and targeted consumers more efficiently and effectively, and with very quantifiable measures of return on investment. Revolutions are painful and costly, but considerably less so than consumers putting you out of business.

PART 3

THE MASTERS

CHAPTER 10

THE MASTER MODEL

OMNI-BRAND TO CONSUMER

The Omni-Brand to Consumer model will accelerate in Wave IV and become the dominant, or master, model in every product category. We believe the power of the model will compel more pure e-commerce sites to open physical stores and more brick-and-mortar retailers to expand their e-commerce and mobile capabilities. While there are many variables for the relative success or failure of any one of the omni-channel brands, in the aggregate, the very reason for their tremendous success is the strategic foundation of their model. Its entire focus is on connecting with their consumer neurologically with incredible experiences; highly differentiated, unique and personalized product; and superior service, all tightly aligned with the six major consumer desires in Wave IV. The model's focus is also on ensuring the brand quickest and easiest access to its customers (preemptive distribution). And because the brand name on the door and its digital platform is the destination brand, they have total and/or dominant control over their value chain (not dependent on any third party), particularly those functions that touch the consumer, both in getting direct input from them (the co-creation of their desires) and the final connection at the point of sale. It is this totally controlled and integrated omni-brand value chain that enables the neurological connection and preemptive access in the first place. Finally, combining these inherent advantages with the new technology enablers and enhancers of Wave IV does make it the master model, poised to continue growing faster and gaining more share than all other retail models.

What follows is an analysis of the competitive advantages of this model, based on our three operating principles of neurological connectivity, preemptive distribution and value-chain control.

Better Potential for Creating the Neurological Connection

Because the entire presentation and environment are controlled by the omni-brand, and the entirety of its imagery is consistent, these brands can more easily create the desired experience. However, it's important to note that while purely digital brands like Net-A-Porter may connect neurologically with consumers, the connection cannot be made as powerfully as when the brand embraces and surrounds the consumer in the physical store. Conversely, all those brands that launched in the physical world and that have now become omni-brands (like J. Crew, Victoria's Secret, Coach and more) have discovered that it's a challenge to replicate the same powerful neuroconnection online. However, for both, there is a synergy to be achieved as an omni-brand.

For example, one might go to an Athleta store or to Warby Parker's website to sense and see the imagery, lifestyle and essence of the brands: the workout lifestyle and pictures of in-store events at Athleta; and the hip, modern and funky imagery of Warby Parker. Consumers may feel connected in a compelling way and may make the purchase online. However, it is the enticement online for them to come into the store and to feel the experience in all "six senses," including the mind, that makes the indelible, impervious connection. Finally, there are new technologies that will augment reality and further enhance these experiences. And, if consumers first connect with the brand in the physical world, it automatically compels them to the website at home as they remember the yoga class or whatever experience they had in the Athleta store. This is also why it is imperative to have a completely integrated and interchangeable omni-channel, so that consumers can order online and pick up in the store at their convenience.

Because of these neurological experiences, consumers will pay more, stay longer, return first to that store or website (thus preempting competitors), come back more often and remain loyal longer.

Easier and More Intimate Shopping Experience

Most of the omni-brands occupy 3,500- to 5,000-square-foot physical stores. This provides a smaller, casual, more intimate and less frustrating shopping environment than department-store or big-box models. Therefore, the Omni-Brand to Consumer model accommodates either a personalized, relaxed shopping experience or a quick in-and-out if the customer so desires. And of course the retailers, through analysis of their new technologically aggregated Big Data bases, will know when the customer walks into the store or keys into the site whether they are a relaxed shopper wanting a personalized experience, and what that experience is, or if they just want to make a quick purchase.

And, again, this experience will carry over in their minds as they shop online or when they are mobile.

Single Dedicated Space for Cohesive and Total Lifestyle Presentation

Since all their space is devoted to one branded lifestyle (again, every brand from Eataly to Apple to Piperlime represents a lifestyle), omni-brands can present their total lifestyle concept, including all the products representing it, in one place and on one site. Conversely, many lifestyle brands carried in traditional, generic stores find their various product categories spread throughout multiple departments and on different floors. The omni-brand model also allows the presentation of a broader mix of products and deeper, better-edited assortments.

More Focused, Knowledgeable and Effective Associates

This focused model simplifies the hiring, training and retention of sales associates. Most omni-brand models hire associates who match the profile of their core consumer. In fact, the majority of associates at Chico's, Abercrombie, Apple and many other omni-brands are hired directly from their consumer bases through in-store "Help Wanted" signage. Obviously, the learning curve for these associates is shortened because of their familiarity with the products, the service and the whole shopping experience. They can immediately relate to the customers, and because they already love the brand, they find it easier to share that love when they're working as associates. Furthermore, as mentioned above, the associates can now personalize the experience for each customer through the use of Big Data, as well as in-store tracking of each customer's characteristics and shopping behavior.

For all these reasons, employee turnover is lower in the omni-channel-brand sector. Experts estimate that turnover is about 50 percent annually, compared to the industry norm of 75 percent.[1]

Real-Time Research and Relationship Building

Finally, since consumers are essentially stepping into the brand when they step into the store or key into the site, there are no competing brand distractions. Customers are captive. This provides an opportunity for the associates to do real-time research to determine what's hot and what's not and, most important, whether their customers are satisfied (and if not, why not). In many cases, moreover, the associates will become friendly enough with their loyal customer base that they interact with them freely about the arrival of special new products, sending birthday cards, wishing them well and so forth. All this real-time research will be augmented by the aggregated customer data mentioned above.

Smaller, Flexible Footprints for More Accessible Locations

Thanks to a single lifestyle focus and smaller physical footprints, these brands have maximum potential for moving their physical stores closer to consumers' neighborhoods, providing even more convenience. And while many of them are currently mall-based, as mall traffic declines and "B" and "C" malls get shuttered (as we predict), replaced by the faster-growing neighborhood shopping centers, these brands will also move, further strengthening the omni-channel synergy for preemptive distribution. And perhaps the biggest part of the omni-channel synergy for preemptive distribution is, of course, the ability to reach out 24/7, digitally, through smartphones and all the many different preemptive apps available in Wave IV technology.

Neurologically Defined Experience as Preemptive Destination

The omni-brand is *the* brand; therefore, the entire store and website, and everything in it, are *the* destination, including the neurological experience. This is much more effective than having a single brand or product category located within the complex maze of a department or big-box store. This element also enables the brand to develop and present itself more quickly, clearly and cohesively on all possible distribution platforms, both offline and online.

Control of One Simpler, Branded Value Chain

The omni-brand model has maximum control, even if not outright ownership, of its entire value chain from creation through consumption. This is what makes the neurological connection and preemptive distribution possible. It also affords maximum efficiency, flexibility, reduced cycle times for more new lines, the ability to localize the product offerings and control over inventory and excesses, all without the time, complexity and compromise that come with a multiplicity of vendors and/or suppliers.

Finally, the value chain in Wave IV has never been as technologically enabled as it is today. Having been more focused on the back end of the chain in Wave II and III, technology in Wave IV has fully connected and integrated every link in the chain, particularly (and most importantly) the final link that connects with the consumer. It is now possible to have optimum control over the value chain in order to provide the consumers with whatever they desire, newer, quicker, cheaper, how and when they want it.

Approaching a New Paradigm in the
Omni-Brand to Consumer Model

A new truth universally acknowledged in the Omni-Brand to Consumer sector is that the days of the megabrand—one brand covering all product categories and consumer segments—are over.

Indeed, the paradigm is shifting in favor of an infinite number of finitely segmented consumer niches, being served by an infinite array of finitely focused brands.

We've mentioned previously some examples of this paradigm shift in the apparel category: A&F's spinning off the Hollister-branded chain, targeting different consumer niches; Chico's acquiring White House | Black Market and launching Soma Intimates; Urban Outfitters with its Free People and Anthropologie offshoots, all three positioned to target different consumer segments, with different lifestyles and shopping experiences; and J. Crew launching Crewcuts for kids and Madewell casual-clothing stores.

But why is this new paradigm evolving? It is the result of three dynamics working in tandem:

- Because of unlimited selection, consumers are seeking exclusivity. They want things that are special, just for them. Mass markets are in decline.
- The consumer's ability to achieve exclusivity is being enabled by an infinitely fragmented and dispersed media and marketing infrastructure, including the explosion of new channels of distribution, the Internet and mobile commerce.
- Technology is further enabling the consumers' demands for exclusivity. Superior information, logistics and distribution technologies are elevating supply-chain capabilities to support multiple market and brand segments and smaller exclusive niches, including different line mixes according to geographic preferences.

The Model to Beat or Imitate

Based on the strength of this omni-brand model and its rapid growth and share dominance in some categories (particularly apparel, primarily taken from the department-store sector), one could argue that some of the major department stores are fighting back with the same weaponry used against them.

For example, there is no question that Macy's, Bloomingdale's, Belk, Nordstrom, Lord & Taylor, Neiman Marcus and others are all focused on elevating their respective shopping experiences (friendlier, more attentive associates, better lighting, less clutter for quick and easy scanning of the entire store, greater use of mannequin displays for outfit suggestions, smaller vignettes, music, videos and colorful graphics, cooking and other classes, restaurants, celebrity and designer fashion shows, etc.). They are also increasing their use of augmented-reality technologies (digital enhancement of the real-world environment) to heighten the in-store experience and of Big Data to personalize service and assortments based on local consumer preferences. Again, the neuroexperience achieved in each case will be different, consistent with its brand image and customer expectations.

If the experience is strong enough, those stores will preemptively get their customers back to their stores before they go to a competitor. Beyond this, they participate on all distribution platforms, including staking out a presence in the social networks such as Facebook, Twitter, etc.

As predicted, and as some are already doing, they will roll out smaller neighborhood store formats, as Bloomingdale's has done, for both preemptive distribution and localizing the product mix and experience. We also predict a direct attack on the specialists by the department stores rolling out their own private brands into the Omni-Brand to Consumer sector (e.g., Alfani or INC from Macy's or Stafford or Arizona from JCPenney).

Finally, their pursuit of more private and exclusive brands will eventually give department stores even greater control over their entire value chains.

We believe that this is the kind of transformation traditional department stores must make to survive. More optimistically, if they do it right, they have the potential to claw back much of their lost apparel share. Furthermore, the Omni-Brand to Consumer model will provide these bigger stores an advantage, thanks to the greater breadth of their product and experiential offerings.

JCPenney, under CEO Ron Johnson in 2012, had a vision that essentially would have transformed the national chain department store into an enclosed mini-mall as an entertainment destination, with streets of shops, all as omnibrands to consumers. Although it was a great strategy, the implementation of the vision was a catastrophic failure.

However, we have also speculated that that perhaps Macy's is methodically and brilliantly evolving into such a visionary model. Indeed, it would be a great irony if the department stores pulled a "back to the future" move and once again became the palaces of consumption they were known as at the beginning of Wave I.

CHAPTER 11

IDEAS FROM THE GREAT ONES

During our comprehensive research on some of the most interesting and successful companies in retailing today, several emerged that have developed differentiated applications of one or more of our strategic operating principles in exceptional ways. We present their stories here, not only because they support our thesis but also because they provide applicable ideas for all businesses.

VF Corporation

With $11 billion in sales, VF Corporation is the largest and most diversified apparel, footwear and accessories company in the United States. Though often flying stealth, under the radar of most consumers, it is one of the best examples of a company executing our three imperative strategies in tandem with the four-wave history of the retail industry described in this book.

Founded in Wave I, VF was a production-driven, wholesale apparel company with one brand, Vanity Fair intimate apparel, distributed solely in the United States through department stores. Today, it is a marketing-driven wholesaler and retailer with a portfolio of more than thirty brands and subbrands distributed through all channels, including its own retail stores and the global marketplace (from 2001 to 2012, international sales grew from 19 to 37 percent of revenues). VF's stable of brands includes Wrangler, Lee, Seven For All Mankind, The North Face, Kipling, Vans, Reef, Jansport, Nautica, Timberland and many others. Five of their brands contribute an average of $1.5 billion each to VF's revenues, or almost two-thirds of the business.[1]

The global behemoth's headquarters is tucked away in laid-back Greensboro, North Carolina, where its executives can be found wearing many of the company's branded casual apparel. The culture, however, is anything but relaxed. VF folks are fierce competitors, roughly doubling their collective business in the past seven years and sailing through the Great Recession with barely a hiccup, with revenues dipping only slightly in 2009.

Consumer Responsiveness and Value-Chain Control

VF has excelled not by trying to get big, but by trying to get different. The company's evolution toward our three operating principles has been timely and steady. In the 1980s the company, led by then-CEO Mackey McDonald, realized the impact that consumer power and its changing demands were going to have on its business. Accordingly, it began to change its strategic direction and business model. It launched a major, company-wide initiative to become a leader in consumer responsiveness. Attached to that goal was the need for a totally integrated, highly collaborative value chain—one that it could totally control.

The philosophical and strategic reimagining of transforming a behemoth business like VF Corporation is one thing; to succeed in implementing the vision is quite another. The road to what might be called a Fortune 500 graveyard is filled with the good intentions of just such attempted transformations. Needless to say, VF is not only alive and breathing, it's winning all the speed and scale records.

In 1980, VF owned the manufacturing of its two major brands: Lee Jeans and Vanity Fair intimates. By the mid-1980s, it had added Wrangler, Jantzen and Jansport, ensuring control of the back end of the value chain. However, VF realized that a paradigm shift was occurring that could not be ignored. Manufacturing was seeking the lowest cost possible to stay price competitive in the heated battle for consumers. Thus all manufacturing in the textile and apparel industries inevitably started to move to Mexico, Central and South America and eventually to Asia.

Understanding the vital link between its goal of total responsiveness to consumers and the need for the entire value chain to support that goal, VF realized it had to manage what would become a totally outsourced function in the chain.

VF's early understanding of this game-changing combination of events helped it focus on strategically adapting, internally and externally. Let's examine some of the key initiatives that helped the company become the industry leader it is today.

Focus on Consumers: From Single-Product Brands to Lifestyle Brands

First, VF was one of the first major apparel manufacturers to identify the trend of consumers seeking so-called lifestyle brands (e.g., Ralph Lauren and Abercrombie & Fitch) over single-product category brands like its heritage brands, Lee jeans and Vanity Fair intimates. This sparked an aggressive acquisition strategy, and in 2004 VF launched a plan to transform itself into a global lifestyle apparel company with a high-growth portfolio of diversified brands.

In 2000, VF's heritage brands accounted for 90 percent of revenues. By 2008, however, that number had dropped to 56 percent, with lifestyle brands reaching 44 percent of total sales. Today they account for around 60 percent of sales.

Value-Chain Control: From Vertical Control to Managed Collaborations

The expertise gained from VF's original vertically owned manufacturing served it well as it transitioned to the necessary collaborations with manufacturers and suppliers around the world.

During its early stages, offshore sourcing went to the lowest-cost countries. But because of VF's commitment to consumer responsiveness as the driving force in the value chain, it was quick to understand that the "lowest cost" was not enough of a differentiator. It evaluated the other aspects it considered important, such as speed to market, better material utilization, lower inventories, less work in progress and lower cost to quality. While lower price was, naturally, still high on consumers' list, they had raised the bar. Low prices were just the price of entry.

As conceptualized by a VF supply-chain executive, reducing the amount of "needle time" that applies to making a garment is no longer a competitive advantage. It's about managing the entire supply chain, and this is where McDonald felt VF was excelling and gaining great advantage over competitors.

Accordingly, VF came up with its Third Way sourcing strategy, a hybrid of complete supply-chain control and relationships with suppliers. (The "first way" is to produce in the company's owned factories, the "second way" is to manufacture in someone else's factory, and the "third way" is to collaborate with a manufacturer to provide VF's expertise in engineering, equipment and even capital investments). VF and its suppliers would make the necessary investments to produce, on an exclusive basis, agreed-upon quantities or a particular product line or lines, committing to a volume forecast over a number of years. The supplier would own the factory and the equipment and be responsible for managing the workforce. VF would make investments in specialized equipment and other capital expenditures when necessary. The Third Way helped reduce costs and lower inventory while increasing productivity and better integrating acquisitions. It also gave VF maximum control over the supply chain, which quickly became the most advanced, efficient, technologically superior and best-managed supply chain in its industry.

VF's supply-chain management has been a competitive weapon for many years. Current CEO Eric Wiseman clearly understands the importance of maintaining that advantage: "We sell about 450 million units of apparel and footwear per year," he said. "So when you divide that back into 365 days a year, we have to sell and ship one and a quarter million pieces a day. So, when we talk about our supply chain as a competitive weapon, it starts with how incredibly diverse and sophisticated we have to be to do that, and serve our customers at a high level."[2] VF, with 29,000 employees, owns just 38 of the 1,500 factories that make their product at various times of the year. Sourcing, therefore, is an enormous, well-run, complicated piece of the company.

VF has also taken its Third Way sourcing strategy beyond just a competitive weapon. In the wake of several factory tragedies and lost workers' lives in Bangladesh in 2013, VF took a leadership position in applying its Third Way engineering and manufacturing expertise in the construction of a new factory that is intended to set the standard for worker safety. Ultimately, the goal is for this standard to spread into the renovation of older factories and future new construction.

Furthermore, the structure of VF's portfolio provides an inherent synergy between the front and back ends of the business. The front end consists of its multiplicity of brands, all decentralized. Each is autonomous, run by its own management, tasked with maintaining the brand's integrity, entrepreneurial culture, focus and connectivity with its core consumers. Meanwhile, the back end is centralized (with the corporate experts using the efficiencies and productivity afforded by scale) and is able to support the front end's all-important need to be consumer responsive.

Preemptive Distribution and Neurological Connection: Each Brand's Role

VF's lifestyle brands currently account for less than half of total sales. However, they make up the fastest-growing segment of the business, and VF's stated goal is to continue acquiring lifestyle brands. More important, it seeks only those brands that also have a retail component, since it expects this retail, direct-to-consumer business across all brands to grow faster than its wholesale business. Lifestyle brands are projected to increase to 75 percent of the business by 2015.

Wiseman projects that the international business will grow to 40 percent by 2015, primarily in Europe, China, India, Brazil and Mexico. And a big driver of the company's global growth, and consistent with VF's obsessive consumer focus, is its commitment to invest in understanding local consumers' desires and shopping behavior across a wide and diverse range of global markets. They call it "smart localization." And as has been proven domestically, VF views this as a huge strategic advantage.

Other big accelerants for global growth will come from VF's major outdoor and action sports brands such as The North Face, Vans, Timberland and Kipling, as well as jeans wear: Wrangler and Lee (which launched in China in the early 90s and is considered an upscale brand). As Wiseman pointed out: "Activities like mountaineering or surfing and skating are global activities, so you can speak to people in many countries."[3] Furthermore, these lifestyle brands fit VF's direct-to-consumer strategy and expansion through e-commerce and retail stores.

With almost 1,200 owned and operated retail stores, and its e-commerce business growing at around 35 percent, VF's direct-to-consumer revenues are expected to reach about 25 percent of its total business by 2017.

While this goal suggests an intention to increase control over its distribution, VF's decentralized business model requires that strategic decision-making on all consumer-touching points in the value chain be made at the brand level. For example, all The North Face consumer research, brand positioning, marketing, advertising, brand imagery, distribution and creation of the brand experience are the responsibilities of The North Face management team alone. This applies across VF's entire portfolio of brands.

However, consistent with VF's strategic growth strategy, the common thread that runs through all its brands is the use of all relevant distribution platforms (the omni-channel model), in pursuit of a strategy of preemptively reaching its consumers ahead of the competition. And since most of its lifestyle brands, like The North Face and Kipling, control their retail component, they also control the brand experience and the neurological connection with the consumer. In fact, even when those brands, along with VF's wholesale brands such as Wrangler and Lee jeans, distribute through retailers like Walmart, Kohl's, JCPenney, Macy's and others, they insist on a strong collaboration to ensure their brands' appropriate merchandising, presentation and strategic integrity. Industry experts have explained VF's strength in its retail partnerships as springing from its deep consumer knowledge, coupled with its superior supply-chain control and rapid responsiveness. To reiterate one of the most illustrative examples, VF is able to distribute two different line mixes of Wrangler jeans to two different Walmart stores that may be just across town from each other.

Innovation and the Future

In 2010, CEO Wiseman initiated a push for innovation at VF. To stimulate innovation, he asked VF leaders to "go outside for new ideas" to other companies and organizations around the world outside apparel and footwear, including labs, scientists, universities and cultural leaders. The journeys have ranged from a trip to a botanical garden to study fire-resistant plants to a meeting with Robert Redford and other people at the Sundance Institute to sharpen storytelling skills.

The company plans to develop three innovation centers for technical apparel, footwear and jeans, located near, but not at, existing offices.

When asked recently how to describe VF, Wiseman called it a dynamic and innovative growth company that's the best environment in the industry to work in. He said: "A couple of years ago, Fortune magazine and Aon Hewitt, the global human resources consulting business, conducted a survey to rank North American Top Companies for Leaders. All the typical names you'd expect were on the list; GE, Intel, P&G, McDonald's. And out of the blue, we were in the top 25. We said 'Wow! How'd that happen?' We were 22nd, and last year, we moved up to 17th. There's no other apparel company mentioned anywhere on these lists. To be 17th is a confirmation of all of the investments we make around rich talent development here; we invest millions and millions and millions of dollars into developing our people every year, and giving them the experiences they are going to need to achieve their personal and professional potential. It certainly has paid off, because our people are delivering like crazy."[4]

Amazon

It's a store. It's a TV and movie producer. It's a book publisher. It's a mall. It's a technology company. It's an electronics manufacturer. It's a fulfillment and distribution company. It's a payment system. Although nobody knows how to accurately and succinctly describe Amazon, other than Amazing, suffice it to say that when considering its role as a retailer, and how rapidly it is shifting the way consumers shop and buy by accelerating the effects of Wave IV and changing the face of retail today, we feel it necessary to explicitly underscore how Amazon has adopted and embodied our three principles. As it continues to expand, Amazon will ultimately be every retailer's main competitor, if not worst nightmare, and certainly the scariest approaching image in Walmart's rearview mirror.

At $74 billion in sales and growing at double-digit rates, Amazon has built its brand and unique position on its enormous array of merchandise, competitive pricing and exceptional service. These powerful competitive advantages have helped it establish a culture of convenience and trust with its customers.

Amazon has grown from being the biggest bookstore on earth when it launched in 1994 to the biggest marketplace on earth, where anybody and everybody can set up shop, by taking on every product and service category it can. With more categories, brands, styles and SKUs than its next five-largest competitors combined, Amazon's convenience has become top-of-mind for shoppers thinking of making a purchase, a preemptor unto itself. The site's one-click-buying capability, free shipping through Amazon Prime and superior ease of shopping, selection and service create an experience that is often more enjoyable, convenient and time efficient for consumers than shopping at an understaffed mall or hard-to-navigate big-box store or strip-mall center, where the ability to find what they are looking for is increasingly uncertain.

The mantra of the company is to put the customer at the center of everything it does. This customer-centricity has led it to areas that founder Jeff Bezos would never have imagined were possible back in the early days of Amazon, when it was an online bookstore.

Let's face it. The company has single-handedly changed consumer behavior. "Running an errand" has been replaced by "going online." Instantaneously price-shopping from one location, or even while on the run with a mobile device, has actually brought retail closer to a perfectly competitive marketplace. Amazon also paved the way for meteoric e-commerce growth for all other retailers by making consumers comfortable with it. In what is probably just the beginning of a trend, it has already put Borders and many other retailers out of business.[5]

Amazon has been the highest-rated online services company in the Satmetrix Net Promoter Industry Benchmark report for the past four years, ranking highest for all loyalty drivers, including "useful reviews and ratings" and "breadth of products available."[6] All this has forged a deep consumer connection and has made the site the go-to destination for anything and everything.

The strength of Amazon's competitive advantages is based on the interplay of our three principles. By controlling the value chain and using innovative preemptive distribution strategies, Amazon has clearly established a deep neurological connection with consumers.

Neurological Connectivity and the Online Experience

Neurological connectivity with consumers has been established by exploiting the six shifts in consumer desires (experiences, customization, democracy, new *and* now, community, technology for life), combined with its tight control over shipping costs and speed and superior management of returns. Amazon was the first to realize that the combination of people wanting better experiences rather than more stuff and wanting things more quickly and easily (new *and* now), with a heavy dose of personalization, would be a game-changer. Therefore, to trump largely mediocre shopping experiences, all Amazon had to do was to make people trust the online shopping process. Aided and abetted by initial cost-structure advantages (e.g., no taxes, the accepted anomaly of not having to make a profit and access to unlimited cheap capital), it used the book category to kick off the long march into every aspect of commerce possible. And the march has been helped by the launch of Amazon Prime, in which for a flat membership fee $99 per year, customers get free standard and two-day shipping on many items, movies on its streaming service and a huge assortment of Kindle e-books, among other perks. This has increased traffic and revenues across the website and has also monetized a core group of regular customers and gained more international business. Prime members tend to shop on Amazon more frequently and spend more money once there. Even for those consumers who do not purchase Prime, cheap shipping and the ability to find whatever they're looking to buy have proven irresistible. And talk about an example of preemptive distribution—since Amazon knows what you like, it provides suggestions for other purchases, eventually customizing the site to the individual consumer's tastes and behavior.

The Preemptor of All Preemptors

Amazon has also been impressive for its preemptive scale. Its distribution investment is immense and expanding. With almost 100 huge distribution centers totaling more than 35 million square feet and 10,000 smaller distribution sites in the United States, a rapidly growing presence overseas and its state sales-tax advantage gradually disappearing, we see a simple and logical extension of those centers into small neighborhood "showrooms" as stores, stocked with samples of locally preferred items. We envision these as futuristic stores that reinforce the experience users have when shopping online and that have low or nonexistent inventory, but that are really cool—maybe showcasing the highest-selling items around the world with terminals to order from. These stores will also be pickup sites for customers who may be ordering online.

Imagine 3-D screens for shopping and ordering, coffee, music and a place for friends to network. In fact, a former top executive of Walmart has admitted that Amazon's opening physical stores is one of the global giant's greatest fears.

Amazon is a key tap away, 24/7, in front of millions of consumers' faces, first, faster and more often than its physical and virtual competitors, and it can deliver overnight through its distribution centers' proximity to its shipping vendors. Another preemptive potential for Amazon would be to expand into new areas that connect with its consumers on an almost daily basis. For example, with its logistics capability, it is already testing its Amazon Fresh concept of same-day delivery in some cities—and why not?

Amazon serves all consumer segments and is thus truly a democratic model, offering everything from discount to luxury goods, with nary a scratch on its image. It has been bold in coming up with new ways to get products in front of customers ahead of its competitors, either by introducing new products and services or acquiring niche websites. It spends billions of dollars on shipping each year, which indicates how important a focus it is for the company.

With the release of the Amazon Kindle, the company popularized the digital-reading device and essentially changed the game in the publishing and bookselling industry, largely decimating the physical retail space. It also furthered Amazon's role in the consumer-electronics industry, allowing people to carry their digital libraries in one device on Amazon's gargantuan "bookstore." The company has also started to work with colleges and universities to supply e-textbooks. With the introduction of the Kindle Fire tablet and set-top box, and a smartphone in the works, the game changes again. One tech industry consultant called them "purchasing devices that put Amazon on the coffee table so consumers can never escape the tantalizing glow of a shopping screen."[7]

In 2009, Amazon acquired online shoe retailer Zappos.com, a business that shared Amazon's own "customer-obsessed" values. The acquisition made Amazon a major competitor in the footwear and apparel industry practically overnight, with substantial ability to leverage shared cost structures and consumer data. Many brands that had previously decided not to distribute product on Amazon could not resist the innovative Zappos model and its potential sales volume, and were forced to rethink their position.

The picture is even more complex because of what Amazon has done with its new technology and fulfillment models. Amazon's ten-year, $2 billion investment in developing its large and sophisticated cloud-computing infrastructure,

Amazon Web Services (AWS), was initially done to keep track of its massive number of online orders. Soon the company figured out it could also expand that infrastructure to store data and run websites for lots of outside companies and other entities. Netflix, one of its competitors, runs on AWS, which will soon be Amazon's biggest business. Most importantly, Amazon has created the next great revolution in B2B (business to business) supply-chain management, which is part of the reason no other retailer will ever catch up with it in the field of e-commerce. A host of web services are targeted toward small- and medium-size companies that may benefit most from Amazon's leveraged web-information capabilities. Using its already developed infrastructure, Amazon is able to fulfill third-party products without incurring significant operating costs. This program has evolved into the Fulfillment by Amazon business, which Amazon uses to help increase its own shipping volume and expand its presence in the online retail sector.

Quite simply, Amazon allows vendors multiple ways to get their products into the hands of Amazon's huge consumer population, from Amazon purchasing the product and selling it on the site to consumers, all the way to Fulfillment by Amazon (FBA), in which a vendor owns the product but stores it at Amazon's distribution center and Amazon does the fulfillment once the sale is made. This provides the fast delivery that is a cornerstone of the Amazon strategy, yet Amazon never actually owns the inventory. Amazon takes a commission for the sale plus a fee for processing the order. With the explosion of mobile shopping, the sky's the limit for Amazon. Recently, it launched Login and Pay, which allows Amazon's 215 million active customers to use Amazon's technology for payment of purchases on other sites. Amazon earlier unveiled Checkout by Amazon for physical retail stores.[8]

Value-Chain Control: Big Data, Big Advantage

As previously mentioned, Amazon as host to third-party retailers or brands can easily become a competitor as the third party's data gets captured by Amazon's own Big Data base, which is greatly enhanced by its cloud-computing capabilities. This kind of "intelligence," so to speak, can be used by Amazon to gain competitive advantage. Furthermore, the hosted brands and retailers are relinquishing an important part of value-chain control: their ability to interact with their customers and their shopping behavior. So, ironically, while Amazon achieves greater competitive advantage, it also risks alienating the third-party companies and potentially losing them to eBay, which is growing its own third-party platform, but with a more third-party-friendly structure, as we will discuss in the following section.

Given this potential problem, we still believe one of Amazon's biggest assets, which will transfer into Wave IV, is the infinite amount of customer information in its enormous Big Data base, an asset that has barely been mined.

Amazon's superbly managed and controlled value chain, its enormous complex of detail and technology and its equally intricate operational structure developed to implement and deliver on their promises make it an über-master of all of e-commerce.

Amazon's logo features an "underscore" of a little yellow arrow connecting the first and fourth letters of the company name, which many people feel is just a smile, but which was originally intended to symbolize "From A to Z." However, in our opinion, the alphabet is too limiting when referring to the possibilities for the company.

Like Jeff Bezos' vision and Amazon's business model, they are limitless.

eBay

It may be a little premature to warn Amazon that there are some loudly accelerating footsteps just behind them. But in today's wide-open world of warp-speed innovation, disruption and fiercely competitive races to preemptively establish dominant positions, even front-runner Amazon has to be on ready alert. And the disruptive noise is coming from a recent victim of disruption itself that has since been revitalized: eBay.

Founded in 1995 as an online auction platform, or an online flea market as some called it, by Pierre Omidyar, a French-born programmer who was inspired by his wife's interest in collecting Pez candy dispensers, it has grown from a scrappy start-up to a bona fide e-commerce juggernaut, along the way changing how Americans shop.[9]

Few other companies have embraced the challenges and opportunities of Wave IV as fully or clearly as eBay has. With a spate of acquisitions, and the strategic leadership in the payments system space, eBay has begun the process of both helping other retailers deal with the major shifts in consumer desires and shopping behavior and positioning itself as the anti-Amazon for those retailers.

eBay's CEO, John Donahoe, who took the helm in 2007, has a similar view of his business model as Jeff Bezos does of Amazon's. Neither is limited to the confines of traditionally defined "retailing," or in eBay's case, to simply being an auction house. Instead, each of them professes to an unlimited scope of being a "marketplace" that provides real estate, or a distribution platform, or a set of services for any or all sellers and buyers around the world, providing all support services necessary to pursue and complete transactions, including the delivery of the value to the end consumer.

Under Donahoe, revenues have grown from $9 billion in 2008 to $16 billion in 2013. Of course, this makes eBay a distant challenger to Amazon's nearly $74 billion. But the real-world corollary between distance and time is not in the lexicon of the cyberworld.

There are three distinct businesses in eBay, and many smaller ones in the works.

eBay Marketplace includes the original eBay.com auction site and some 300 million listings, along with Shopping.com, Half.com and the StubHub ticketing business. Marketplace has 24 million active users buying 500 million items each year through the company's website and mobile apps. eBay trades about $2,000 worth of goods every second. It has about 100 million active users doing transactions, millions of merchants using one or more of its platforms and a developer community with more than eight hundred thousand members using its application programming interfaces, or APIs. While the original auction model transactions were primarily of secondhand items, today 70 percent of the items are new and sold at a fixed price. Also, more than 50 percent of its business is done outside the United States, with a major presence in forty countries. In the United States, a flatscreen TV gets sold on eBay every six minutes.

The PayPal Payments business, which represents half of its revenues, was a losing business when eBay acquired it in 2002, even though it had established itself as a safe way to transfer money online between people who didn't know each other. Newer parts of that business include Bill Me Later (a deferred-payments service) and cellphone payments provider Zong. The company is actively moving PayPal into brick-and-mortar stores, trying to make it the preemptive payment distributor. Its PayPal subsidiary recently announced a service offering free two-day shipping (just like Amazon Prime) for purchases made on third-party retail sites.[10]

eBay recently responded to rising competition in online payments by paying $800 million for Braintree, an online payments-processing company popular with mobile developers and growing start-ups like Airbnb, a digital platform that connects people looking for places to stay with those who have space, and Uber, which connects riders and drivers. Donahoe has said that the acquisition will strengthen PayPal's global presence in mobile commerce. And just recently, eBay bought London-based Shutl to help it offer same-day deliveries in as many as twenty-five cities by the end of next year. PayPal Beacon, which uses widely available low-energy Bluetooth technology, will ultimately allow people to swap their wallet for a smartphone, and it is now in thirty store systems with large retailers at one hundred thousand locations, and growing rapidly.

Donahoe no doubt had his "friends up north," as he calls Amazon, in his crosshairs with his acquisition of GSI Commerce in 2011 for an astounding $2.4 billion. Even though it's still a relatively small part of eBay's total revenues, eBay Enterprise (as GSI was renamed) provides another growth engine, ultimately scalable to a position directly competitive with Amazon.[11] It will not only enhance eBay's Marketplace business through its e-commerce and interactive marketing services, it will also extend eBay's relationships with major brands and retailers, including Toys "R" Us, Aeropostale, Kenneth Cole, Adidas, Calvin Klein and others. These collaborations are now possible with eBay's capabilities in website development and maintenance, order fulfillment, customer-service functions and online marketing campaigns, among other functions. It is the ultimate in community building—using its infrastructure and expertise to help other retailers in their omni-channel efforts. Independent retailers and up-and-coming brands will benefit greatly from this, because one of the deeper purposes of Enterprise is to help retailers improve and manage relationships with their customers.

In the company's Commerce and Innovation Centers, in a test mall that demonstrates the future of shopping, eBay Enterprise shows other retailers how it's done. With its digital wallet, a consumer can pay for something without even handing money or a credit card to a sales associate. With Connected Glass, he or she can order an item from a touchscreen store window without even entering the store. Not only can you ask, "How much is that doggie in the window?"; now you can also buy it.

From Pez Dispensers to Touchscreen Walls and Mobile Payments

Meg Whitman, a former Disney and Bain & Company top executive, was hired and appointed CEO in 1998, and stepped on the accelerator. In six months she took eBay public at an initial market value of $700 million, small by today's standards but significant back then. Between 2000 and 2004, revenues were rising at the blistering rate of 77 percent a year, fueled by acquisitions and aggressive global expansion.

By 2004, the stock had soared to a high of $58 a share. eBay under Whitman was one of the great business success stories of the modern era. She built a powerhouse with a collection of assets that placed the company well for the next wave in retailing, but the transition was not without bumps. In January 2005, eBay announced the first quarter in which its revenues rose less than 50 percent over the prior year.

A big part of eBay's decelerating growth could be attributed to the increasing competition in the online auction space as well as the increasing build-out of online capabilities by retailers. Yahoo had built a more comprehensive retail offering; Amazon by then was no longer just a bookstore and was selling everything from designer apparel to electronic devices; Google was also advancing its platform for businesses to buy ads and sell products for free; and Walmart and others were building a reliable transactional platform. And today, there are many competing auction platforms, fixed price-models and online payment services.

On top of a decline in listings, eBay's search engine for users to sort through its more than 2 million products was in need of an upgrade. In fact, some experts referred to eBay's site as chaotic.

So, by 2007, mounting competition and maturity were pressing down on the online auction business, eBay sellers and buyers were unhappy, growth was decelerating and its stock was in decline. Enter John Donahoe on the cusp of the Great Recession. And whether or not John saw the signs as he took the helm at eBay, he certainly did not let the oncoming recession go to waste.

It was to be a time of stabilizing the decelerating growth rate; revitalizing the core businesses, including a "cleansing" and greater discipline, control and transparency in the buying and selling operation; and the development of new growth engines for eBay—all designed to reaccelerate eBay's trajectory. Over the next six years, under Donahoe's leadership, eBay would acquire thirty-four companies and transform itself into a tech powerhouse.

From Disruptee to Disruptor

One of Donahoe's first priorities in revitalizing the core business was to up-grade its "chaotic" website for both buyers and sellers. Also, the model increasingly shifted from a pure auction site to one that highlighted both "Buy It Now" and at a fixed price. With so much choice and price compression available elsewhere, consumers no longer wanted to be tied solely to the classic auction model. This was coupled with a realization that delivery cost and reliability were central to the consumer's experience. eBay systematically started upgrading the delivery-fee structure and sellers' tracking requirements to compete. The core business is once again well positioned, but this is only step one. eBay has a grander vision—one that just may reshape the future of retail.

eBay Bets Heavy on Mobile

Perhaps the most significant win for Donahoe arising out of his growth strategies was his big bet on mobile retailing, which, he feels, continues to be a game-changer: "Mobile technology is really the catalyst of the integration of online and in-store into a seamless shopping experience."[12] The bet on mobile's future dominance is focused on redesigning and adding enhancements to its website to compel mobile shoppers to make eBay their destination of choice. Perhaps more significantly, eBay's PayPal business, as the leader in facilitating safe and secure mobile payments, provided another competitive advantage to its enhanced site with its one-click-payment capability. PayPal also has more active accounts than Discover and American Express, and is accepted by more than sixty of the top hundred online retailers in the United States, including Walmart and Home Depot, among others.

eBay acquired Critical Path, a software developer that gives it mobile-app development expertise. Donahoe largely attributes eBay's recent earnings improvements to his early bet on mobile, and on his vision of how revolutionary mobile would be in terms of how people shop and pay. Analysts predict that at current growth rates, PayPal will soon surpass its core Marketplace's revenues.

eBay's mobile apps have been downloaded more than 100 million times around the globe, and sellers are now posting 2 million items per week from their smartphones, with hundreds of thousands of new users making their first eBay purchase from a smartphone. It is estimated that a woman's handbag is purchased on eBay mobile every thirty seconds.[13]

Preemptive Distribution

And, in another swipe—no pun intended—at Amazon, eBay is currently testing a new mobile app called eBay Now. In test markets of New York, Chicago, Dallas, San Francisco and San Jose, it allows customers to buy products from retail partners using their phones and, for a $5 fee, promises to deliver the very same day.

eBay has been opening physical pop-up stores with partners in London, New York and San Francisco, including a Kate Spade store in New York. So far, they have been for special occasions and holidays, and some have been tie-ins with celebrities and designers during fashion weeks. Same-day shipping is inevitable, according to John Donahoe.

While eBay's same-day-shipping program, eBay Now, may be available in just a handful of US cities, Donahoe foresees a day when customers can get thousands of items from partners like Target, Home Depot and Urban Outfitters everywhere within an hour, from Portland to Peoria.

That means exploring other third-party shipping and transportation systems to exploit excess capacity. For example, just as uShip connects truckers and shippers with shipments and Uber leverages the downtime of limousine and taxi drivers, eBay Now could utilize the excess capacity of shipping services like UPS.

So how does this all fit together? eBay understands the huge shifts in consumer behavior that the rapid spread of the new technologies has facilitated. Its consumer is now mobile, looking for unique product and experiences with great convenience. eBay has all the elements to bring these together for both the retailer and the consumer. If you own the customer wallet (PayPal), you have access to lots of data on purchasing history. If you can see what people have searched for (eBay core site and apps), you know what they are also dreaming about; if you have geo-location data through PayPal, you know where they are and can recommend where they should shop (you and your retail partners); if you know what inventory your retail partners have (acquisition of product research site Milo), you can guide the consumer there or deliver it from the store (eBay Now and Shutl); and finally, through eBay Enterprise you can provide all the e-commerce capabilities, including fulfillment.

So quite simply, if eBay has many of the great connect points that link the retailer to the consumer, it can motivate many retailers to sign up for the entire eBay system.

Neurological Experience

Can eBay create a sufficiently unique and compelling shopping experience to neurologically connect with consumers so that they will go out of their way to return again and again? Even though eBay is roughly five lengths behind Amazon (one-fifth the revenues), given John Donahoe's strategic moves and vision, not the least of which was his bet on mobile and his goal of enabling the 90 percent of the retail trade that is still brick-and-mortar with Enterprise, we believe eBay is indeed poised to break out of the pack, to accelerate its pace and to press heavily on Amazon's lead, ultimately becoming the anti-Amazon of Wave IV.

Burberry

Ask anyone at European fashion house Burberry which other retailer the company most resembles, and the answer might surprise you. It's not Prada, Chanel, Coach or Louis Vuitton. It's Apple.

The connection makes sense when you think about the fact that both retailers are brilliant design companies determined to become leading lifestyle brands with technology at the heart. However, Apple is a technology company that became a lifestyle brand, and Burberry is a lifestyle brand that has transformed into a $3 billion digital pioneer.

Burberry is taking high-tech, high-touch to a new level. At its London headquarters, a larger-than-life video of two of-the-moment Hollywood stars frolicking in the sun while wearing the brand is projected on huge screens in the building's lobby. In the building's huge glass atrium—which Chief Design Officer Christopher Bailey designed with the help of top architectural firm Gensler, and which uses the weather, something that both the English and this quintessentially English brand are obsessed with, as a backdrop—Burberry-clad employees pass by new and old products displayed on many of the walls and hallways of the building. Everything is on-brand.[14]

Customer Experience

Nowhere is the technological bent more apparent than at the company's Regent Street store in London, Burberry's biggest in the world. Walking through the doors is like walking into a website.

The store completely immerses visitors who opt into its magic in a high-tech, high-touch multimedia experience. More than 500 speakers and 100 screens are synchronized to disperse information and allow customers to engage with the brand.

A network of little elevators behind wood paneling shows a moving display of product. There is a huge screen on the main floor of the store, on which the runway shows are streamed live, allowing customers to come to the store and watch them in real time.

Clothing is embedded with RFID chips, which can be read by screens and mirrors. When a customer picks up an item, the RFID tag triggers the nearby screen or mirror to reveal multimedia content about the item—how it was made, fabric, stitching, craftsmanship, how it can be worn. Like the brand, the store fuses history and innovation.

The store has no cash registers. Store associates carry iPads with a log of the customer's previous purchase history, to mimic the online world. The information helps drive up the average transaction value and will begin to build for Burberry an immense trove of customer behavioral data.

When customers walk into the London store and opt in, it is the ultimate in neurological connection. In fact, it's not only a blurring of lines between physical and digital, it's a merging of neurological and technological. The store is a model of digitally advanced consumer commerce that is a harbinger of the next wave of stores to compete in an increasingly online world.

Digital-First Thinking

How did the 150-plus-year-old British brand with a heritage in trench coats accomplish this technological transformation? In 2006, after CEO Angela Ahrendts ascended to the top job at Burberry, the company began to go after millennials because that was the white space in the luxury market. Once this target was determined, the tech part was a no-brainer, because that was the best way to reach this demographic. Then, as projections materialized that there would be 7 billion smartphones—one in almost everyone's hands—in the next five years, digital was suddenly no longer a niche marketing strategy. And now Burberry is already way ahead of everyone else in luxury.

Ahrendts is not your typical modern European luxury chief. One of six children from a middle-class Indiana family, she started sewing her own clothes as a young girl and dreamed of a career in fashion. After graduating from Ball State University, she headed to New York City, where she worked at Liz Claiborne and Henri Bendel, eventually becoming president of Donna Karan.

Ahrendts explains "the digital thing" this way: "I grew up in a physical world. I speak English. The next generation is growing up in a digital world. They speak social."[15]

Burberry Chat, an in-house communication platform, is one way management talks to all eleven thousand Burberry associates. It's a unifier of the culture. Each month they each do a three- to four-minute chat on an important topic—marketing, design, product, a new digital tool rollout. Sometimes they use the platform to interview a young talented staffer as inspiration to his or her peers. It gives associates pride about where they work, and it communicates—albeit tacitly—that this could be them one day.

Blurred Lines

Mobile, according to Ahrendts, has been the game-changer. The challenge the company has taken on is to make the in-store and mobile online experiences equally exciting.

Everything's coming through this device. Burberry had a runway show in London that was mobile-first, simulcast in 3-D in New York, Los Angeles, Dubai, Paris and Tokyo. Burberry viewers at home anywhere in the world could watch the show streamed over the Internet in real time and feel as if they had a front-row seat.

Burberry's design team designs for a mobile landing page, and that landing page dictates what the store window will look like, not the other way around. Creative media now shoots photography for digital, and then reverts it to print.

Said Ahrendts: "We used to be doing everything for print, then converting it for desktop, then converting it for mobile. Now it's mobile first, then the conversions."[16] And social is huge. Burberry has a strategy for every platform—Google, Facebook, YouTube and others.

Some categories are available online months before they arrive in stores. The brand has more than a million Facebook fans, a fan website called ArtofTheTrench.com, social media, Burberry Acoustic music available for download. It's more than just the commerce. Burberry is about building a community.

Value-Chain Control

Out of desperate necessity, Ahrendts's predecessor, Rose Marie Bravo, began a process of controlling the company's massive supply chain that continues today. Over the span of many years, Burberry had lost control of its brand. The company was a licensing shell with a trench coat with an iconic check lining at its core. The product line was relatively small, but distribution was unfocused. In 1997, the brand was available in more than sixty different stores in central London but was not stocked by the city's most prestigious retailers such as Selfridges, Harvey Nichols or Harrods. Bravo started cleaning up the brand's licenses and taking ownership of a dizzyingly complicated network of retail franchisees and manufacturing licensees. She restructured the brand hierarchy with clear positioning for the flagship-tailored Burberry London, the lower-priced casual Burberry Brit and higher-end Burberry Prorsum collections, and it brought brand identity and positioning functions in-house.

After the plaid design had been knocked off by everyone and his brother, and even appropriated by gangs of hoodlum teens, Ahrendts realized that its ubiquity, and the way it had become almost a caricature of the brand, would hurt it. She removed the pattern from all but a small percentage of the company's lines. Someday, it was hoped, that plaid could rise like a phoenix from the ashes, which it has now started to do.

Some licensees designed and produced goods that bore no resemblance to what was going on at headquarters, but it has taken years to purchase back all the licenses, which included eleven in menswear alone.[17]

Omni-Channel and Preemptive Distribution

Burberry doesn't plan to blanket the world with stores. It is retaining its relationships with other key retailers—reinforcing them, in some cases, as its participation in the $400 million renovation of Macy's flagship Herald Square store indicates.

Burberry's product line is descended from its outwear legacy, what Ahrendts calls "Born from the Coat," a blend of function and fashion that makes it democratic and accessible. Accessories and outwear represent the largest businesses, though the men's tailored business is enjoying double-digit growth. As part of its ongoing mission to elevate product, the company has been exiting lower price points.

Beauty is not viewed as a stand-alone business, but as a fifth fashion product division after women's, men's, accessories and children's wear. The company is making the bold move of putting beauty products on a fashion cycle, and of having the colors match those in the clothes.

It also made the audacious move to bring its fragrance and beauty business in-house, and it started down the digital path with marketing that business as well. A new fragrance was launched via outdoor digital advertising, using footage from live music performances in London, New York and Singapore.

In what is probably the biggest twist of irony in retail in a long time, Angela Ahrendts recently left Burberry, ceding the reins to Bailey, who will take over as CEO. Where did she go? Well, Apple, of course.

TJX Companies

For the brand-conscious consumer seeking value, there is no greater rush of dopamine than the one unleashed while a shopper pulls into the parking lot of one of the TJX companies' stores. Few retailers deliver the shopping thrill of the hunt better than Marshalls, T.J.Maxx or HomeGoods, whose businesses are based on the principle of sell low, buy lower.

By default or design, the off-price business model totally dominated by TJX has, in a stealthy kind of way, been untouched by the "perfect storm" of an overstored, intensely competitive retail environment, omnipotent consumer and resulting madness of the mainstream retail share wars. How has it done this? Well, TJX stays above the fray by simply taking the best of the spoils from each of the warring brands and retailers around the world and putting them all together in the TJX stores, making them the largest purveyor of upscale brands in the world. And, since the products consist of overruns, order cancellations and closeouts, retailers and brands are happy in most cases to sell them to TJX for whatever they can get above cost. Plus, TJX buys less-than-complete assortments, pays promptly and asks for neither advertising funds nor markdown allowances.

Thus, the TJX stores, with the strategic advantage of their off-price business model, are able to provide consumers with "more for less" of everything branded fashion, apparel, accessories, fine jewelry, footwear and home, for up to 60 percent below traditional department and specialty stores, all the time. Although you can't count on finding anything particular at any given time in their stores, you know you'll find high-quality product at unbeatable, irresistible values. And shoppers keep coming back for more.

One might find boots at Marshalls priced at $125 that sold for twice that amount at Coach or UGG, or a pair of $29 Ralph Lauren jeans that were originally priced at $99. Fitness enthusiasts make frequent visits in search of Under Armour shirts, which, though rarely discounted, occasionally make an appearance at T.J.Maxx priced at $24.99—50 percent off regular retail. And it's hard to walk through a Marshalls without seeing a sea of Michael Kors at 40 percent off the price that Macy's charges. During the holiday selling season, designer-branded cashmere sweaters are offered at $79, a quarter of the price at luxury department stores.

For consumers now addicted to (and largely responsible for) the relentless discounting, unprecedented outlet-store expansion, couponing, mobile e-commerce "daily deal" onslaught and whatever other "race to the bottom" pricing gimmickry is being employed, the TJX stores are nothing short of shopping nirvana. Rather than hunting and pecking from one store or website to another and fumbling through coupons and store circulars, shoppers can meander through some sixteen thousand vendors' brands from around the world, all in one location.

The Treasure Hunt, Fast Fashion and Localization

The shopping experience is likened to Costco's popular "treasure hunt," except that rather than finding a designer brand or other unexpected item that Costco offers only once every few weeks, the thrill of the hunt—and surprise findings that delight—occurs every day in the TJX stores. This is the result of another incredible strategic advantage TJX has over all other retail sectors, which is its totally flexible business model, both operationally and structurally. The company's eight hundred merchants are sourcing from vendors in more than sixty countries, continuously on the prowl for an opportunistic buy and able to pounce at any minute on a find. These buyers buy opportunistically, all the time, as opposed to seasonally and limited to a narrow list of vendors. TJX defines itself as a "value-driven global sourcing machine."[18]

Delivering value—a combination of fashion, quality, brand AND price—to its customers every day is what drives the business. Value is not just about price—it has to be the right product, delivered at the right time, with all the elements that make up the value equation. The off-price business model, while greatly flexible, takes relentless attention to execute well. And TJX executes better than anyone else. Its buyers are in rapidly changing marketplaces, reading and reacting to market and fashion trends. They must constantly monitor the various macro environments that affect the business.

And, because it is not buying full lines, its merchandise flow is similar to that of the fast-fashion giants Zara and H&M, introducing new merchandise, brands, styles and fashion at least once a week, rather than every month. Scarcity is therefore built into the process, compelling consumers to visit more often to hunt for what's new, and when finding it, to buy it, since it will probably be gone in a day or two. And since TJX is buying all the time and closer to each season, it has a better idea of what consumers are looking for, which also enables it to localize its assortments.

Finally, to fill in some of the broken assortments or missing categories, TJX has goods produced for its own private and licensed brands. It is also astute in selecting lines it deems to be more fashion-right several seasons into the future, which it will buy and "pack away," as it defines the process.

And make no mistake about it—though the company keeps much of what it does under wraps, this kind of stellar execution, moving hundreds of thousands of units through its system every day to thousands of stores, obviously requires top-notch purchasing, inventory management and distribution technology—in short, preemptive excellence in distribution.

And not only is TJX demographically democratic, it is also attracting younger millennial customers like crazy and has focused on selecting more contemporary brands and styles and on marketing through social media sites Facebook, Twitter, Pinterest and Instagram.

Less than 15 percent of the merchandise is from prior seasons, a particularly important feature for younger consumers. The company changed its marketing to emphasize details like this because it realized its old strategy was talking to existing customers, when it really wanted to attract new ones. Price tags say "past season" if it is.[19]

Unlike in the old days, when it sourced primarily from agents and jobbers, 85 percent is now purchased directly from manufacturers. Much is identical to what the brands sell in department stores. A very small portion is irregular. These distinctions are more significant than ever for consumers looking for a good buy in a sea of deals.

To attract those who feel off-price stores can be a lot less appealing than department stores for some manufacturers and shoppers, the company has remodeled most of its stores over the past few years and is on a mission to make the in-store experience better and better.

Structurally, to accommodate the more rapid turnover and constant flow of newness, the TJX stores are easily adjustable. Since there are no walls formalizing a branded or category segment, they are continually resetting the floor areas to accommodate the rapidly flowing new merchandise and brands. This also heightens the thrill of the hunt and provides a continual new shopping experience for consumers.

The TJX Rewards credit card allows customers to accumulate points for expenditures that can be redeemed for reward dollars to be spent at TJX stores, further cementing its relationship with customers.

For all these reasons, the TJX nameplates are go-to destination brands in the minds of consumers.

Executing Its Way to Preemptive Excellence

Led by Carol Meyrowitz, who has been with TJX for about thirty years, rising from a buyer in 1983 to CEO in 2007, the chain has turned into a retail powerhouse, with more than three thousand stores in six countries. T.J.Maxx, Marshalls, HomeGoods and the smaller chains share buying, merchandising and administrative functions.

Net sales have risen like a rocket from about $2 billion in the early 1990s to $27 billion in 2013, with eighteen consecutive years of earnings-per-share growth. The company's consistently positive financial returns are among the highest in the retail industry, and TJX has generated a significant amount of cash, which raises the question of whether it might seek future growth by acquisition—for example, of its next-largest but much smaller competitor, Pleasanton, California–based Ross Stores, whose sales totaled $10 billion last year.

And there's still room to grow. Management thinks it can expand its store count of some three thousand by at least 50 percent, with a total of five hundred stores in the United States. The company's fledgling businesses in Germany and Poland have been very successful so far. These markets hold huge potential for TJX, provided the company can successfully navigate local commerce laws, which can sometimes make it difficult for discounters.

Meyrowitz, who keeps an exceedingly low profile, has set the tone from the top and believes TJX can be at least a $40 billion company.[20]

Untouched? How about Untouchable?

Because of the TJX business model, its strategic and structural advantages and flexibility, the story is that not only is it untouched by the traditional warring marketplace, it is close to untouchable.

TJX has been catapulting through the share wars for the last twenty-plus years, and like a meteor it continues on that blistering trajectory, with nary a hiccup during the Great Recession. In fact, company management believes the recession may have caused a paradigm shift in consumer behavior in the United States to a greater focus on value. So, TJX is in an even better place at the right time. Not surprisingly, TJX has seen its store traffic increase by double digits as the intense price competition in the rest of retail has intensified its customers' thirst for bargains. For thirty-six of the last thirty-seven years, TJX has delivered same-store sales increases, including at many T.J.Maxx and Marshalls stores that are twenty years old.[21]

E-Commerce: The Five-Hundred-Pound Elephant

Until very recently, TJX has not wanted to—and given its success, may have felt it didn't have to—recognize the five-hundred-pound elephant in the room: its lack of progress in e-commerce. It may have believed, understandably, that its focus had to be on managing and scaling its store growth. Because while it has no real direct competition, other than the off-price chain Ross (whose e-commerce efforts are no better), it woefully trailed its consumers' desired access to its brands wherever and whenever they wish to have such access. Though TJX's sales have grown virtually every year, the competition for bargain-hunting shoppers is coming from an increasing number of sources. Between outlet stores, pure-play e-commerce sites like Overstock.com and flash-sale sites like Rue La La, The RealReal, One Kings Lane and eBay, you have a consumer bombarded with discount offers.

At long last, after acquiring off-price Internet retailer Sierra Trading Post and converting it to TJMaxx.com, the company has finally launched an e-commerce site that will complement the "thrill of the hunt" luxury- and designer-deal model that is experienced in the stores, thereby implementing a segmented strategy that provides a distinct and unique role for each of its distribution platforms. Many of the branded deals offered in the stores cannot be replicated online without alienating the brands that liquidate through this channel. TJX has come to believe that to win in Wave IV you need to be on every platform, even if that means with different product from the stores, though as of this writing no news has yet been released regarding its success. Will TJX come to realize something that the well-run omni-channel retailers have discovered—that consumers shopping both channels spend three to four times more than those shopping one? Or will it find that its model, which revolves around the "thrill of the hunt" and the delight to the senses that its physical stores provide to the neurological connection, obviate the need for omni-channel retail? Only time will tell. Until then, bargain shoppers will continue to enjoy visiting the stores that are, as one of its old advertising campaigns called them, "never the same place twice."

Costco

It's virtually impossible to have a discussion about top retailers without including Costco, the second-largest retailer in the United States behind Walmart. Revered by Wall Street and obsessed over by its 71 million member-customers in 40 million households, the Issaquah, Washington–based warehouse-club operator with $105 billion in annual sales and $2 billion in net income is considered not only one of the best-run retailers around but also one of the best-run companies.

What Costco sells is outsized value, pure and simple. And that value is so compelling and enjoyable that it gets folks to plunk down $55 per year to participate ($110 per year for an executive club membership.)

Yes, you read that right. In today's overstuffed, highly competitive, über-saturated retail environment, the equivalent of almost a fifth of the US population is *paying* for the privilege to shop at a particular store. And not just as a one-off, let's-see-what-it's-like kind of thing. Costco's membership renewal rate is a whopping 90 percent each year—indicating that the Costco experience is truly an addictive one. Not only is the retailer's main source of profit recurrent, it's growing. In 2013, there was a 6 percent increase in memberships.[22]

Each of the club's 630 no-frills stores (450 of which are in the United States, with the balance in Canada, Mexico, the United Kingdom and Asia) is a massive yet austere warehouse the size of two and a half football fields (143,000-plus square feet) devoid of signage in the aisles and stacked floor-to-ceiling with steel shelving, enabling it to carry about four thousand items in huge quantities. What isn't on shelves is piled on pallets throughout the store, requiring less labor for setup, making Costco almost the anti-Apple. After accounting for fixed costs like real estate and salaries, the company barely breaks even on many of its products, using them essentially as loss leaders as a service to members, another way of enhancing the customer experience.

Each store's main aisle is in a racetrack layout, which leads customers to circle the entire floor and view the entire mix of product offerings, often enticing them to buy things they didn't necessarily set out to buy.

Its product categories range from tires to diamond rings, with food, clothing, electronics, cleaning supplies, home décor items and everything else in between. More than 66 percent of sales are food. Approximately 75 percent of merchandise sales are in what the company calls "triggers"—staple products like cereal, ketchup, detergent and paper towels—that people use day in, day out. They buy these products in bulk at Costco. Need twenty pounds of sirloin steak or five pounds of whole cashews? Then Costco is your place. Eggs come in cartons of ninety. Diapers are ten dozen to a box. You can buy Colgate Advanced Whitening toothpaste, but only in a pack of four eight-ounce tubes. The other 25 percent of sales are in so-called treasures—opportunistic finds that Costco stocks to surprise and delight its customers. Electronics, appliances and other infrequent purchases at extremely good prices, and then the fun stuff, like Waterford Crystal, Coach handbags, Omega watches and Lacoste shirts, some of which are acquired from distributors rather than the brands themselves. These are sold individually, not in bulk, and often sell out quickly.[23]

Eighty percent of Costco's gross margin and 70 percent of its operating income are derived from membership fees, which means Costco collects most of its profits twelve months in advance, not at the eleventh hour of the fiscal year like most other retailers.

Price and Productivity

How does Costco manage to offer such down-and-dirty prices? For starters, it has economies of scale. Costco buys more apple juice, diapers, pasta, towels—in fact, more of any product it decides to offer its members—than just about any other retailer, allowing it to negotiate the lowest prices from vendors and to set the standard for the lowest pricing in the industry so that not even Amazon can beat it. As a result, the Internet has disrupted Costco less than it has other retailers.

It keeps margins razor thin, with markups at 15 percent or less, compared to 25 percent for supermarkets and 50 percent for department stores. Costco's prices are on average 30 percent below large supermarket chains.

Because of the relatively low number of SKUs that Costco carries, the Costco model is simpler, cheaper and easier to execute, and it is inherently more productive than that of the average retailer. It requires less time to sort, restock, reorder and deliver product.

Costco eschews carrying multiple brands of products that are similar or essentially the same, except of course when it has a private-label brand to sell, typically its Kirkland Signature label. Think about it: A major supermarket chain like Kroger's might offer forty different peanut butter SKUs, Trader Joe's has ten, and Costco's number is two. The resulting lower marketing and distribution cost enables it to charge even lower future prices and to send out monthly books of coupons to members for new and exciting deals.

After a brief experience with customer self-checkout, the company returned to using cashiers. And even though its customers' only real major complaint is long checkout lines, Costco maintains that the cashiers are more efficient for high-volume transactions. However, it also saves money by not stocking extra bags or packing materials. To carry out their purchases, customers bring their own bags or use the boxes used to ship the product from the company's outside vendors. To further save on expenses and energy, lighting costs are reduced on sunny days by the use of skylights in most Costco locations. An electronic light meter measures how much light is coming in from the skylight and turns off an appropriate number of the interior lights.

Costco turns over its entire inventory twelve times per year, a demonstration of incredible value-chain control. Its 17-million-square-foot distribution centers, or depots, allow for cross-docking of product, which means reduced lead times between the suppliers' warehouses and when the product ends up in one of the Costco stores. The depots receive container-based shipments from manufacturers and reallocate them to stores in less than 24 hours. The company usually sells merchandise even before it has to pay its vendors for it, drastically reducing its need for working capital. Its cash-conversion cycle is less than a week, compared to a month for most traditional retailers.

Costco's shoppers are college-educated homeowners with an average income of $100,000 per year—not surprising, given that the stores are located mostly in affluent suburbs. It is also not surprising, then, that Costco is the country's largest purveyor of fine wines. The parking lots contain as many late-model luxury cars as ten-year-old minivans. The company targets people who have the disposable income to make large purchases.

The 3 million shoppers per day who visit Costco stores are some of the most neurologically connected consumers on the planet. Many admit to falling prey to "the Costco effect," shorthand for "spending more than they planned to spend." The deals are so good that they're hard to resist. Shopping at a warehouse club gives its members license to spend, and they feel compelled to go back again and again, giving rise to the term "Costcoholic." One of those very connected customers, Kimberly Peterson, started a blog in 2006 to share news of what she bought at Costco with her mother and sister. Today, AddictedtoCostco.com has 2 million readers and generates enough ad revenue that Peterson was able to quit her job and run the site full-time.[24]

Out of what it calls immense respect for its customers, and unlike its main competitor, Walmart's Sam's Club, Costco has lenient return and payment policies, so if you are unhappy with your six-pound wheel of Brie, you can get a full refund. AddictedtoCostco.com's Peterson recalls once standing in line behind a man who was trying to return a violin a year and a half after buying it because his daughter didn't want to play anymore. Costco cheerfully gave him a full refund for the instrument. The retailer has expanded the number of payment methods it accepts, though for credit cards it still accepts only American Express and its own private-label card, and it has added gift prizes for frequent purchasers.

Respect for People

Though the physical plant might be spartan, the way Costco treats its employees is anything but. At a time when many retailers are cutting staffs and reducing employee hours to cut costs and avoid paying benefits, Costco, the second-largest retail employer after Walmart, is an anomaly. It sees employees not as a cost to be minimized but as an asset to be respected and invested in. Former CEO Jim Sinegal told *Stores* magazine, "We've always had the attitude that if you hire good people, provide good jobs, good career opportunities and good wages, good things will happen in your business."[25]

Costco pays its hourly employees an average that is more than two and a half times the minimum wage, and almost twice what Walmart employees make. Almost 80 percent of its employees have company-sponsored health insurance. With initiatives such as those, Costco earns incredible employee loyalty, which in turn also results in fantastic productivity.

While other big retailers like Walmart and Amazon have implemented sizable campaigns to actively keep unions out, Costco is okay with the fact that the Teamsters represent some of its employees.

Costco's labor-friendly attitudes date back to its origins. Price Club, which was acquired by Costco in 1993, was founded in 1976 by Sol Price, a left-leaning attorney from New York who embraced organized labor. He marked everything up a flat small amount because he felt retailers added only limited value to the consumer purchase equation. He also believed firmly in treating employees, customers and vendors well, with respect—and in the process, rewarding shareholders.

Sinegal, one of Price's top executives, brought the Price Club model to Seattle in 1983 to start Costco. The two merged in 1993 and went public in 1995. Wall Street repeatedly begged the retailer to reduce wages and health benefits. Sinegal, in a nod to his former boss, instead increased them every year, including during the recession. The company's attitude was "The economy is bad, we should figure out how to give people more." To preserve the company culture, it will not hire business-school graduates, but prefers to grow executives from within. The many MBAs working at the company earned their degrees while working there. Said Sinegal: "Culture isn't the most important thing, it's the *only* thing."[26]

Costco is not without its challenges. Although its online sales are running at about $2 billion, the site's popularity lags behind that of its physical stores. Also, much of the company's growth has been in food, so Amazon's entry into the grocery business might be cause for concern. And some social media postings complain that Costco still has a distance to go before it matches Sam's Club's excellence in fresh food, particularly produce.

With limited success, the company is courting luxury brands like Coach, Ralph Lauren and Louis Vuitton to allow sales of their brands through Costco.

Global expansion is in the works. The company hopes to open hundreds of more warehouses in the next decade, with two-thirds of them planned in foreign markets, where there are still untapped pockets of value shoppers. It has plans to open its first locations soon in France and Spain. Costco has begun to request that its suppliers give it global deals, even if that means upsetting their current local retail relationships. Costco's plan is to export not only its unique value proposition but also its corporate culture as well.

Trader Joe's

The first thing one notices when entering a Trader Joe's grocery store, other than the thirty-bottle mountain of spiced apple cider, stacks of two-pound tubs of fresh strawberries, and wall of fresh-cut flowers, is the signage. Seemingly done by hand, every one of the signs is a whimsical work of art with friendly, bold, hand-lettered-like copy. They don't advertise a sale or invite you to use coupons. Instead, they tell you a little something about the store or the product and its affordable price. One of them says: "At Trader Joe's, S-A-L-E is a four-letter word."

The next thing you notice is the people who work there. The manager ("Captain") and assistant manager ("First Mate") wear brightly colored, Hawaiian-style shirts. Sales associates dressed in hibiscus-print T-shirts smile as they hand stickers out to fidgety kids and chat about products with customers. If you're unhappy with a purchase, they'll cheerfully refund your money—no questions asked, even if it expired months ago. Ask one of them where to find a particular item in the store, and he or she will not just tell you but likely walk you over to its location and even open a package to let you sample.

Trader Joe's, you see, is no ordinary grocery chain, but an offbeat and fun discovery zone that elevates food shopping from a chore to a cultural experience. Positioned as "a unique neighborhood grocery store," it sells basic, gourmet, imported, organic, health and vegetarian foods, frozen and fresh vegetables and meals, appetizers, desserts and more. Where the law permits, the stores also have domestic and imported beer and wine, including its now-world-famous "Two Buck Chuck" made by the Charles Shaw wine company, sold for $1.99 per bottle, and a growing collection of tantalizing craft beers.

It's a place that appeals to all demographic groups, from starving artists to yuppies. In the mornings the store is full of senior citizens on fixed incomes, scouring the ingredients list for the healthy stuff that will satisfy their low-sodium and other restricted dietary needs. They like the store because of its prices, which are lower than most health-food stores, and its small footprint, which is easier to navigate with a walker or cane. In the evening, in come the families, anxious to pick up frozen mandarin orange chicken, boeuf bourguignon or chicken tikka masala for dinner, and single people, who love the small-package-size options.

Trader Joe's sells things you can't find anywhere else—literally. Approximately 80 percent of company sales are of its private-label brands. Ethnic or global products are given names like Trader Jose (Mexican), Trader Giotto (Italian) and Trader Ming (Chinese). "Joe's Os," the TJ version of Oreos, is a best-seller. Its products contain no artificial colors, preservatives, MSG or trans fats and are sourced from non–genetically modified ingredients. Dairy products are made from the milk of cows not having received the growth hormone rBST.[27]

The store offers accurate pricing (everything is unit priced, which reduces the amount of time to check out), small formats, well-edited assortments and value pricing. The whole shopping experience is created to encourage increasing frequency of shopping trips. Impulse purchases make the trips particularly appealing and rewarding, reinforcing the neurological connection. A sample station located at the back of the stores distributes tastes of the latest delicacy to waiting guests, encouraging customers to tour the entire place before leaving.

Trader Joe's ranks highest in the United States in customer satisfaction, with a net promoter score that is the best of any grocery chain. The unique friendly experience and atmosphere are key benefits.[28]

It's no wonder that Trader Joe's is one of the hottest retailers—let alone food stores—in the country. The four-hundred-store privately held chain based in Monrovia, California, has estimated sales of more than $11 billion. Since 1990, the chain has more than quintupled its store count and increased profits tenfold. *Supermarket News* estimated that, at $1,750, TJ achieves more than double the sales per square foot of Whole Foods.[29]

Trader Joe's has managed to grow along with America's increasingly sophisticated, ethnic and healthy tastes. It pioneered the democratization of the discriminating palate by showing Americans that you don't have to be wealthy or pay a lot to appreciate or have access to great-tasting food. The company takes niche products, once considered gourmet and highly discretionary and found only in a specialty shop (such as white-cheese popcorn, artisanal ciabatta bread and bruschetta spread) and brings them to a wider audience, making them mainstream. Some products have such a cult following that people buy up all of an item as soon as it comes off the truck. The genius of Trader Joe's is in preemptively staying one step ahead of the increasingly inquisitive American palate, with interesting new items that will add up to volume.

The chain has a deliberately scaled-down strategy, both in reach and footprint. Its eight- to twelve-thousand-square-foot stores, tiny by grocery store standards, allow penetration into neighborhoods that can't support a large supermarket. While a typical grocery store carries fifty thousand items, TJ's stocks four thousand, giving it much higher turnover and the ability to buy large quantities from its suppliers and secure deeper discounts. It makes the whole business—from stocking shelves to checking out customers—more streamlined. With its global foods and localized décor (aisles are sometimes named for local streets or landmarks), Trader Joe's looks special while being affordable.

Strip-mall operators and consumers alike aggressively lobby the chain to open a store in their towns. When Trader Joe's opens a new store, not only does it create new jobs, but its presence is like an affirmation that one is living in a nice, worldly, secure and smart community.

According to its employees, it's also a great place to work. Associates are paid more than average industry wages and are provided generous benefits. An entry-level employee will earn an average of $10–$20 per hour, and store managers can earn in the low six figures. Employees work everywhere in the store, which makes them very knowledgeable about products, which in turn helps the customer experience. Employees often come in on their days off to say hello to their colleagues.

Part of the customer experience is the low-tech *Fearless Flyer*—part newsletter, part magazine. A sort of cross between *Consumer Reports* and *MAD Magazine,* it is a small monthly booklet printed on what looks like old newsprint that describes new and existing products and how to enjoy them. Using self-deprecating humor, it tells stories about the products and their origins, thereby personalizing and "de-commoditizing" them, and imparting personality, mystery and whimsy to the brands. While Whole Foods customers may consider themselves serious "foodies," TJ customers have the whimsical air of the brand itself, which seeps into every aspect of the shopping experience.

A challenge facing the company is how to keep growing while maintaining its personality and keeping the neurological experience intact. The term "national chain of small-town neighborhood specialty grocery stores" sounds a little oxymoronic. However, in the case of Trader Joe's, it's not so much mom and pop, but eccentric uncle.

The company has not yet ventured into Wave IV territory, however. There is no e-commerce or company-run social media, and no sign of any on the horizon. Facebook, Twitter and other social messages are run by fans, and never responded to by the company. Over time, this—and the company's refusal to engage in e-commerce—will no doubt change, if only because its customers eventually demand it. Ditto for expansion into Canada and other countries. Out of frustration, a very entrepreneurial third party launched a website called Pirate Joe's. He purchased Trader Joe's products in stores, paying the full retail price, then turned around and sold them on Pirate Joe's at a premium. TJ's sued Pirate Joe's and won, forcing the site to close. However, it's only a matter of time before someone else is more successful at knocking off the quirky chain online and internationally.

Trader Joe's exercises control over its value chain through its small group of top buyers, called product developers, who scour the world looking for the next successful item before its competition finds it. The product R&D budget is largely for travel. Lower-level buyers field calls from the hundreds of would-be suppliers each week desperate to sell to Trader Joe's. The company reportedly pays all its bills on time and doesn't charge the slotting or marketing fees usually associated with grocery retailing. To do business with the company, though, a supplier has to work under the cloak of secrecy, so that no one knows the source of its products. That doesn't stop the buzz on social media and fan websites about which major brands are hiding under those private labels.

How, then, does one describe a local/global, healthy/gourmet, small yet big, whimsical yet serious, reliable yet ever-changing grocery shopping experience?

How about: always an adventure.

HSN

Anyone who tours the sixty-six-acre campus in St. Petersburg, Florida, that is the headquarters, broadcast studios and operating heart of HSN Inc. (formerly Home Shopping Network) becomes immediately awestruck. There's the HSN brand across all platforms—television, Internet, mobile, interactive TV, gaming. Then there are the eight e-commerce and catalog brands in its Cornerstone division: Frontgate, Ballard Designs, The Territory Ahead, Garnet Hill, Travelsmith, Improvements, Smith + Noble and Grandin Road.

What is perhaps most impressive, however, is what one might call its "store," a gargantuan building that houses all the mini-theaters where the television, online and catalog sets get changed hundreds of times a day.

HSN Inc. is the $3 billion media, entertainment, technology and retail business that created the television retail industry in 1982 and has truly become an omni-channel retailer in every sense of the word. No longer just television, but a multifaceted interactive shopping platform, it has developed tremendous synergy among all its "screens"—big and small. It offers innovative, differentiated retail experiences digitally and physically, on TV, online, in catalogs, on social media and in brick-and-mortar stores. More than 15,000 videos on its YouTube channel are selling themed products. Online versions of special events or programs are shown on the website for a limited time following their broadcast on TV. Also on the site are 60,000 video demonstrations of products available for sale. HSN was among the first to develop an iPhone app.

HSN has more than 5 million active subscribers, reaches 95 million homes (twenty-four hours a day, seven days a week, 365 days a year), and handles more than 50 million inbound customer calls annually. Almost 40 percent of its sales, or almost $1.5 billion, are now placed digitally. HSN.com ranked twenty-sixth in 2013 among the top five hundred Internet retailers.[30]

Its growth in the mobile channel has been nothing short of meteoric, catapulting it to the ninth spot for global retail in the Mobile 500. In addition to its existing media platforms, HSN is the industry leader in technological innovation, including services such as Shop by Remote, which allows registered members to click on the TV screen with their remote control to order a product, the first service of its kind in the United States, and was also among the first to pioneer video on demand.

Through its Cornerstone Brands division it markets leading home and apparel lifestyle brands through its distribution of 324 million catalogs annually and its eight separate e-commerce sites, and it runs twenty-five retail stores.

A macro view of HSN's evolution from its beginnings could be described as the transformation from a TV show that sold cheap household gadgets and miracle face cream to couch potatoes into a brand inviting modern consumers into Twiggy's living room in London for tea and a fun shopping experience.

Through our research about the company and conversations with Home Shopping Network CEO Mindy Grossman, a thirty-year apparel industry veteran who previously held top jobs at Nike, Polo and Warnaco, we have come to learn that this business model, and the way in which Grossman has transformed it from its original structure, provide a powerful example of a company implementing the New Rules of Retail.

Rather than just sell stuff to its target customers (women over twenty-five with an average income of $60,000), HSN aims to enhance their shopping experience, either on TV or online, and promote customer loyalty by bringing brands and products to life in unique, compelling, informative and entertaining ways.

It sometimes uses celebrities to invite consumers into conversations, fashion shows, cooking lessons or product demonstrations. The show's sets and themes are constantly evolving and can change in real time. For instance, if a cooking show was planned for a specific time, given updated information about what consumers are buying, HSN may change the lineup even within a given day. Consumers are compelled to check in throughout the day, lest they miss something exciting.

HSN has total control of its value chain, from creation of the shopping experience all the way through consumption. Its brand value also promises a broad array of merchandise available across its comprehensive preemptive-distribution platforms, proprietary and/or exclusive brands; designer and celebrity brands; and much more. HSN controls the selection of the merchandise and collaborates with its vendors on presenting its brands according to the brand's positioning.

Grossman told us: "We have new product every single minute, every single hour. We have urgency all the time. But we're not about a discount. We are about exciting great product, and our customer expects that she's getting something valuable and for a great price/value, but not a discount. How do we do that and remain competitive? Seventy percent of the products we sell are exclusive to us. Either the brand is, or we have something first before anyone else does, like in electronics."[31]

Neurological and Preemptively Connecting with Shoppers Where They Live

When Grossman recites her mantra and philosophy about the brand standing for an entertaining, fun and exciting shopping experience that can be accessed anytime and anywhere the consumer wishes to be engaged, we heard two of our favorite phrases: "neurological connection" and "preemptive distribution."

Says Grossman: "The days of trying to get a consumer to come to you are over. You really have to be in the consumer's world, wherever, whenever and however."[32]

Grossman decided early on to deemphasize Veg-O-Matic slicers and instead focus on things like designer handbags and celebrity chefs, elevating HSN's wares from needs to wants and solidifying its customer relationship. When she first joined the company, it had what she calls a "big audacious goal" to be a disruptive force on the retail and consumer landscape. Now the intention of her team is to lead and pioneer the future of boundary-less retail—their term for omni-channel, which they've trademarked, by the way—a world devoid of artificial barriers where collaboration and community all come together to create a unique and seamless experience for consumers.

The brand roster runs the gamut from mainstream labels to luxury brands, and includes fashion authorities like Carmen Marc Valvo, Josie Natori and Vince Camuto, home and lifestyle leaders like Martha Stewart, Nate Berkus and Emeril Lagasse, and legendary consumer brands like Neutrogena, Coty, Bissell and Lladro.

HSN even creates its own brands, such as Firm-A-Face, a technologically advanced product from one of its largest proprietary beauty brands, Serious Skin Care.

Designers are clamoring to show their stuff on the network. With opportunities to grow top-line sales becoming increasingly rare in other channels, can you blame them? HSN's strategy of bringing the entire shopping mall to living rooms, offices and people on the go everywhere is obviously working, and in many ways represents the future of retailing.

HSN operates under the principle that if you're not constantly moving, not incredibly connected and inquisitive, you will be left behind in the dust. If you think you're going to do everything yourself, "on an island," then you're not being realistic. The company forges strategic collaborations and win-win and eschews not-invented-here, opting instead for great partnerships.

More significantly, the way in which HSN has combined its preemptive-distribution strategy with the experiences the brand promises to (preemptively) deliver creates a powerful synergy. In fact, the synergy of the two creates a strong neurological connection with the consumer. Indeed, the distribution platforms and the neurological experiences become one.

With top designers and celebrity television hosts romancing products like Lancôme moisture cream and Badgley Mischka ready-to-wear, and selling tons of it in the process, the company has shed a lot of its down-market image and become a go-to distribution channel for brands wanting to tell a story.

The neurological experience, or the "high" consumers get when thinking about HSN, comes from their anticipation of the new and exclusive merchandise and experience that HSN promises them every day. This neurological rush is essentially a preemptive distributor for HSN because the consumer can't wait to get to the brand ahead of its competitors.

HSN's distribution platforms are highly integrated to achieve maximum cross-shopping benefits, and its rapid growth in mobile has coincided with its skew toward younger consumers.

The brand also seeks new distribution models. The company launched the first live in-flight shopping service, giving customers access to signature entertainment, lifestyle content and commerce during air travel. Its recently announced collaboration with Spanish cable operator Univision will bring HSN's products to Hispanic consumers—*in Spanish.*

Further strengthening all three operating principles, HSN does not merely buy products. It partners with visionaries, experts and design authorities to build proprietary brands and bring them to life in unique and compelling ways. Says Grossman: "Our mission is to partner and be not just a commerce or transactional partner but a strategic marketing partner for brands to tell their stories, to translate the voice of their product. And I think that's why we've been able to attract brands and businesses. I say to everyone you're not going to win by just telling someone that you can sell more of these in ten minutes. But if you say to someone I will bring the DNA of your brand to life, I will tell your story, I will be your partner in the long term and make it relevant and modern and fun and informational, treat it with respect and create a bond with you and your consumer base, that's a little bit more compelling. That's an experience."[33]

Nothing proves the soundness of HSN's collaboration strategy and storytelling ability more than an event that took place two years ago, when R&B star Mary J. Blige debuted her fragrance My Life exclusively on HSN, and sold out of 60,000 bottles during her six-hour appearance, busting previous HSN fragrance records, and making it one of the most successful prestige fragrance launches in history.

A few years ago, HSN decided it really needed to rev up the entertainment factor and be a part of popular culture. It needed to evolve the entertainment to the next level. So Grossman went to California and met with heads of movie studios, TV studios and music companies to educate them on HSN and its customers. Grossman told them: "You want to engage women. You want to get women into your theaters, to watch your shows. We have those women, and they're very passionate and very engaged in what we're doing." HSN's first promotion with Sony Pictures was a seventy-two-hour extravaganza around the feature film *Eat Pray Love,* with twenty-four hours on Italy, twenty-four hours on India, and twenty-four hours on Bali, using the story of the journey as the storytelling vehicle. Sony provided trailers, behind-the-scenes clips and even the makeup artist who worked on the film, while HSN created an entire magalog, web landing site and programming. Entertainment e-zine *Deadline Hollywood* credited HSN for driving women to the theaters on opening weekend. After that, the floodgates opened, bringing more promotions around films such as *The Help, Footloose* and others.

Grossman sums up HSN's success by relating everything back to the most important person in the business: "Our customer—nobody, in fact—wants to be sold. They want to be inspired. We're about great product, a great story, told by a great storyteller."

Nordstrom

If the consulting buzzword "customer-centric" had a mother, it was Nordstrom. *The customer, the customer, the customer*—repeat it like a mantra. No lip service, no fancy strategic PowerPoint presentations, no hyperbole. The entire Nordstrom team, simply and pragmatically, has one goal burned into its DNA: to delight yet another customer, a goal that continues to be driven from the very soul of the company.

However, while the term "customer service" is now used everywhere, it has a deeper strategic meaning within the Nordstrom organization. Not unlike the core philosophies of Apple's Steve Jobs and Jeff Bezos of Amazon, the entire Nordstrom organization, across its entire value chain, will not develop any strategy or implement any tactic that does not have an absolute benefit for consumers. And, like Apple's and Amazon's, Nordstrom's growth is evidence of that core commitment. Since 2008, revenues have grown by more than 50%, to $12.5 billion. However, as Nordstrom grows into Wave IV, that commitment takes on a whole new dimension.

Accordingly, over the past several years, Nordstrom has invested millions of dollars to perfect its omni-channel capabilities and is now widely acknowledged as a technology leader among its peers, including its direct competitors. Yet, to CEO Blake Nordstrom, it's just Retail 101: delighting customers beyond expectations. All aspects of the business, throughout the value chain, including technology and the omni-channel, are merely supportive tools for accomplishing and enhancing that number-one goal.

One of the major reasons Nordstrom has been so successful in becoming what could be considered "best in class" in developing its omni-channel was that it did not build it from the "inside out," to the customer, based on some detached business objective. Rather, every step of the very complex, seamless integration of the online and brick-and-mortar businesses was made with total focus on what would deliver greater satisfaction to the customer, from the "outside in." This operating principle is not lip service. Its distinction is enormous. Everything it does starts with the question "How will what I do end up delighting the consumer?" So, the beginning is from the consumer, "outside," and is then brought "in" to the organization, and executed accordingly across the value chain. Or, according to Blake Nordstrom, "It's about doing what's best for the customer right now, and since the customer is always raising the bar in setting the standard, we're continually resetting ours upward."[34]

Preemptive Distribution

These stellar achievements are not only a result of an ecstatic customer, buying more and more often; they are also driven by the fact that Nordstrom is not a promotional department store—because it doesn't have to be. With a seamlessly integrated online and in-store business, inventory is unified across both channels. Thus, an online order from New York could be shipped from the floor of a California store. Orders are simply directed to stores with excess inventory, reducing the need for markdowns.

Furthermore, while some experts believe the growing Nordstrom Rack store business provides Nordstrom an outlet to discount excess inventory, Nordstrom views its Rack strategy as proactively responding to consumers' desires for off-price fashion, which is indeed the fastest-growing sector in retailing. Its acquisition of HauteLook, the online flash-sale site, is another example of serving the customer first. Again, being totally responsive to changing consumer desires and behavior, Nordstrom identifies and becomes strategically positioned on multiple distribution platforms, all creating synergies.

In fact, Blake Nordstrom has said, "What we've learned is that our Racks do well when they're closest to our flagships. But our flagships also do better closest to a Rack! We think there's a great synergy."[35] While that seems coun-terintuitive, because the stores differentiate their product they attract either different consumers or the same consumer for a different occasion (hence in-creasing their share of wallet). The Rack's pricing is lower, and stores are about a third of the size of the full-price stores, but with much lower operating costs, they're highly profitable.

It's also believed by some experts that the Rack is targeting the younger end of Nordstrom's core consumer segment, enabling Nordstrom luxury at an affordable price. The stores also appeal to younger tastes: urban locations; one-floor design; and a faster, more convenient shopping experience, enabled by mobile checkout devices. It's also serving as a training ground for store managers. Most of the full-price store managers started at the Rack.

In fact, a much more aggressive growth strategy is planned for the Rack stores to double in number, to 230, by 2016. There is not a current plan to add to its almost 120 full-price stores in the United States, however.

Other preemptive distribution moves creating synergies are Nordstrom's partnering with Bonobos, Brooks Brothers and Topshop, and a newer initia-tive to launch themed in-store designer shops, all being presented as almost pop-up shops within the Nordstrom stores.

In another move that ultimately gives Nordstrom yet another preemp-tive connection with its consumers, the company plans to ultimately invest more than $1 billion to accelerate the personalization of Nordstrom's e-commerce operations: mining individual customer information to be able to proactively (yet unobtrusively) reach out to each customer with personalized recommendations.[36]

One indication that its philosophy is working comes out of a Market Force Information survey of more than 6,800 consumers. Nordstrom was cited as North America's overall favorite fashion retailer. The Seattle-based chain earned significantly more votes than all the other chains, and frequently ap-pears on other consumer favorites lists.

Market Force also looked at why shoppers prefer one store to another and, not surprisingly, Nordstrom was a favorite across many of the service-oriented attributes. It ranked highest for store atmosphere (64 percent), return policy (59 percent), helpful associates (56 percent), friendly associates (52 percent), knowledgeable associates (50 percent) and having a website that complements the store (27 percent).[37]

Neurologically Connecting Experience

Already widely known and understood as one of the greatest tools in Nordstrom's belt are its roughly 65,000 sales associates, including the growing number of 1,300 personal stylists, all of whom are personalizing service for each and every customer. This team is Nordstrom's widely recognized competitive advantage, its "secret sauce," using the most fundamental play in retailing: satisfying customer needs.

And Nordstrom gives its sales force complete autonomy and authority to do whatever they believe is necessary to satisfy customers' dreams. And in Wave IV, during which the only way brick-and-mortar stores will survive is to provide awesome, neurologically connecting experiences, Nordstrom's superior associates team already provides an enormous competitive advantage.

On top of this, Nordstrom is employing all the technology enablers and shopping enhancers being launched into the industry on a daily basis. Associates have iPads for quick and immediate checkout, and transparency across distribution platforms will provide identification and delivery of products not found in the store.

The "outside in" process has also led Nordstrom to add "Free Shipping, Free Returns, All the Time" as part of its e-commerce offering, again leading its sector of the industry. The company has experienced several consecutive quarters of online sales growth that is almost three times the industry average, according to Forrester Research.[38]

Supporting such individual empowerment and incentivizing associates' goals to provide outstanding service "one customer at a time," Nordstrom's compensation program is commission based on performance. In addition to the commission formulas, there are other incentives, including a generous 401(k) program, awards, bonuses, stock-purchasing advantages and other programs.

Management's encouragement of an aggressive commissioned sales force focused on exceeding customers' needs, as well as its tendency to promote from within, resulted in a reputation for stellar service. There are countless stories of associates unquestioningly accepting returns, paying shoppers' parking tickets and personally delivering product to customers' homes after hours.

Think about it. Each and every square foot that is occupied by a Nordstrom or Rack associate engaging a customer is yielding huge top- and bottom-line returns, all based on that associate's priority goal to satisfy their customer's dreams. Yes, superior customer service is a simple concept and imperative in today's intensely competitive marketplace. It is unanimously declared a priority by every retailer. However, truly accomplishing it requires execution that is not easy, and Nordstrom, by the numbers, keeps achieving it.

The importance of the associates as the core of the shopping experience in Wave IV cannot be overstated. The most important moment in retailing is the moment when the customer's dream can be tipped into reality—the moment of purchase. If that moment becomes more than just a physical transaction— if it comes not just with a smile, but with over-the-top engagement, empathy, interest and warmth—then that customer will stay longer, buy more and will come back, over and over again. Indeed, not only is this human "touching and tipping" point Nordstrom's competitive advantage, it is a neurologically connecting experience. When a retailer like Apple, Trader Joe's, Lululemon or Nordstrom provides an overwhelmingly compelling experience, it goes beyond just connecting emotionally with customers—it connects with their minds, strongly enough to compel them to keep coming back to that experience, making them, for lack of a better word, addicted.

That is what also turns Nordstrom's dreams into the reality of winning the trifecta of same-store sales growth, sales per square foot and over-the-top operating income.

Nordstrom's strategy was clearly summed up by Blake Nordstrom in the *Wall Street Journal* back in 2004, and his words still resonate today: "It doesn't sound very glamorous to say that what's next is to continue to improve on the little things in front of us, but that's what we're going to do."[39]

Not brain surgery; not rocket science. But it works.

Home Depot

When Frank Blake became CEO of Home Depot in 2007, he faced many challenges. Although the home sector hadn't yet felt the devastation wrought by the recession, the consumer experience inside Home Depot was challenged by self-inflicted wounds arising from reductions in service that had occurred under prior management, along with competitive pressure from elevated experience levels at Lowe's and from e-commerce.

Of e-commerce, Blake said: "The threat is real. It's hugely convenient for the customer. It's going to transform the way they feel about a physical store. If I can shop in the convenience of my home, why should I put up with rude associates and dirty stores?"[40]

Home Depot was already rising to the challenge of Wave IV, and it had a number of the critical elements under way to build upon its already impressive asset base.

Value-Chain Control

Founded in 1978, the Atlanta-based company, with its 2,220 cavernous stores averaging 100,000 square feet in size, is the preemptive distributor of building supplies, hardware, paint, electrical and plumbing fixtures, tools, kitchen cabinets and appliances in the country.

Home Depot is in the final stretches a long-overdue renovation—of itself. During its first thirty years, the retailer didn't focus much on its supply chain. It grew by opening new stores, which doubled as distribution centers. The strategy was hard to criticize, given its history of double- and even triple-digit annual growth in the go-go years. As that sales growth slowed, fuel costs rose and competition intensified, however, it realized it had fallen behind its competition, particularly Lowe's, in operational efficiencies. Then, in 2007, the housing sector crashed, and spending on remodeling plunged by double digits. The home-improvement giant knew it had to make its next big move. It decided to improve productivity and profits by retooling—if you'll pardon the pun—many of the business practices that never changed during the meteoric growth years of Wave III.

Home Depot's original supply-chain model involved having 80 percent of its inventory shipped directly from suppliers to stores, with store managers placing 70 percent of orders. As the business grew, this resulted in an expensive, inefficient logistics infrastructure that was wasteful and inefficient, with lots of half-empty trucks traveling to stores, but that didn't necessarily reduce out-of-stocks.

In 2009, the company began the most dramatic supply-chain revamp in its thirty-five-year history. At the core of the project was the construction of eighteen highly automated rapid deployment centers, or RDCs, each designed to serve about a hundred stores. The facilities enabled the cross-docking of large volumes of merchandise, with little actually stored in them, because most of the products in the RDCs are shipped out within twenty-four hours of arrival. Centralized procurement and distribution were designed to reduce the amount of inventory vendors were shipping directly to the stores. Since RDCs came online, inventory levels have fallen, out-of-stocks have plummeted and vendors have seen the improvement—they have fewer shipments to send to Home Depot. Hundreds of purchase orders per month were reduced, in some cases down to one.[41]

Although the impact on costs has been huge, the benefit to consumers is even greater. Store managers and associates, who before had spent too much time working on the loading dock coordinating inventory flow, could now go back to helping customers. There is increased flexibility, and products can be rapidly sent to the stores, increasing accuracy and arriving closer to need.

The company has put the brakes on new store openings—a gutsy move for a retailer—and invested in customer service, value-chain improvements and employees. With most of the major markets already containing its share of Home Depot stores, there is less white space in which to grow. In fact, the opening of smaller stores in secondary markets was exactly the chink in the wall that exposed the operating inefficiencies of the old supply-chain model. Many of these stores have been closed.

E-Commerce

Home Depot management saw early on that big-box growth would be stymied by store saturation and the rise of pure-play e-commerce competition. With Amazon nipping at its heels, it has set about rethinking its digital offering amid Americans' changing needs. Its e-commerce business, begun in 2001, was inadequate, it decided. Home Depot does about $1 billion annually in on-line sales. Although that is less than 2 percent of its total revenue, it's a bigger chunk, percentage-wise, than Lowe's, and the fastest-growing segment of the business.

However, it has lots of catching up to do. According to Forrester Research, online sales for the home-improvement industry are around $200 billion, a number that is growing at double digits, or 9 percent of the total, and are expected to grow to about 15 percent of the market by 2015. The company has dedicated hundreds of millions of dollars on Information Technology to shore up its digital foundation, including mobile. The company knows that almost half of all home-improvement projects begin online. Consumers visit the website and then travel to the store. The RDCs were not designed to be stock, pick and pack centers, however, so they could not be used to support its growing online-fulfillment strategy. For that, Home Depot is in the process of building three huge distribution centers—one near its headquarters about thirty miles from Atlanta, another in Ohio, and the other in the Los Angeles area—each of which will hold about 100,000 SKUs and help the company's five other distribution centers that support the company's direct-fulfillment operations.

Home Depot offers more than 600,000 SKUs online, compared to an average of 30,000 per store. It is also streamlining some of its most profitable areas, like kitchen design. Now customers can schedule appointments online with kitchen designers, rather than wait in the store for one to be free, and work out design changes. A decade ago a new kitchen design could take three months and up to twenty store visits. Today it can be done much more efficiently.

The challenge facing the company is to figure out how to use the site to draw traffic into the store, and to convert shoppers into buyers.

When asked how he was thinking about that relationship and how to work across the digital/physical space, Blake responded: "Our first stage was to say ' . . . We have to take this stuff seriously.' We worked on the site, making the experience on it really great. This has taken a lot of time and effort. Then we asked ourselves 'Okay, how does this site help me draw traffic into the stores, and vice versa?' Because if we can't figure that out, it's like having a foot on the boat and a foot on the dock, and that's not a comfortable place to be."[42]

Currently, customers can order an item online and have it shipped directly to them, or order online and pick up in the nearest Home Depot store. The latter option is extremely popular, since shipping is free, and it drives traffic to the store, often resulting in additional purchases. Home Depot's more than 2,000 stores in the United States, Canada and Mexico already serve as de facto distribution centers. The average large home Depot store carries about 35,000 SKUs. For some products, the store is the fulfillment center for online orders shipped directly to customers. The key to making the relationship between the digital and physical environment work was to change the incentive structure so that full credit for sales either online or in stores accrued to the sales staff (not just the store manager).

Blake explained how the process works. To encourage employees to sell things online, HD began to credit e-commerce sales to individual stores, and the individuals within them, instead of counting them separately. He said: "Yes, first we figured out we had to give the stores credit, but the next thing was we had to get it to the individual associate level, because what was happening was, you're in the store, and I'm an associate, and I'm measured by my sales in my department. You're not finding what you like in the department. I could help you find what you're looking for in the online assortment, but unless I get credit for that, I have less incentive to do it. I like the company and my store, but I like my compensation, too. So we've made it so that if the associate helps the customer in the store, and buys it right there, the associate gets credit for the sale."[43]

Blake also indicated that customer experience is going to be fundamentally shaped by the integration of technology and the experience in the store. And we believe that Home Depot is moving exactly in that direction.

Mobile

Mobile, or m-commerce, with mobile apps for e-commerce, and in-store navigation for both consumers and trade, will be the next big area of focus for Home Depot.

About mobile, Blake said: "Wow, mobile is really easy to say and really hard to do. Our mobile applications are good, and answer some of the basics for their customers when they're in the store, but fall short of being compelling retail experiences. Knowledgeable associates is what Home Depot always sold. In the old days, we would have customers come to the store to ask how to fix a leaky faucet. Now those customers go to YouTube. Having sales associates stay ahead of customers in the knowledge department is an interesting challenge."

The company spent a reported $60 million on handheld devices that help workers check on the spot whether something is in stock.

The restructuring has come at a great time, helping the company recover margin lost during the downturn. Leveraging those improvements as business recovered has been a huge boost to the bottom line.

Home Depot figured out how to do the store experience in the physical world, with better associate service, do-it-yourself clubs and classes, etc., but the challenge now is to do it digitally. Then it would have both, which Amazon does not.

Foot Locker

If you were to ask Foot Locker CEO Ken Hicks what he does for a living, he'd tell you, "I sell sneakers." The self-effacing, plain-talking, West Point– and Harvard Business School–educated former army artillery captain has led the athletic footwear retailer since 2008. As is usually the case with Hicks, his answer would be an understatement. Last year, the 3,500-unit mall-based athletic footwear chain sold more than $5 billion worth of sneakers—along with more than $1 billion worth of active apparel and other products.[44]

Before Hicks' arrival, Foot Locker had allowed itself to become, to use his description, too finite. It had become too specialized in basketball, and in so doing had overly narrowed its customer profile. When the recession hit, Foot Locker's core segment, the minority male aged fifteen to twenty-five, got hit pretty hard, and sales plunged by a billion dollars. Foot Locker had to close stores, cut staff and figure out how to grow all over again.

The company set its sights on becoming the leading global retailer of athletically inspired shoes and apparel. It needed to become once again the go-to place for sneakers. To do that, it had to become a focused power merchandiser, which meant developing a distinct positioning for each of its key store nameplate brands (Foot Locker, Lady Foot Locker, Kids Foot Locker, Champs, Footaction, Eastbay and CCS), for developing product assortments that are compelling and exciting and for integrating the two into a shopping experience that would keep its customers coming back more often.

Neurological Connectivity

Foot Locker's secret sauce is a relentless focus on product, product, product. By forging a powerful connection with suppliers, it can deliver the latest and greatest top-brand sneaker styles before anyone else, with the biggest selection of styles, colors and sizes, most of them unique to Foot Locker—wherever and whenever its customer wants it.

Footwear is the aspirational product for young males, their special luxury. Sometimes these customers even forego something they need so that they can buy the sneakers. Many of Foot Locker's customers are minority and moderate-income customers. Whether they pay $150 or $200 for the latest pair of Nike foamposites isn't a function of the price of the shoe. It's a function of whether they can scrape the money together. Hicks claims that sneakers are the "Louis Vuitton of Middle America."[45]

Foot Locker works with vendors on exclusive styles and colors. "We have athletes like Kobe Bryant come for events for Footlocker and House of Hoops. We did a shoe with Taboo of the Black-Eyed Peas for Footaction, which has a more street customer. It's a product category that's always exciting, always changing."

Hicks' team is working relentlessly to make the stores and Internet sites interesting and engaging places to shop, to really improve the customer experience. House of Hoops, the in-store basketball shop, is very inviting. There's a basketball floor, as well as great product. There are lots of mannequins to show how things go together and to make the environment more exciting—to create the neurological connection.

Said Hicks: "At one Foot Locker in Toronto, we've got an invisible wall which has all the shoes, to show that we've got a lot of shoes. At Lady Foot Locker and Champs, we're showing a lot more apparel and how things go together. But I think the most important thing is to have great product, so we work with our vendors to have new exciting products, exclusive products and to have great service through the associates."

Using Brick-and-Mortar for Value-Chain Control and Preemptive Distribution

Nike is Foot Locker's biggest supplier. More than 65 percent of its sales are of Nike footwear and apparel. Foot Locker has become very skilled at inventory management and visibility, which are particularly challenging and critical for footwear since there are so many SKUs.

Foot Locker views each of its 3,500 stores as preemptive distribution or inventory staging points, and locations for merchandising, marketing, sales and service. Customers can buy online, ship to store, pick up in store and return to store. Direct-to-consumer results in higher return rates, so making it easier to return and replace is key. Increasingly, associates have scan guns and tablets to determine if an item is in stock, and if so where it can be found.

Product availability has become an increasingly critical means to enhance the customer experience, to deliver on the retail promise and to meet customer expectations. For a mall-based store, driving traffic is essential. Without confidence that the store will have the product they want, customers will be less likely to make the trip. Loyalty is being undermined at every turn. Once customers go elsewhere, it's very hard to get them back.

In the omni-channel world, visibility is no longer about simply whether the product is on the shelf or in the back room. Foot Locker management understands that this issue becomes more nuanced, a question not only of "Do we have it in stock" but also of "Can I promise it?" and "Where is it?" Said Hicks: "In a business like ours, where 20 percent of your customers drive 80 percent of your margins, keeping customers is really important."[46]

Apparel as Add-On

Part of becoming the go-to place for sneakers involved strengthening Foot Locker's apparel assortment. People generally buy apparel more frequently than shoes, so they come to the stores more often. Whereas most specialty retailers have apparel as their main product line, Foot Locker finds it a natural add-on to the business. If it sells a new pair of LeBron James or Carmelo Anthony signature Nike basketball shoes, the sales associate will point out the T-shirt that goes with it, and the hat, and so forth.

Said Hicks wryly about Foot Locker's apparel offering when he first joined the company: "I tell people: 'We always wanted to do apparel in the worst way, and that's exactly what we were doing.'"

He then added: "We didn't have any apparel merchants, we had shoe people trying to do apparel, so we went out and hired people who knew apparel.

"We realized apparel should be sold at a higher margin than branded shoes, which it wasn't. The apparel margin was less than the shoe margin. We weren't turning apparel; and the apparel we had was very inexpensive stuff. We were selling $5 polos. Walmart doesn't even sell $5 polos. We've upped the quality, and are selling it for higher prices. We're turning it faster, and doing a better job replenishing it."[47]

Apparel, it turns out, also helped the retailer get a foothold, so to speak, with running shoes. Running was one of the businesses Foot Locker wanted to get into in a bigger way. It found that if customers bought a pair of running shoes but the store didn't have running shorts, they would end up going to a competitor, where they would end up buying their next pair of shoes. So developing a good running-apparel assortment helped Foot Locker sell more shoes and keep more customers.

Foot Locker's top-selling footwear brands are Nike, Adidas, Reebok and Asics. While basketball was its dominant category, it was seriously underpenetrated in the technical running segment, a huge market opportunity. Now it has the Nike lightweight running collection, as well as Mizuno, Asics, Brooks, New Balance and other brands.

Hicks also saw early on that apparel was a great visual stimulant for the stores: "As you walk by the store, the thing that defines the banner that you can see easily is the apparel. I walk by a Foot Locker, I see more performance apparel. I walk by a Champs, I see the NBA stuff in the store. I walk by the Footaction store, I see Jordan or some Levi's jeans, I see something up there that changes more frequently than the shoes and is more visible than shoes. I can only put so many shoes into the store, and it would look kind of strange because with the shoes on the wall, I wouldn't have anything in the middle of the store, so it helps me utilize the real estate that I have. It allows me to accommodate the customers and give them service."[48]

Teamwork: Key to Success

Another key to the successful execution of the Foot Locker playbook is the way the company develops and uses its people. It works to enhance communication, knowledge and skills across the organization to help everyone sell more sneakers.

Hicks told the *Harvard Business Review* that being in the military helped prepare him for a career in retail: "When I took over my artillery battery at age 25, I could shoot a cannon better than any of my section chiefs. And I had six guns. The only problem is, I could only shoot one gun at a time. I realized that what I had to do was train my section chiefs to be better cannoneers than I was. Because shooting 18% of the battery isn't going to be effective. And my job really wasn't to shoot a cannon, it was to develop an entire artillery battery. So I learned that you're very dependent on your people to be their best. You train and develop and motivate them."[49]

Foot Locker's successful evolution has been partly due to the shifting the role of its sales associates, known as "stripers" because they wear black-and-white-striped shirts similar to those worn by basketball referees, from simply being stock pickers and cashiers to product experts with strong sales and customer-service skills and a true belief in what the company is trying to do.

Foot Locker was one of the few stores in the mall with a full sales staff. It had to take advantage of having people there to sell, to make it an interesting, exciting place to shop.

Foot Locker's sales associates, whose average age is twenty-three, must stand toe-to-toe with its powerful consumers if the retailer is to be successful, so the company works with vendors to develop training programs for its sales associates. It uses short videos primarily, activated by QR or bar codes on the shoe's tag that pulls up a video message that talks about the shoe. The company also has two informational websites. One is Sneakerpedia, a blogger site for sneaker enthusiasts, and the other is Striperpedia, an information site, that answers questions like "If I pronate, what would be a good shoe for me?" It also has ratings for shoes. Technology has been a major disruptor and has caused major changes in the business. The customer is more informed than ever and often enters a store knowing as much about product, if not more, than the sales associate.

To respond to the needs of the increasingly demanding customer, who wants more sizes, colors, styles and features, it's no longer okay to debut a hot new item in urban areas only. They want it everywhere, and they want it *now*. They want to see the latest, so they first come to the website to find out about a new design, then they visit the store.

Staying Ahead of Competition

How does Foot Locker stay competitive and move forward? According to Hicks, it's about being flexible, listening to customers and associates and shopping the competition. "Competition used to be just the other mall-based athletic footwear sellers," he said. "Now it's an infinite competitive environment. I'm in multiple stores every week. Because I do that, everyone in the organization does it. You need to monitor Twitter and Facebook to see how you're behaving, how your sales associates are behaving. I once worked with a retailer who said, 'Retail is war without blood.'"[50]

Strictly speaking, the last point is not exactly true anymore. Sneakers seem to have become such an emotionally charged and symbolic item that several new product introductions have resulted in brawls, fights and worse at Foot Locker stores. In December 2011, a young man was fatally stabbed outside one of the company's London stores in a sneaker-related disagreement. Foot Locker stores have also been targets during riot-related lootings in London, Paris and Dublin, as well as in Oakland and other US cities. In 2012, after a disturbance broke out in an Orlando, Florida, mall, Foot Locker canceled the release of a $220 Nike NBA All-Star sneaker in several US malls, citing safety concerns.[51]

The company is making substantial capital investments into new store formats, technology and people development. It hopes to increase sales and earnings by 35 percent in the next few years, to $7.5 billion and $525 million, respectively.

According to Hicks, Foot Locker management is also prepared to fail in order to be more competitive: "We're willing to try anything. We'll test things as a prototype and see if it works and if it's financially viable. To move forward, you can't refuse to change, but you can't change everything, either. You have to find that middle ground.

"But I'll buckle my chinstrap and go up against anybody and compete, and compete well. Like the old joke about the two guys in the woods, and they see the bear, and the one guy starts tying his shoelaces. We'll outrun the other guy."[52]

Apple

We could not end this chapter without tipping our hat to the true master: Apple.

With so much having been already said about this company, there is no need to repeat its history or the story of its growth. Apple may be the world's most valuable technology company, but one pillar of its amazing success is decidedly low-tech: its brick-and-mortar retail stores.

Apple's decision to open stores was a brilliant strategy, in which it's providing an unequalled neurological experience and gaining preemptive distribution. (And, of course, it totally controls its value chain.) Microsoft, Samsung and others are now only playing catchup. The question is whether they can execute to the Apple standard.

Apple realized that it could control, shape and determine the emotional connection that customers have with its brand by opening stores. In doing so, every channel of distribution—online sales, sales through third-party retailers like Best Buy, etc.—would be enhanced, and the connection with the consumer intensified. Whereas other tech leaders might say, "Let's sit down with the engineers and figure out what awesome technology we have and then figure out how to market it," Jobs would ask instead: "What incredible benefits can we give the customer?" He would say that the answer isn't in having more engineers. All of them come up with brilliant ideas in their specialized areas all the time. It's figuring out which ones, and how they will benefit and excite the consumer. In other words, they can come up with more gizmos and gadgets than one might be able to count, but they are useless if they do not enhance the consumer experience. This provides a very clear picture of Jobs as a bridge, interpreter and visionary in converging the art and science of retailing, in holistically connecting with consumers.[53]

As we mentioned earlier, we believe that Amazon, eBay and other pure e-commerce sites will open stores, and that retailers will one day create branded mini-malls within their four walls. And every successful retailer or consumer-facing company will accelerate its investments in creating a great in-store experience.

Starting with their customers' anticipation of a fun shopping experience, when they get to the Apple store, their first step is into the "box," branded with the iconic Apple logo. It is the beginning of what founder Steve Jobs called the "Apple user experience." Apple Stores have a distinctive futuristic interior and interactive, pristine display tables. All stores share glass and anodized aluminum paneling.

Once inside, customers are met by friendly, enthusiastic and technologically sophisticated sales reps who engage and put them at ease while they introduce them to products and explain any of the attributes the consumer needs help with. The white interior with splashes of the color wheel evokes the user-friendly, yet vibrant, experience of owning a Mac product. The experience is never dull.

Even though all the stores are relatively new, they are constantly being improved. The Genius Bar supports the advertised user-friendly factor. Serving as Apple's tech support and repairs team within every store, it is so popular that customers must make an appointment or wait at least an hour, sometimes two. The so-called Geniuses are exclusively trained to troubleshoot products and help people with their technological questions.

Like the retail stores, the simplicity and style in product offerings and physicality are competitive advantages of Apple's brand. We don't want to downplay the genius of the product development at the heart of the company. That feature is obvious. When the iPod/iTunes launched, it was a game-changer in the consumer-electronics and digital-music industry. The push forward into physical stores, however, was not obvious even with that product's success. Only if you believe that you need to control the consumer experience to achieve extraordinary success would you have made this move. We believe that the data are proving this to be true in every consumer business.

Apple Stores aren't designed merely to sell products, but to give a halo effect to its brand. Each one sells an average of $50 million per quarter.[54]

And of course, control of the value chain has also been crucial to Apple's success. For example, Apple's five-year exclusive partnership with AT&T gave Apple unprecedented control over the development and branding of the iPhone. Value-chain control extends to maintaining tight licensing structures around all Apple's products.

Apple has changed people's expectations of what retail should be. After they've experienced an Apple store, they'll never look at a supermarket, drugstore or the jeans section of a department store the same way again.

Apple has just launched a new location-based technology called iBeacon that will do things like help customers find products, learn about products they walk past in the store, pick up information if they're coming to the store to get a device they ordered online, provide indoor mapping services or find out if they qualify for an upgrade.

The company estimates that 84 million people now visit its 400 retail stores in a single quarter—more than the 60 million who visited Disney's four biggest theme parks last year. Sales per square foot have soared to more than $4,400, the most of any retailer. Add in online sales, which include iTunes, and the total soars to $5,900.

At the time the first Apple Store was built, electronics stores resembled warehouses, with sky-high shelving stuffed with accessories, pamphlets and cords. Apple, by contrast, chose an open plan with a clutter-free look, using natural materials like wood, glass, stone and stainless steel.[55]

Apple's control of the customer experience extends down to the smallest detail. Sales associates are trained on what to say to customers who are upset or emotional. They are told to listen and limit responses to simple reassurance—to say "Uh-huh," "I understand," etc.[56]

In a highly symbolic, if not poetic, move, Apple recently hired Angela Ahrendts, who transformed Burberry from a faded British iconic brand to the epitome of global luxury, to retool Apple's physical and digital retail efforts so that they are both equally admired.

Although the company has added many upgrades to its physical stores over the years, the e-commerce site has, ironically enough, not changed much. It hopes to make this Apple shopping experience the same wherever a customer is shopping. It is also rumored that Apple wants to evolve from a technology innovator to a luxury lifestyle company.

On all three principles, neurological connectivity, preemptive distribution and value chain control, we see Apple as the true master.

CHAPTER 12

LESSONS FROM SEARS

FROM SUCCESS TO STRUGGLE

Two of the most frequently asked questions from retail executives, employees and investors during our research were:

1. Are there examples of major retailers that responded to the vast consumer and market shifts from Wave I, II and III and that successfully transformed their business strategies and models accordingly?
2. If a retailer fails to successfully transform its business in Wave IV, according to your thesis, how difficult is it to turn the business around?

These questions are not academic. While we have provided many examples throughout the book of retailers and wholesalers that are transforming themselves in Wave IV, with varying degrees of success, you always need a benchmark to measure yourself against.

Our research led us to an obvious choice for closer analysis.

Sears, Roebuck and Co., founded in 1886, embodies the successful shift from Wave I to II, making its struggle to navigate Wave III and its worsening condition in Wave IV even more instructive. Some experts believe its current management, as of this writing, has determined that the Sears and Kmart businesses are not salvageable, and is therefore "managing" them into liquidation. However, its meandering search for a relevant value proposition through Waves II and III is a lesson to every company wondering whether it can turn itself around.

We also chose Sears to explore these questions because, although like every company it has its own quirks, the Sears story also has many universal components.

As we discussed in Chapters 1 and 2, Sears was arguably the most successful retailer during both Waves I and II, responding to the marketplace characteristics that drove success in both waves. Among the most notable shifts were two in particular.

From Catalogs to Stores to the
Mass Markets of Wave II

In the late 1800s, before the Internet was even imagined, the famous Sears catalog gave it the same advantage that innovative e-commerce sites have over brick-and-mortar retailers today. Essentially, Sears was distributing its entire store into the living rooms of America's middle class, whose shopping options were slim, and in many cases too impractical. As we pointed out in earlier chapters, the catalog contained everything those families would ever need, from cradle to grave, at affordable prices. And if they couldn't pay it all at once, Sears would help them out with payment terms.

Those families also could not wait to see the new catalog every season in anticipation of exciting new products. More and more of those products were exclusive to, and some even produced by, Sears. In this, Sears was truly on the leading edge of vertical integration and value-chain control.

Because its different aspects were so closely intertwined, Sears grew just as rapidly as America's middle class. Then, as the population began migrating from rural areas to the newly forming towns, cities and then suburbs, and particularly after the construction of the interstate highway system, Sears adjusted its preemptive strategy to ensure that its stores were the first ones to reach consumers in their new neighborhoods. In fact, Sears was the developer and ultimate anchor for the very first shopping centers in the country, and it expanded along with the mall movement across the United States.

Sears thus expanded its strategy through multidistribution platforms and physically demonstrated the extent of its investment in the consumer. Sears was beginning to become untouchable.

From Retail Marketer to Branded Mass Marketer of Lifestyle Brands

In the early 1960s, Sears' merchandising supervisor was James Button. Schooled in research psychology at the University of Chicago, he brought the concept of marketing to Sears. Known as a bit of an enigma, Button had a view of marketing that embodied all the activities of value creation, including research and development, branding/imaging, communications/advertising, publicity and distribution. These functions were arguably nonexistent in most retail businesses at the time.

Button increased the size of Sears' R&D lab, introduced a market-research department and process and advanced the company's understanding of advertising. He firmly believed that relentless consumer research and product development and testing (as opposed to gut instinct) were the only sure paths to successful innovation.

And successful they were. A constant stream of brands and products was rolled out through the largest distribution machine in the world. The number of "firsts" and private and exclusive Sears brands were mind-boggling: the first steel-belted radial tire; Craftsman tools; DieHard batteries; Kenmore appliances; Toughskins jeans; Cling-alon hosiery; the Comfort Shirt; the NFL and Winnie-the-Pooh exclusive licenses; and many others. These exclusive brands were made possible by Sears' unique merchandising structure and process. As the owner of many of its suppliers, and as the primary buyer from others, Sears possessed a vertical integration that facilitated a continuous process of joint research, innovation, testing and therefore a continuous stream of new and exclusive products and brands. It provided the foundation of Sears' value proposition and gave it an enormous advantage over competitors.

A vital characteristic of these relationships was the mutual reverence, loyalty and trust that bound Sears' merchandisers and suppliers. In fact, Sears would often fund suppliers' production or buy ingredient products in volume for several suppliers, reducing costs for the benefit of both. Sears also used its knowledge of suppliers' costs, along with a promise of huge-volume orders, to negotiate the lowest-possible price for the goods.

Button's genius gave consumers some of the greatest products and brands the world has ever known, all exclusive to Sears. And his underlying strategy—which went largely unnoticed, even by Sears management and consultants at the time—was to pursue product innovations for *all* consumers. His open acknowledgment of their desires for better quality and better performance, and for honest, low prices, made Sears a "democratic" retailer. It was a resource for all Americans, not just the middle class. High- and low-income consumers of all ages and genders shopped at Sears. Thus, it had a unique niche—in the sense that it wasn't niche at all. Button's approach reflected the outlook of then-CEO Robert Wood, who said, "The customer is your employer, and the moment we lose their confidence is the beginning of the disintegration of the company."[1]

Sears did not have to compete head-on with the department stores (because it had its own exclusive brands) or with the discounters (they couldn't operate on the higher cost structure necessary to match Sears' offerings). Most important, Sears' sales associates were the early equivalent of Best Buy's blue-shirted Geek Squad or Apple's Geniuses. They were thoroughly trained and proficient in the Sears rule book; they could instruct customers how to use every brand and product in their area.

Furthermore, all Sears stores were decentralized when it came to merchandise decisions. Therefore, store managers ordered and bought the products and quantities according to their local consumers' preferences. Through this localization, there was a clear competitive advantage.

In Wave II, Sears was the equivalent of Walmart today. And it powered into the 1970s as an unparalleled master of retailing, bigger than the next five-largest retailers combined, with nine hundred large stores and more than 2,600 smaller retail and catalog outlets, accounting for 1 percent of US gross national product.[2] More than half the households in the country had a Sears credit card, and a survey at the time confirmed that it was the most trusted economic institution in the country.[3]

Then, in the mid- to late 1970s, the unraveling began. Tragically, after eighty-four years of building one of the greatest brands the world had ever seen, it would take Sears just a few years to lose its unique competitive position and veer into a quarter century of decline that continues to this day. What happened?

Misreading the Tea Leaves

Sears conducted a major study in the early 1970s that alerted it to the following major shifts, which were exacerbated by growing market saturation and the slowing economy:

- Sears' customer base was getting older and turning into two-income families, and women were becoming the most important shoppers.
- The youth of America were not getting married as early as their parents had, and they were seeking their own shopping sources, such as the rapidly growing specialty chains.
- Sears' profitability was shifting from merchandise, which had been contributing 80 to 90 percent of profits, to services, which were contributing 75 percent by the end of the 1970s (including installation, credit extension and its Allstate insurance business).
- Competitors were closing the gap—JCPenney in the malls and Kmarts on every corner. The specialty-store upstarts were also staking a claim in the malls, and Walmart was a preview of coming attractions.[4]

The result of this study, along with many other internal issues that were coming to a head, included political infighting between stores and merchandising management; mounting costs; and a calcifying culture, ultimately forcing Sears management to seek a new direction. It began to believe that the key to growth was not to be found in the core competencies that had driven the success of the company. It started to look into new businesses that would be complementary and synergistic. (Not coincidentally, this was also the period in Wave II when the trends and drivers that would fuel the growth of the successful retail models in Wave III began to emerge.) Sears moved in a completely different direction.

This was the critical juncture in Sears' history. Had the visionary leadership of CEO Arthur Wood and the brilliant James Button remained in place, Sears might have successfully executed the necessary strategic changes to meet the challenges and maintain its unique competitive position. This did not happen.

Wood's successor, Edward Telling, was plucked from store management (or "the field," as they called it, as opposed to the "parent," where the merchandising and marketing departments resided). The field had grown to five powerful regional organizations that operated like fiefdoms, and their infighting with merchandising and marketing grew proportionately. Telling, the most powerful of the five heads, in charge of the Northeast region, was the first CEO to be selected from the field.

With Telling in charge, it did not take long for the field heads to begin gaining in the turf wars and for the influence of James Button to be diminished. Then Button became ill and resigned toward the end of the 1970s.

Even as the Sears Tower was going up as the company's new Chicago headquarters, the tallest building in the country, much of its world, inside and outside, was starting to crack. And to make matters worse, the larger economy was tanking.

While Sears' profits were plummeting in 1979 and 1980 because of the combination of inflation-raging interest rates, rising operating costs, loss of direction, mounting competition and organizational disarray, Telling determined that the retail business had matured, and retreated to the Tower with his new team to work on building what he called the "Great American Company": Sears as a diversified conglomerate of financial, real estate and insurance services. At the same time, he elevated Edward A. Brennan, another field man, to head up the retail business. Ironically, Brennan was charged with saving what truly *was* the Great American Company—the Sears retail business. At this crucial crossroads in Sears' history, the chief executive was leaving the scene of the disaster to chase his dreams.

That dream was of a great synergy between financial services and the core retail business. Sears already owned Allstate Insurance, and it went on to acquire Dean Witter Reynolds financial services, Coldwell Banker real estate and, later, Discover Card. It also created the Sears US Government Money Market Trust Fund and formed the Sears World Trade Company. The synergy was to come from Sears using its stores, catalogs and Allstate Insurance offices as additional locations where they could insert the financial services businesses. It expected to lure the millions of Sears customers across the aisle to purchase financial services, and vice versa. Telling boasted to the press about its "socks and stocks" strategy.

Chief among the several factors necessary for this grand strategy to work, however, was a successful and growing core retail business to generate the crossover and new traffic expected. But this was not the case. Not only was the core business beginning to decline during this period, but the customers also questioned Sears' authority on financial skills and management, citing confusion about where in their lives Sears now belonged. What was it—retailer, banker, financier, real estate mogul or the "money store"? What did it stand for?

In the end, rather than an inspired synergy, Telling's so-called Great American Company was one of the first major strategy missteps that sent Sears into its long decline. In fact, the strategy likely caused a reverse downward synergy. Along with the already daunting task of turning the retail business around, Telling's idea to tack on a completely different business just compounded the complexity and confusion of accomplishing either.

Carol Farmer, a retail consultant at the time, declared: "If Sears executives can't run the business they know—retailing—why should we think they'll be able to do any better running a business they don't know?"[5]

So Telling's dream did not come true. In fact, the financial services businesses might as well have been independent entities of a holding company. They ended up contributing only incrementally (with the exception of Allstate, which Sears held even before Telling, and eventually the Discover Card). By the early 1990s all the financial services, real estate and insurance businesses were sold off as Sears entered another decade-long search for direction.

The 1980s: Up Again, Down Again, Part I

The new head of retail, Edward Brennan, did make some bold moves in the early 1980s, enough to achieve a short-lived spike in business and confirm his promotion to CEO in 1984 upon Telling's retirement. Some of his initiatives for a "new Sears" included improving stores and merchandise presentations; adding national brands; trying to strengthen apparel lines; launching a "Store of the Future" concept as a template for refurbishing stores over a five-year period; rolling out Business System Centers and paint and hardware specialty stores (a beginning probe for competing in the specialty tier); and the launch of a national ad campaign.

However, all these initiatives turned out to be merely opportunistic tactics. The ad campaign's underlying message said it all: *Sears has everything.* So while Sears gained a momentary boost through Brennan's initiatives, it had definitely lost its once-supreme position and still lacked a clear strategic direction.

The once-proud culture turned arrogant, then bureaucratic. The constructive balance between stores, merchandising and marketing deteriorated into constant infighting. This conflict, along with the loss of Button's private and exclusive branding strategy (giving way to national brands) and cost-cutting, led to the unraveling of Sears' fully integrated (and/or exclusively controlled) product development and production sourcing. This was further exacerbated when it shuttered its R&D and consumer-research departments.

Sears' small-store strategy, also initiated under Brennan, would prove to be too little too late, as well as underfunded, since more capital was being infused into the financial services business. Finally, it was confronting the arrival of Walmart as the new, hot discounter in small towns. Cutbacks in store expansion also left many of its original stores anchored in declining locations.

For ten years, Sears focused on the so-called synergy for growing financial services while ignoring the store. The Store of the Future was a flop. An everyday-low-price branding strategy failed. During the 1970s and '80s total retail space doubled in the United States, while Sears concentrated on closing and remodeling. It halfheartedly dabbled in specialty-store concepts that turned out to be too late and insufficiently funded.

Sears' return on equity (ROE) in 1984 was at 14 percent. In 1992, it stood at 9.6 percent. Virtually all Sears' earnings between 1985 and 1992 came from the financial services businesses. And, despite its cost-reduction efforts in the 1980s, Sears' cost-to-sales ratio continued to be almost double that of Walmart, and well above the rest of its competitors.

Finally, with the $3 billion sale of the financial services business, which at the time was claimed to have reduced debt, many pundits said there would not be enough left for capital spending on the stores.

Sears was not only on a severely declining revenue and income trajectory, it was also waffling on a strategic positioning in the no-man's-land of "everything to everybody." Therefore, it was competing against the discounters from below, the department stores from above, the specialty stores in front and the newly emerging big-box specialists. In the process, Sears had become a traditional retailer instead of the greatest brand and marketer with the strongest consumer connection the country had ever known.

It was time for a new leader.

The 1990s: Up Again, Down Again, Part II

In 1992, Arthur Martinez became only the second leader from outside Sears in its history (after Robert Wood). By then, Sears had shed all its financial services businesses.

Martinez came in with a strategic vision for Sears and developed a plan for fundamental transformation, primarily focusing on women's apparel, with an advertising slogan emphasizing "The Softer Side of Sears." Having come from the Saks department stores, he would also move Sears into more of a department-store positioning. This and other strategic initiatives showed initial success. By 1997–1998, revenues had increased about 30 percent to roughly $36 billion, and profits rose from losses of close to $3 billion to a profit of more than $1 billion.

However, when sales and income started to drop in 1998, there was speculation that the seemingly spectacular turnaround may in fact have been due to Sears' aggressive focus on growing its credit-card business, beginning in 1993. By 1997, 60 percent of all sales transactions were done with credit cards, and experts suggested that more than 60 percent of Sears' bottom line was coming from the credit business.[6]

Despite the potential of the credit business as the growth engine for the retail business, though, Martinez simply could not change the culture of Sears. In fact, in the book he would eventually write, *The Hard Road to the Softer Side: Lessons from the Transformation of Sears,* Martinez stated that toward the end of his tenure, he felt Sears was falling back into the same trap he inherited when he took over in 1992: "Just do more of the same, only work harder." He was also asking himself the same question as when he arrived: "What is this company going to be? What does it stand for?"[7]

At the end of the 1990s, then, Sears had no more of a strategic compass than it had ten years before. It was time for yet another leader.

The 2000s: Slowly Sinking during Wave III

When Alan Lacy was made CEO in 2001, he immediately moved to grab the low-hanging fruit by doing what he had done best as CFO under Martinez. He slashed costs and further pumped up the credit business. Lacy would be the fourth non-merchant in a row to run the company, and the second, after Martinez, with a primarily financial background.

In less than a year, the *Wall Street Journal* reported that Lacy was considering abandoning the apparel business altogether, after a 25 percent drop in net income in the first quarter of 2001. He himself admitted at an analyst meeting that Sears could not find its place in fashion, stating, "We almost don't have any personality."[8] As apparel growth slipped, critics increasingly took shots at Martinez' efforts, which now appeared short-lived. However, Lacy realized that the cost of radically changing stores and replacing lost clothing sales (stagnant, at about $8 billion) would be too steep.

By 2003, Sears had experienced eighteen consecutive months of sales declines, and the credit business was responsible for more than two-thirds of total net income. In reaction, Sears bought Lands' End, thereby going deeper into the apparel category, where it had had no success since the late 1970s.

If Martinez lost his control of the culture, Lacy was losing it on all fronts. Sears still didn't know what it stood for. Indeed, Sears seemed to be poised for its final descent. Adjusted for inflation, Sears' volume declined about 20 percent from its pinnacle in the late 1970s, and it continues to drop today.

The Lessons Learned So Far

We believe Sears' successful migration from Wave I into Wave II occurred because it evolved across three key business dimensions:

1. The shift from a production-driven model to one of marketing and demand creation (with a flow of new and exclusive products and brands, and developing sophisticated marketing and advertising strategies)
2. Expanding its distribution platforms (catalogs, stores), initiating and anchoring shopping centers and malls; all following the population migration from rural areas to towns, cities and then suburbs

3. Building the infrastructure and supplier relations necessary to support this model

Interestingly, these principles are in many ways early versions of the principles we believe drive success today. And Sears' original model implemented these strategies far more effectively than its competitors did, much like Walmart does today.

However, as the major Wave III consumer, competitive and marketplace shifts began to occur, enabled by technology and globalization, Sears made three fundamental errors:

1. It concluded that market saturation meant growth had to come from businesses outside its "core." This did not have to be fatal; however, it starved the resources (capital and management) from the retail business, leaving it unable to respond and adapt to the evolving needs of the Wave III consumer and marketplace.
2. It allowed the emergence of a bureaucratic culture, which slowed decision-making. When the unraveling began in the late 1970s, Sears' culture became characterized by infighting and significant strategic redirects. This cultural sclerosis is a disease that cripples many large, older companies in need of change for survival.
3. It stopped investing in new distribution formats.

We believe these are key lessons for all retailers attempting to make a successful shift into Wave IV.

Sears as It Struggles into Wave IV

In 2004, a strategic financial visionary named Edward "Eddie" Lampert came to the rescue. Head of his own hedge fund, ESL Investments, and a former Goldman Sachs risk arbitrageur, Lampert has a genius for spotting great deals among distressed companies that he considers to be undervalued. He then buys a major stake at a bargain price.

Having made such a deal for the equally distressed Kmart a couple of years before his move on Sears, he combined the two companies under the name Sears Holdings (to be owned by ESL Investments, with Lampert owning 41 percent of the stock). He and his newly appointed team declared to Wall Street and the world that they were going to return Kmart and Sears to their rightful positions as successful, iconic retail brands.

In keeping with his track record, Lampert and his team slashed costs across the board to boost per-share earnings and improve returns on capital, even though both retailers were hemorrhaging before he bought them. Comparative store sales were, and still are, declining month-over-month. However, by cutting people, advertising and research costs and slashing store maintenance and capital improvements, he improved profitability and share prices. Lampert could then leverage the earnings and cash to invest in more promising growth opportunities with higher returns—not necessarily back into the dying businesses.

After several years of cost-cutting, even amid a flurry of tactical initiatives, in our view Sears Holdings still does not clearly stand for anything so compelling that consumers make Sears (or Kmart) their destination of choice. And perhaps that was never Lampert's true intention; the press and some industry pundits conjectured that Lampert's financial expertise was being used to create larger profits as opposed to creating real retail value.

Is There a Sears in Our Future?

Today there are many focused "masters" competing in each of Sears' many businesses. Indeed, Sears' thirty-year quest to regain its former glory has certainly eroded its relevance to consumers, or at least severely tested their patience.

Simply put, Sears is still in the middle of a perfect storm. The seminal question is whether the following three storm fronts will allow Sears the time to find its position:

1. Consumers: Today they have unlimited equal or better shopping choices, and their attitudes, behavior and demographics have changed in favor of Sears' competitors, many of whom are located closer to where the consumers live. This raises the attendant issue of Sears' captivity in malls and how it will deal with this issue. The challenge

for Sears is to create experiences for the consumer and build a strong emotional connection that propels them into the stores—even if that's a little farther than the consumer would normally go. And, as of this writing, because of CEO Lampert's early decision to cut store-maintenance costs, eschewing any investment in creating a compelling shopping experience, the stores are in miserable shape.

2. Competitors: Sears must focus on competitors that have more efficient and effective business models, positioned with dominant value promises and elevated shopping experiences, attacking each or several of the conglomeration of Sears' arguably waning businesses (appliances and tools included). This includes competitors such as Walmart, Kohl's, Target, Home Depot, Lowe's and the multiplicity of specialty chains, all of which have a major advantage because of their lower operating costs and real estate flexibility. Thus they gain more pricing leverage and greater profitability, as well as better proximity to the consumer. Between 1998 and 2010, the number of competitors within a fifteen-minute drive from Sears grew from 1,400 to 4,300 stores. Furthermore, during this period, Sears has barely developed an e-commerce strategy, much less a preemptive one, and it lags behind in the application of other leading-edge distribution platforms (e.g., mobile technology).

3. Economy and Industry Dynamics: A slowly recovering, postrecession economy, an oversaturated retail industry and the overall downtrending of the channel that Sears competes in all provide very little wiggle room and no more time for drifting.

We believe that for Sears to survive, it will have to revisit its roots and the strategic drivers that made it the paragon of retailing throughout the world. It must reposition its model, based on our three New Rules: a neurologically compelling shopping experience; preemptive, precise and perpetual distribution; and optimum control of the value chain, without which the first two are impossible. The question is, does Sears have enough time and capital to execute this change? Or will the clock run out first?

CONCLUSION

MODELS FOR THE FUTURE

The marketplace has arrived at Wave IV after a century-long roller-coaster ride of strategic and structural shifts. The unparalleled growth of the US economy over the last hundred years has resulted in market saturation, despite exponential consumption growth due to the widespread availability of an unprecedented selection of goods and services. In essence, consumers today have thousands of equally compelling stores, websites, products, brands and services—right at their fingertips. They have the power of total access.

Due to globalization, technology and increased productivity, consumers have faster and cheaper access to more products. They utilize a multitude of rapid, responsive new distribution platforms (e-commerce, kiosks, in-flight shopping, in-home events, etc.), and they communicate information freely and easily on the Internet and mobile electronic devices.

Mobile access in particular is a twenty-first-century game-changer, making that old retail real estate adage for success—"location, location, location"—a nonstarter. Simply identifying the center of town or a space in the mall as a high-traffic area doesn't cut it today. The location must now be mobile, both physically and electronically, even to have a chance. And, in the greatest challenge of all, retailers, brands, products or services can no longer just approach their customers. Today companies must be invited or otherwise permitted into their customers' lives.

And if a retailer or brand is permitted into the consumer's space, or if the consumer chooses to go to a particular store, website, or TV channel, the experience must be overwhelmingly compelling, or the company risks never getting the consumer back. In fact, we posit that the experience must be neurologically addictive, causing a release of dopamine in the consumer's brain at the very thought of the brand for a business, as Apple, Starbucks, Trader Joe's and J. Crew have done, so consumers will rush back to those brands without even considering competitive options.

Overabundance of choice enables consumers to demand more, which in turn drives competitors to perpetually innovate with new products, services and features around the shopping experience. So even having compelling "stuff," however new, is also a nonstarter on its own. Retailing *must* also be a neurologically stimulating experience, both in the store and online.

All this is meant to underscore that, in the current environment, which we have defined as retailing's Wave IV, retailers, wholesalers, brands and services must completely transform their business strategies and models to survive.

A good framework for this transformation would be the six major shifts in consumer desires that have occurred in recent years. These are the dynamics that retailers and all consumer-facing industries must understand, respond to and deliver on. These shifts are:

1. **From Needing Stuff to Demanding Experiences**—the "thrill of the hunt" offered to brand-savvy bargain hunters at T.J.Maxx and Marshalls, and the Apple Store turning electronics shopping on its head.

2. **From Conformity to Customization**—specialized, personalized and localized niche brands, like Nike ID and Keurig single-serve coffee machines that are rapidly gaining share from large megabrands, the continued growth of special sizes in apparel and footwear and the rapid growth of 3-D printing.

3. **From Plutocracy to Democracy**—accessible luxury for all: Missoni at Target, Vera Wang and Rock & Republic at Kohl's, Karl Lagerfeld at Macy's, Isabel and Ruben Toledo at Lane Bryant and the explosive growth of Michael Kors' "affordable luxury."

4. **From Wanting New to Demanding New *and* Now**—what's new today is cloned tomorrow, favoring "fast fashion" brands like Zara and Forever 21 that create two new lines every week, the convenience of e-commerce, free delivery and neighborhood stores.

5. **From Self to Community**—proliferation of social media, social shopping, community interests such as sustainability, global initiatives like human rights and safety; all are trends, no longer simply commercial promotional gimmicks.

6. **From Technology for Work to Technology for Life**—technology enabling the blurring of lines between "life" and "work," people are working during their "off" hours and playing during their "work" hours, getting what they need to get done whenever and however they can, using technology to save time and money and to enhance entertainment.

The Three Imperative Strategic
Operating Principles for Success

To respond to and satisfy these consumer demands—and thus survive and grow—businesses must excel in all value-chain functions, including marketing and innovation, just to achieve competitive parity. However, they must achieve *superiority* in the following strategic operating principles:

Neurological Connectivity

Today, as consumers expect the moon and stars—because they can—the retailer or brand must far exceed their expectations. They must co-create, with the customer, an experience that indelibly connects with their mind. It must be a holistic experience, consisting of pre-shopping anticipation, shopping ecstasy and consumption satisfaction, and it must be so emotionally compelling that the customer wants to repeat it upon the mere mention of the brand or retailer's name. Even when established, however, it is not static, and it requires constant reinforcing, often with subtle changes. But executed correctly, the brand–consumer connection preempts competition.

Preemptive Distribution

This is the necessity of gaining access to consumers in front of the multiplicity of equally compelling products or services—by existing precisely where, when and how the consumer wants you. Preemptive distribution relies on speed, agility and the ability to reinforce the neurological connection, or brand promise. By definition, this requires an integrated matrix of all possible distribution mediums, the most important ones being those driven by the new, rapidly evolving technologies as well as distribution into faster-growing international markets.

Value-Chain Control

No consumer-facing business can achieve the highest levels of a neurological connection and preemptive distribution without complete control of its value chain, from creation all the way to consumption. This control is especially important in those parts of the chain that touch and connect with the consumer: namely, market research, where knowledge about the consumer and his or her dreams is determined; production and marketing, where the dream experience is created; and finally, the point of sale, where the experience must be competently delivered. Furthermore, in Wave IV, it is imperative that retailers incorporate technology into every aspect of their process in order to remain competitive. This defines a vertically integrated and controlled, though not necessarily owned, business model.

The retailers and wholesalers that understand how these strategies ultimately satisfy and win consumers are transforming their business models right now. Some of the steps they are taking include:

Value-Chain Integration

- Retailers integrating backward (accelerated pursuit of private and/or exclusive brands)
- Wholesalers integrating forward (opening their own branded retail chains)

Structural Realignment

- Segmentation (to compete in an infinite number of finite market niches)
- Consolidation (to leverage back-end supply chain for scale and productivity synergies)

Multidistribution Formats

- Smaller stores as neighborhood extensions
- E-commerce sites
- Social networks (including transactional platforms)
- Mobile devices (smartphones, for example)
- In-flight shopping services
- TV
- Pop-up stores
- Catalogs, kiosks, in-home, door-to-door and others
- Nontraditional platforms of opportunity (ballparks, museums, etc.)

Market Expansion

- Niche branding by specialty chain brands
- Brand proliferation—accelerated line/style cycles
- Growing globally

New Names for New Models

Our thesis predicts that the traditional definitions of "retail" and "wholesale" will be irrelevant in the future because only those that transform their business models based on our three strategic operating principles will survive in the future. Therefore, those that do will simply be perceived by consumers as brands. The retail or wholesale distinction will no longer be meaningful to consumers. Distinct brand names will provide the only worthwhile definition of value, whether it's the nameplates of stores or the labels on the products in the store. The new business models for retailers and wholesalers alike will be those that can best implement the three imperative strategic operating principles defined earlier.

Essentially, transformed retailers and wholesalers, now defined as brands, will render value chains seamless, with value controlled, managed and distributed by its creator all the way from creation to consumption.

In cases where it is absolutely necessary to collaborate with a second party at some point in the value chain, we predict that the creator will still manage and control its value within the second party's sphere. Bloomingdale's, for example, in the midst of transforming its business model, would grow its own private brands as well as demanding brand exclusivity from outside branded vendors—the combination of these two facets eventually making up 80 to 90 percent of the merchandise it sells. We believe it will also lease the remaining space to (or make some other financially collaborative arrangement with) designers such as Ralph Lauren or globally powerful brands such as The North Face, which will manage and control their brands in the hosted Bloomingdale's space.

Likewise, we predict that 80 to 90 percent of strong brands' revenues will come from their own retail outlets. Finally, retailers such as Macy's and others will have some form of leasing space to other strong retail brands, as many European and Asian retailers currently do. Perhaps department stores will invite powerful traffic-creating brands to operate "shops" in those categories in which they have been underperforming. For example, Victoria's Secret, Soma and other brands might be more compelling in Macy's historically share-losing intimates space. Not only would the department store gain the synergy of two go-to brands, they would also increase space productivity. And of course, the branded retail "renters" would get immediate preemptive distribution (department-store locations everywhere) for a relatively low capital investment. As we noted earlier, this synergistic strategy is already being employed by Nordstrom with Topshop, Brooks Brothers and Bonobos shop-in-shops.

All new business entities will be strategically conceived to provide maximum access to consumers and positioned to gain maximum access for the business. Therefore, they will operate in a multitude of distribution channels (mobile, clicks, bricks and catalogs), with a multitude of different formats (from small, convenient and flexible to larger, all-inclusive destinations), and all will compete in as many consumer, product and retail sectors as the brand or service entity can credibly pursue. However, all retailers will fit into one of our three newly defined Wave IV sectors: the Commoditization sector; the Omni-Brand to Consumer sector; or the Liquidation sector. Also, the back-end functions—operations, production, logistics and distribution—will be tightly centralized for maximum-scale leverage and productivity synergies, as well as to support the enormously complex and segmented front ends of their businesses.

Incidentally, this redefinition of retail favors what we defined as the Omni-Brand to Consumer model. Because of its optimum alignment with the New Rules, this model is best positioned among all sectors for preemptive distribution and the delivery of a neurologically connecting experience.

Finally, we predict that e-retailing in all facets, including mobile commerce and the linkage to stores through omni-channel initiatives, will continue to grow. Every large chain will begin to see its stores as either a distribution center or an experiential palace. There will be no neutral ground. However, we also believe that players that currently operate exclusively in this space, such as Amazon and eBay, will eventually open brick-and-mortar stores for the purposes of preemptive distribution and enhanced delivery of the neurological experience. These competitors will also continue to redefine the value chain with a set of capabilities and relationships that will make the realization of same-day delivery a feature in every major metropolitan market and will therefore further challenge those stores without any clear point of differentiation.

If there is one thing that we must reemphasize from all our work, it is that Wave IV requires massive differentiation for a retailer or brand to survive. This differentiation has to exist throughout the entire business model, from sourcing to delivery, and most importantly in the eyes of the consumer. If you are not clearly differentiated, even unique, then you are vulnerable to extinction in Wave IV. The highlights below of the transformed traditional models encapsulate all the foregoing, and essentially represent the New Rules for successful change and the effective implementation of our three strategic operating principles.

Rules for Transforming Traditional Retailers

Change the Retail Value Proposition
Become a branded neurological experience, not a store.

Adopt a New Structure
Reorganize around lifestyles.

Accelerate Private/Exclusive Branding or
Lease Space to Compatible Brands
Cede control to other powerful brands, but exercise total control over your
own.

Results
Synergy-creating organic growth.

Preemptively Access Consumers with:
- Larger urban "lifestyle experiential emporiums"
- Smaller freestanding neighborhood stores
- Private branded specialty chains (e.g., INC and Arizona Stores)
- New channels of opportunity (pop-ups, in-home, etc.)
- Integration of all distribution platforms (clicks/bricks/catalogs)
- Investment in new technological channels of distribution.

Rules for Transforming Traditional Wholesalers

Change the Wholesale Value Proposition
Become a portfolio of lifestyle-branded retail specialty chains providing neurologically connecting experiences.

Adopt a New Structure
- Reorganize around preemptive distribution strategies through all possible platforms and mediums (clicks, bricks, catalogs and more), including providing exclusive brands to transformed retailers and selecting
  compatible transformed retailers to lease space for total management
  and control of individual brands.
- Pursue cobranding joint ventures with compatible retail specialty chain
  brands.
- Create a clear distribution strategy that has exclusive, segmented product by retail partner and price point.

Results
Synergy creating fundamental new growth.

New Rule for E-Commerce and Mobile Pure-Play Brands

This newest and fastest-growing retail sector, which includes Amazon, Zappos, eBay, flash sites, social networks and the older QVC and HSN, must also transform its models to embody our three operating principles. As suggested throughout the book, the most successful brands, such as those just mentioned, are all striving to create great experiences as opposed to simply providing convenience. The newest rule for this sector will be driven by its need for greater preemptive distribution. This will mean faster and faster access through mobile purchasing and rapid delivery. We believe this will ultimately lead to e-commerce expanding its distribution to include brick-and-mortar stores, within which they can better provide the neurological experience, particularly for those products requiring a more high-touch experience such as apparel.

Regardless of operating on all distribution platforms, all will attempt to control, if not own, as much of the value chain as possible, from Amazon's cloud to eBay's PayPal payment system. All of this will be further intensified as Google, Facebook and others begin to enter the retail world at scale with even more diverse business models.

Others that will excel in Wave IV will do so because they embrace the technology of this era to create a seamless shopping experience across all platforms that evolves and delights customers faster and more often than their competitors do. This is what is driving the permission-based marketing era: greater access to the consumer, and thus ever-greater competitive advantage. For many the price of entry will be high, and for some it will be too great.

Back to the Future? Not Really

Many experts and colleagues of ours today, as well as you, our reader, could argue that the department-store palaces of consumption of Wave I and Sears' early mall dominance and catalog strength were operating on our three strategic principles, although then unarticulated. To a limited extent, we would agree.

Sears was providing an enjoyable shopping experience, although not to the level of neurologically addictive. Its distribution was as good as could be expected, given the economic and distribution infrastructure of the United States at the time, as well as the lack of globalization and technology advancements. Therefore, the term "preemptive distribution" did not exist, because the reality of it couldn't. Finally, total control of one's value chain was impossible without the enablers of technology and globalization.

Waves II and III were like a harmonic convergence of equal parts economic growth, consumer demand, infrastructure building, marketing and advertising, innovation, mobility and geographic expansion and the leading edges of new technology and globalization.

Then the seemingly equal parts of the convergence, which were all harmoniously driving unprecedented prosperity for all, became unequal. Abundance grew to overabundance, which provided consumers with unlimited selection and thus the power to demand more from suppliers. This imbalance of overcapacity chasing slower population and demand growth set the stage for Wave IV, and the necessity for businesses to transform their models around our operating principles merely to survive.

However, neither our New Rules nor their transformation would have been possible without major advances in technology, including the Internet and globalization.

Wave IV finds consumers in the center of the universe, with all parts focused on pleasing them—*period*. Furthermore, while consumers may go to stores or tap into sites or order from a catalog, the term "retail" is meaningless to them. And while they may buy wholesale brands, they do not know or care where the brand was made or by whom. Therefore, those that do survive and succeed, transforming their models to our New Rules, neither will be, nor should they call themselves, retailers or wholesalers. In the minds of the consumers, which are the only minds that count in Wave IV, they will all simply be brands.

At the end of the day, those who succeed will be brand managers whose sole responsibility is to manage and control the preemptive distribution of their neurologically addictive and highly differentiated brand from its creation all the way through to consumption.

NOTES

Chapter 3 Wave III: Approaching Total Consumer Power

1. Venkatesan Vembu, "Transforming Giants," *DNA,* February 3, 2007, http://www.dnaindia .com/lifestyle/special_transforming-giants_1077797.
2. International Council of Shopping Centers data, "The Economic Impact of Shopping Centers," 2013.
3. Apparel manufacturing cost data, Olah & Co.
4. International Council of Shopping Centers data, "The Economic Impact of Shopping Centers," 2013.
5. www.internetlivestats.com, maintained by Netcraft Internet Research and Security Company.
6. Peter Lyman and Hal R. Varian, "How Much Information," 2003, http://www.sims.berkeley .edu/how-much-info-2003.

Chapter 4 Wave IV: Technology Explodes:
The Jobsian and Bezosian Era

1. Forrester Research, "Marketing to Millennials: The Next Generation of Purchasing Power," 2011.

Chapter 5 Wave IV: The Transformation

1. US Census Bureau, Historical Income Tables, http://www.census.gov/hhes/www/income /data/historical/index.html.
2. Pew Research Center, "A Portrait of the Millennials," 2010.
3. Kurt Salmon review, "Five Trends to Know," www.kurtsalmon.com.
4. Richard Easterlin, "Will Raising the Incomes of All Increase the Happiness of All?" *Journal of Economic Behavior and Organization* (1995): 35–47.
5. E. Diener and R. Biswas-Diener, "Will Money Increase Subjective Wellbeing? A Literature Review and Guide to Needed Research," *Social Indicators Research* 57 (2002): 119–69.
6. Daniel Kahneman, "Would You Be Happier If You Were Richer? A Focusing Illusion," Princeton University, CEPS Working Paper No. 125, May 2006.
7. Abraham Maslow, "A Theory of Human Motivation," *Psychological Review* 50 (1943): 370– 96. (The hierarchy of needs includes, in order, physiological, safety, love/belonging, esteem and self-actualization.)
8. Travis Carter and Thomas Gilovich, "The Relative Relativity of Material and Experiential Purchases," *Journal of Personality and Social Psychology,* Cornell University, 98:1 (2010): 146–159.
9. Barry Schwartz, *The Paradox of Choice: Why More Is Less* (New York: Ecco, 2004).
10. Unpublished interview with the authors.
11. David Moin, "Bloomingdale's Opens Store in Dubai," *Women's Wear Daily,* February 1, 2010.

12. Ben Fischman, "Retailers Can Transform Operations by Creatively Integrating New Technology: A Wharton School Conference Explores the Reality of Retailing in a Web 2.0 World," lecture, Macy's Herald Square, New York, March 23, 2010.

13. Kurt Salmon Review, www.kurtsalmon.com.

14. Personal conversation with the authors.

15. Ibid.

16. Pia Sarkar, "Stores Boost Sales with Own Labels / National Brands Face Increasing Competition," *SFGate.com*, May 5, 2006, http://articles.sfgate. com/2006–05–05/business/17 294456_1_wal-mart-private-brandsprivate-label.

17. Private Label Manufacturers Association, *Store Brands Market Profile, 2013*.

18. Personal conversation with the authors.

19. Kevin Lindsay, "How to Make Online Shopping Feel Like 'Real' Shopping," *Apparel*, September 10, 2008, http://www.apparelmag.com/ME2/ dirmod.asp?sid=&nm=&type=news &mod=News&mid=9A02E3B96F2A415ABC72CB5F516B4C10&tier=3&nid=04556E590A4 0483F8B8ADB73F8C1D6A0.

20. Tara Parker-Pope, "This Is Your Brain at the Mall: Why Shopping Makes You Feel Good," *Wall Street Journal*, December 6, 2005.

21. Emily Steel, "Nestlé Takes a Beating on Social-Media Sites," *Wall Street Journal*, March 29, 2010, http://online.wsj.com/article/SB10001424052702304434404575149883850508158.html ?mod=rss_media_marketing.

Chapter 6   Making the Mind Connection: Neurological Connectivity

1. Kasra Ferdows, Michael A. Lewis and Jose A. D. Machuca, "Rapid Fire Fulfillment," *Harvard Business Review* 82 (2004): 104–10.

2. John Luciew, "Hershey Learns at Retail Stores How to Get Its Candy into Your Head," *Associated Press*, February 16, 2010.

3. Ilan Brat, "The Emotional Quotient of Soup Shopping," *Wall Street Journal*, February 17, 2010, http://online.wsj.com/article/SB10001424052748704804204575069562743700340.html.

4. Eric R. Kandel, James H. Schwartz and Thomas M. Jessel, eds., *Principles of Neural Science*, 4th ed, (New York: McGraw-Hill, 2000).

5. C. K. Prahalad and Venkatram Ramaswamy, "The New Frontier of Experience Innovation," *MIT Sloan Management Review Summer* 44:4 (2003), http://socialmediaclub.pbworks .com/f/cocreation.pdf.

6. Ivor Morgan and Jay Rao, "Making Routine Customer Experiences Fun," *MIT Sloan Management Review*, October 15, 2003.

7. Army Experience Center, http://www.thearmyexperience.com/.

8. Manasee Wagh, "Peace Group Protests Army Center at Mall," *The Intelligencer*, November 29, 2009, http://www.phillyburbs.com/news/news_ details/article/27/2009/november/28 /peace-group-protests-army-centerat-mall.html.

9. Robin Lewis, "Q&A with Jim Fielding, President of Disney Stores," *The Robin Report*, March 2012.

Chapter 7   Redefining the Rules of Engagement:
Preemptive Distribution

1. Robert A. Iger, "A Message in Every Medium," Keynote Interview, *Financial Times* Business of Luxury Summit, Los Angeles, CA, June 13–15, 2010.

2. Robin Lewis, "Q&A With Steve Sadove," *The Robin Report*, January 2011.

3. David Moin, "Gap Launching China Strategy," *Women's Wear Daily*, June 24, 2010.

Chapter 8   The Importance of Value-Chain
Control: The Bottom-Line Winners

1. Personal conversation with the authors.

2. Ibid.

3. Ibid.
4. Personal conversation with the authors.
5. NRF Convention Keynote, January 2014.
6. Liana B. Baker, "On the Hunt for the Next Bay Area Delicacy," *Wall Street Journal*, June 3, 2010.

Chapter 9   What It All Means: Today, Tomorrow, the Future

1. The source for these statistics is NPD (National Panel Data), a consumer-panel tracking and research company.
2. Personal discussion with the authors.
3. Susan Reda, "With SKU Reductions Underway, Which Will Survive?" *Stores*, February 2010.
4. Ibid.
5. Paul Ziobro, "P&G to Test Waters Again on a Bargain Tide," *Wall Street Journal Online*, September 3, 2013.
6. IRI Research Report, "Private Labels and National Brands," December 2013.
7. "New Masters of Management," *Economist*, April 17, 2010.
8. Dennis K. Berman, "Lazard's Statesman, a Game-Changer," *Wall Street Journal*, April 13, 2010, http://online.wsj.com/article/SB10001424052702304506904575180363245274300.html?ru=MKTW&mod=MKTW.
9. Jonathan Birchall, "Criticism that Spread Like a Rash," *Financial Times*, May 26, 2010.
10. Melanie Wells, "Kid Nabbing," *Forbes*, February 2, 2004, http://www.forbes. com/forbes/2004/0202/084.html.
11. David Kirkpatrick, "Why 'Bottom Up' Is on Its Way Up," *CNN.com*, January 15, 2004, http://www.cnn.com/2004/TECH/ptech/01/15/fortune.ff.bottomup.econ/.

Chapter 10   The Master Model: Omni-Brand to Consumer

1. A. T. Kearney, "Recasting the Retail Store in Today's Omnichannel World," http://www.atkearney.com/consumer-products-retail/featured-article/-/asset_publisher/S5UkO0zy0vnu/content/recasting-the-retail-store-in-today%E2%80%99s-omnichannel-world/10192.

Chapter 11   Ideas from the Great Ones

1. Company financials.
2. Personal conversation with the authors.
3. Ibid.
4. Robin Lewis, "Amazon . . . From Earth's Biggest Bookstore to the Biggest Store on Earth?" *The Robin Report*, 2012.
5. Ibid.
6. Satmetrix Net Promoter Retail Industry Benchmark Reports 2010 through 2013.
7. Derek Thompson, "The Amazon Mystery: What America's Strangest Tech Company Is Really Up To," *Atlantic Monthly*, November 2013.
8. Company financial reports.
9. "Inside eBay: A Bloomberg West Special," *Bloomberg TV*, December 9, 2013, http://www.bloomberg.com/video/12-6-inside-ebay-~3eButkhSRmr2DwLngYrrg.html.
10. Jeff Himmelman, "EBay's Strategy for Taking On Amazon," *New York Times*, December 19, 2013.
11. Ibid.
12. "Inside eBay: A Bloomberg West Special," *Bloomberg TV*, December 9, 2013, http://www.bloomberg.com/video/12-6-inside-ebay-~3eButkhSRmr2DwLngYrrg.html.
13. James B. Stewart, "Behind eBay's Comeback," *New York Times*, July 27, 2012.
14. Samantha Conti, "Burberry Opens New Headquarters," *Women's Wear Daily*, January 16, 2009.
15. CNN.com video interview with Burberry CEO Angela Ahrendts, http://tech.fortune.cnn.com/2013/10/22/apple-ahrendts-video-social/.

16. Ibid.
17. Rupert Neate, "How an American Woman Rescued Burberry, a Classic British Label," *Guardian,* June 15, 2013.
18. Jayne O'Donnell, "Behind the Bargains at TJ Maxx, Marshall's," *USA Today,* October 26, 2011.
19. Ibid.
20. TJX Cos. Second Quarter 2013 Analyst Conference Call, August 20, 2013.
21. Company financial statements.
22. Ibid.
23. CNBC Documentary, "The Costco Craze: Inside the Warehouse Giant," first aired April 26, 2012, http://www.cnbc.com/id/46603589.
24. Phone conversation with Kimberly Peterson, founder, AddictedtoCostco.com.
25. "All American Retailer," *Stores,* January 13, 2014.
26. Ibid.
27. Beth Kowitt, "Inside the Secret World of Trader Joe's," *Fortune.com,* August 23, 2010.
28. Satmatrix Net Promoter Retail Industry Benchmark Report, 2013.
29. SupermarketNews.com/trader-joe-s-co-2014.
30. Mobile 500 2013, InternetRetailer.com.
31. Personal conversation with Robin Lewis.
32. Brian Stetler, "Up Next: Reruns from HSN," *New York Times,* June 14, 2010.
33. Robin Lewis, "Q&A with Mindy Grossman," *The Robin Report,* 2011.
34. Robin Lewis, "Nordstrom: Ghost of Vince Lombardi Lives On," *The Robin Report,* February 2013.
35. Ibid.
36. Evelyn Rusli, "Stores Go Online to Find a Perfect Fit," *NYTimes.com,* April 11, 2012.
37. Market Force Information Press Release, December 10, 2013.
38. Sucharita Mulpuru, "U.S. Online Retail Forecast, 2012 to 2017," Forrester Research, March 13, 2013.
39. Ellen Byron, "Nordstrom Regains Its Luster," *Wall Street Journal,* August 19, 2004.
40. Personal conversation with authors.
41. Miguel Bustillo, "Home Depot Undergoes Renovation," *Wall Street Journal,* February 24, 2010, http://online.wsj.com/news/articles/SB10001424052748704188104575083081020924838.
42. Geoff Colvin, "Housing Is Back—and So Is Home Depot," *Fortune.com,* September 26, 2013
43. Unpublished interview with authors.
44. Company financial statements.
45. Robin Lewis, "Q&A with Ken Hicks," *The Robin Report,* September 2011.
46. NRF Keynote Roundtable, January 13, 2014.
47. Robin Lewis, "Q&A with Ken Hicks," *The Robin Report,* March 2011.
48. Ibid.
49. Katherine Bell, "'Retail Is War Without Blood': What Foot Locker CEO Learned in the Army," *Harvard Business Review,* November 15, 2010.
50. Ibid.
51. Andy Beckett, "Foot Locker, the Brand that Spells Trouble," *Guardian,* February 17, 2012; Joe Kemp, "Sneak Attack? Release of Nike Air Jordan Gamma Blue 11s Causes Brawls in Shoe Stores Nationwide," *New York Daily News,* December 23, 2013.
52. Personal interview with Robin Lewis.
53. Robin Lewis, "The Jobsian Era Is Upon Us: The Art and Science of Retailing Converge," *The Robin Report,* March 2012.
54. Company financial statements.
55. Walter Isaacson, *Steve Jobs* (Simon & Schuster: New York, 2011).
56. Yukair Iwatani Kane and Ian Sherr, "Secrets From Apple's Genius Bar: Full Loyalty, No Negativity," *Wall Street Journal Online,* June 15, 2011.

Chapter 12   Lessons From Sears: From Success to Struggle

1. Donald R. Katz, *The Big Store: Inside the Crisis and Revolution at Sears* (New York: Viking Press, 1987).

2. Ibid.
3. Rosabeth Moss Kanter, *On the Frontiers of Management* (Cambridge, MA: Harvard Business Press, 2003).
4. Robin Lewis, "Strategic Insight into the Decline of a Great American Icon," *The Robin Reports,* January 2003–April 2003.
5. Ibid.
6. Ibid.
7. Arthur C. Martinez, *The Hard Road to the Softer Side: Lessons from the Transformation of Sears* (New York: Crown Business, 2001).
8. Personal interview with Robin Lewis.

INDEX